The Beatitudes, Discipleship,
and the Justice of God

The Beatitudes, Discipleship, *and the* Justice of God

The Twelve Steps of Discipleship
in the Kingdom of Mercy

Brooks Harrington

CASCADE *Books* · Eugene, Oregon

THE BEATITUDES, DISCIPLESHIP, AND THE JUSTICE OF GOD
The Twelve Steps of Discipleship in the Kingdom of Mercy

Copyright © 2024 Brooks Harrington. All rights reserved. Except for brief quotations in critical publications or reviews, no part of this book may be reproduced in any manner without prior written permission from the publisher. Write: Permissions, Wipf and Stock Publishers, 199 W. 8th Ave., Suite 3, Eugene, OR 97401.

Cascade Books
An Imprint of Wipf and Stock Publishers
199 W. 8th Ave., Suite 3
Eugene, OR 97401

www.wipfandstock.com

PAPERBACK ISBN: 979-8-3852-1871-4
HARDCOVER ISBN: 979-8-3852-1872-1
EBOOK ISBN: 979-8-3852-1873-8

Cataloguing-in-Publication data:

Names: Harrington, Brooks, author.

Title: The beatitudes, discipleship, and the justice of God : the twelve steps of discipleship and the kingdom of mercy / Brooks Harrington.

Description: Eugene, OR : Cascade Books, 2024 | Includes bibliographical references.

Identifiers: ISBN 979-8-3852-1871-4 (paperback) | ISBN 979-8-3852-1872-1 (hardcover) | ISBN 979-8-3852-1873-8 (ebook)

Subjects: LCSH: Jesus Christ—Teachings. | Christian life—Biblical teaching. | Social justice—Biblical teaching.

Classification: BS2415 .H36 2024 (paperback) | BS2415 .H36 (ebook)

VERSION NUMBER 10/10/24

Unless otherwise indicated, Scripture quotations are from the New Revised Standard Version Bible, copyright © 1989 National Council of the Churches of Christ in the United States of America. All rights reserved worldwide.

For all who sometimes doubt the power and goodness of God
in a world of so much suffering, injustice, and evil.

For the clergy and laity of the United Methodist Church
who refuse to demonize and who aspire to see
the image of God in everyone.

Contents

Introduction | ix

Our Need for the Kingdom | 1
The Twelve Steps of Discipleship of Matthew's Beatitudes | 6
First Step: Matthew 4:18–22 | 8
Second Step: Matthew 4:23–25 | 28
Third Step: Matthew 5:1 | 39
Fourth Step: Matthew 5:2–3 | 47
Fifth Step: Matthew 5:4 | 58
Sixth Step: Matthew 5:5 | 69
Seventh Step: Matthew 5:6 | 91
Eighth Step: Matthew 5:7 | 105
Ninth Step: Matthew 5:8 | 121
Tenth Step: Matthew 5:9 | 145
Eleventh Step: Matthew 5:10 | 162
Twelfth Step: Matthew 5:11–12 | 179
Faithfulness for Those of Us Who Remain in Our Boats | 192
Thirteenth Step: Following the God Who *Is* Mercy | 197

Endnotes | 201
Bibliography | 203

Introduction

A few days before Christmas in 2021, I drove to my office in the early morning dark to prepare an application for an emergency protective order for a woman who had been badly beaten overnight by her husband. I am an attorney and an ordained United Methodist minister. My ministry is the Methodist Justice Ministry, through which my colleague lawyers, staff, and I provide free legal representation and financial and counseling support to protect indigent women and children from abuse and family violence. As I arrived at our offices in a downtown church building, my car headlights illuminated a homeless man who had been sleeping on newspapers on the concrete under an overhang outside the front door. He was startled by my lights, jumped up, and began pacing and talking to himself. A wad of his clothes lay next to where he had slept. It was drizzling and he was wet. His hair was damp and matted. He was a tall, thin man, obviously agitated. I was concerned at first to get out of the safety of my car. But I have learned through work with the homeless that fear of them is almost always unfounded.

He moved out of my way so I could get to the locked building door. I asked him how he was doing, asked his name, and introduced myself. He seemed surprised and relaxed a little, but he still put distance between us by moving out into the parking lot. I realized that he was probably afraid I would call the police to report that he was trespassing on church property. I called out to him that he was safe here and asked if he wanted to come inside to use the restroom and get dry and warm. He kept his distance and declined. His words were slurred so maybe he was high or just sleepy. But then he asked if I could spare a few dollars so he could get something to eat. I said yes and pulled out my wallet. All I had were two twenty dollar bills. I hesitated to give him that much, but he clearly needed it. I gave a bill to him. He looked at the twenty in his hand, and mumbled softly to himself in a slurred voice, "Christians, man. Christians." I wanted to talk to him about his situation, but he walked quickly away to find something to eat, leaving his pile of clothes behind. I have never seen him again.

"Christians, man. Christians." He and his words stayed with me. He was living a hard, tragic life. If he was like so many homeless, he was alone and shunned. He had every reason to be despairing and angry with the people who shun him, the injustice of life in general, and the source of that life. But whatever the church has done to dilute and distort the message of Jesus, this suffering, outcast child of God still associated our faith with mercy to those in need.

Surely Jesus' Kingdom of *Mercy* is a faith and a Way worthy of our continued loyalty and commitment. Mercy is the essence of the Way that has touched the hearts, minds, and souls of millions over the Christian centuries. If the church is in decline in America, in attendance, in influence, and more importantly in faithfulness to Jesus' teachings, it is because it has allowed itself to be diverted from the Way of Jesus' Kingdom of Mercy into paths of doctrine, rules, judgment, indifference, and property accumulation. It is because it has compromised too thoroughly with kingdoms other than Jesus' Kingdom.

This book is about what the Jesus of the Gospel according to Matthew asks of disciples of the Kingdom of Mercy.

One issue considered in this book is the promised Kingdom of Heaven, which was and is the Kingdom of Mercy. May we still "realistically" yearn for it in this suffering world? What is and what will the Kingdom be? Why has it not yet fully come? How may disciples help God bring it?

Another issue is discipleship *with* Jesus. What is this discipleship, and who is a disciple? Is every Christian called to be a disciple according to Matthew's Jesus? A main thesis of this book is that the Beatitudes of Matthew's Jesus (Matt 5:3–11) are not randomly ordered blessings, but are the third through the twelfth Steps on the Way of discipleship in the Kingdom of Mercy.

Another issue is the justice of God—what theologians call the *theodicy* issue. *Theodicy* is a Greek word that is formed from the Greek for God, *Theos*, and the Greek for justice, *dike*. If God is good and powerful, why is there still so much evil, undeserved suffering, and injustice? Why has this God of goodness and power not already brought the long-promised Kingdom? Or does the God revealed through the lives and words of the prophets and Jesus lack the power to impose that Kingdom upon the world? Are sin and evil defeating God's will on earth as they cannot in heaven? Underlying all this, what *is* the extent of the goodness and power of God?

At the end of discussion of each of the Twelve Steps of discipleship, I will offer an episode of a twelve-part, fictional story about what that discipleship could look like in our time and place. I emphasize that this story is wholly fictional and does not describe or intend to describe, resemble, or recreate any actual person, church, or event.

Our Need for the Kingdom

Why does the world need the Kingdom of Mercy? Why should the coming of the long-delayed Kingdom remain among humankind's deepest yearnings?

I have a good friend who is a fellow United Methodist minister whose motto might as well be: "Our God makes *sure* that there are *lots* of milk and cookies for *everybody*!!" He loves the saying "God is good, all the time. All the time, God is good." He is personable and *very* popular with the members of his wealthy church. They want to be uplifted at worship and fed encouraging insights and advice about how to be joyful and fulfilled within the prevailing kingdom of consumerism. And, as a matter of fact, there *are* lots of milk and cookies for almost all of these comfortable members. And life is good, and so is God, almost all the time . . . for them.

There are *not* lots of milk and cookies for *everyone* in God's world. Many of us are taking more than our fair share of life's milk and cookies. Evil, through people and institutions, preys upon the poor, elderly, outcast, and particularly children. Life's benefits and curses fall randomly, unjustly, and mostly without remedy for most people in creation—despite the belief in the goodness and power of God that is so essential to many people's faith. Most of our prayers for God to save us from bad health, injury, addiction, family tragedies, injustice, or conflict in the world don't seem to be answered. Every time we pray the Lord's Prayer or the Our Father, we ask: "Our Father, who art in heaven . . . thy kingdom come. Thy will be done, on earth as it is in heaven" (Matt 6:9–10). Well, has it? Is it still coming? Am I missing it?

As I work on this book in late 2023, the leaders of Hamas have just persuaded their followers to respond to the injustice of their plight in Gaza by kidnapping, sexually assaulting, and murdering hundreds of unarmed Israelis, many at an outdoor music festival, many of them women, children, and infants. And the leadership of Israel is responding by bombing homes and hospitals in Gaza indiscriminately, killing and maiming noncombatants whom Hamas fighters may be hiding among, and blockading shipments of essential humanitarian aid to innocent and trapped Palestinians, many of whom are also women, children, and infants. At this writing, 25 percent of the people in the Gaza are starving, and 40,000 are estimated to be dead from Israeli bombs and tank shells.[1] Hamas refuses to release any more of the Israeli hostages until the bombardment stops, and the Israelis refuse to stop shelling until the hostages are released. All this is occurring in what both sides would characterize as a holy land, with many on both sides invoking the will of their God to justify this hatred and inhumanity. Their religious beliefs just seem to intensify their brutality. Despite *millions* of prayers, God has yet to step in to stop the carnage.

In Ukraine, Russian invaders and Ukrainian defenders have reached a stalemate, for now, reminiscent of trench warfare in WWI. Ukrainian land, cities, and towns have been laid to waste by missiles, drones, artillery shells, and tank rounds, while thousands of families have been turned into refugees and thousands of children have been killed and maimed. Yet the leaders of the Russian Orthodox Church continue in loud, public support of Putin's aggression.

The total value of military expenditures worldwide in 2022 reached 2.24 trillion in US dollars (that's $2,240 billion) and growing for the eighth consecutive year, according to the Stockholm International Peace Research Institute.[2] On January 8, 2024, CNN reported that the US Pentagon is the world's largest employer with 2.86 million employees in all military and civilian defense services.[3] There are more than 12,500 nuclear warheads stockpiled worldwide as of January 2023, according to The International Campaign to Abolish Nuclear Weapons based in Switzerland, which was awarded the Nobel Peace Prize in 2017.[4] Russia is said to possess 5,889 of these warheads, the US 5,224, China 410, France 290, the UK 225, Pakistan 170, India 164, Israel 90 (unconfirmed), and North Korea 30 (unconfirmed).[5] Six other European nations host nuclear weapons. There are more than 50 ongoing conflicts in the world as I am typing this page, ranging from drug wars, terrorist insurgencies, ethnic and religious conflicts, and territorial aggressions.[6]

As I type this morning, there are stories on CNN about two more mass shootings—one near Dayton, Ohio, and another in southern Colorado. In the Ohio shooting, a man walked into a Walmart and began killing shoppers indiscriminately before taking his own life. Law enforcement suspected that the shooting was motivated by racial hatred. In the Colorado incident, a man reportedly shot and killed a number of his neighbors because of a dispute over the location of their common property boundary line. These two incidents raised the number of mass shootings in the US in 2023 alone to more than 600.[7] And the response of organized gun manufacturers, sellers, and many gun owners to all such shootings is to advocate for the freedom of even more people to carry even more guns into even more places. *Forbes* reports that just over 24.4 million AR-15 and AK-style assault weapons were manufactured in the US from 1990 to 2020, with 2.8 million entering US circulation in 2020 alone.[8] According to the Centers for Disease Control and Prevention, firearms became the leading cause of death among children from 1 to 19 years of age in the US in 2020.[9] Polls taken by the Public Religion Research Institute and Brookings Institution in mid-2023 showed that 33 percent of one political party, 22 percent of independents, and 13 percent of the other main party agreed with the statement: "Because things have gotten so far off track, true American patriots may have to resort to violence in order to save our country."[10]

In the US and the world, studies show the gap between the comfortable and the poor continues to grow. An article in *The Guardian* in March 2021 states that the top 1 percent of Americans now own more wealth and assets than the bottom 92 percent combined.[11] In the last decade, the percentage of children living in poverty in the US peaked to almost one in four. A recent report on my home state of Texas shows that 852,000 children are without health insurance and 25 percent are food insecure.[12] Eighty-five percent of the children enrolled in public schools in my hometown of Fort Worth, Texas, a city with a population of almost one million, live at or below the poverty line.[13]

The National Alliance to End Homelessness reported in June 2023 that there were 653,104 homeless in the US, and that more than a quarter of that number had no indoor place to stay for more than a year.[14] The Alliance also reported that homelessness rates have climbed by about 6 percent each year since 2017. In 2021 the World Economic Forum reported that 150 million people were homeless worldwide. Among these were 32.5 million refuges—people forced to leave their homes by war, violence, famine, or ethnic cleansing. One third to one half of these 32.5 million refugees were children.[15]

UNICEF and the World Bank Group reported 333 million children in the world lived in *extreme* poverty as of 2022, struggling to survive on less than the equivalent of $2.15 per day.[16] As of 2019, one *billion* children were "multi-dimensionally poor," meaning suffering from at least one area of *severe* deprivation in health, shelter, nutrition, sanitation, or water.[17] UNICEF reported in 2020 that over 149 million children under 5 years old were severely stunted in growth and another 45 million emaciated because of lack of adequate food.[18] Three *billion* adults and children remained locked out of healthy diets, largely due to excessive costs. Nearly a third of women of reproductive age suffered from severe anemia.[19] UNICEF reported in 2021 that 5 million children under 5 years of age died, including 2.1 million newborns, which is an average of more than 13,500 newborn deaths each day, 93 each minute, more than one each second. These deaths were predominantly due to easily preventable or treatable disease, malnutrition, lack of basic vaccinations, foul water, and bad sanitation.[20]

Can anyone believe in good faith that any of the above is within the will of the good and powerful God in whom we believe? And yet all of the above prevails.

Where is God in the midst of the darkness? Will God keep the old promise to save us from ourselves and our urge to evil and indifference . . . on this earth? Or must we who are suffering give up on our earthly lives, think only of our souls, concentrate on believing the various dogmas about Jesus rather than following his Way, insulate ourselves as effectively and selfishly as we can from the darkness here, and only await God's kingdom in heaven upon our deaths?

The response of the Hebrew scripture and of Matthew's Jesus lies in a coming Kingdom of Mercy in which God and God's compassion, justice, and peace reign on earth.

What has God promised through scripture that this Kingdom of Mercy will be like? The Kingdom will be one of community and peace in which God will:

> judge between the nations,
> *and shall arbitrate for many peoples;*
> they shall beat their swords into ploughshares,
> and their spears into pruning-hooks;
> nation shall not lift up sword against nation,
> neither shall they learn war anymore. (Isa 2:4)

The Kingdom will be one in which oppression, slavery, and conquest will no longer occur because there will be "endless peace" (Isa 9:4–7). It will be a Kingdom in which God's messiah will come to bring wellbeing and nurturing community for all through his "wisdom and understanding," his "counsel and might," and his dedication to justice and mercy for the poor (Isa 11:2–4). It will be a Kingdom in which, metaphorically speaking, "The wolf shall live with the lamb, the leopard shall lie down with the kid, the calf and the lion and the fatling together, and a little child shall lead them. . . . They will not hurt or destroy on all my holy mountain; for the earth will be full of the knowledge of the LORD as the waters cover the sea" (Isa 11:6–9). It will be a Kingdom in which God comes to stop the oppression of "workers" and the violence of the "wicked," and "to loose the bonds of injustice, to undo the thongs of the yoke, to let the oppressed go free." It will be a Kingdom in which we are caused by God "to share [our] bread with the hungry, to bring the homeless poor into [our] house," to "cover" the "naked" and to reconcile with our "kin" (Isa 58:3–7). It will be a Kingdom in which God sends the Messiah "to bring good news to the oppressed, bind up the brokenhearted, to proclaim liberty to the captives, . . . to provide for those who mourn" (Isa 61:1–3). It will be one in which people will be "blessed" by God because of their merciful acts toward the poor, hungry, thirsty, sick, prisoner, and stranger (Matt 25:31–46). It will be a Kingdom in which God will dwell with us on earth and "wipe every tear from [our] eyes. Death will be no more; mourning and crying and pain will be no more" (Rev 21:3–4).

According to the Gospels, Jesus is the Messiah who has already brought the dawn of God's promised Kingdom . . . but only the dawn. How long must we still wait for the fulfillment of the creation's and humanity's divinity until the coming reign of the Kingdom of Mercy? Since Jesus walked the earth, how many children have suffered and died from hunger, bad water, disease, war, loss of homes and families, neglect, and abuse? How many times have cruel men exploited the poor and the powerless with inhumane violence, crushing taxation, theft, corruption, forced labor, enslavement, torture, and the many methods of cruel crucifixion?

Yet still we wait, unable to create on our own a kingdom in which mercy and justice reign without God's help, praying that God have the compassion that we have at our best or that we somehow obtain God's reported power to bind up the broken heart of the world.

The Twelve Steps of Discipleship of Matthew's Beatitudes

For most of my preaching career, I have been most engaged by the prophets, Jesus' parables in Matthew and Luke, and the Sermon on the Mount reported in Matthew's Gospel. The beginning of the Great Sermon—the nine Beatitudes—has fascinated me, although I doubt that I have ever given a valuable sermon on any of them. The Beatitudes always seemed to me to be so unrelated to one another that I had a difficult time recalling their sequence when I used them in *lectio divina*.

But during one Sunday afternoon I had set aside for meditation, the Beatitudes and their context abruptly took on meaning to me *as a progression of steps in discipleship*. Like many people who chant and meditate repeatedly on portions of scripture, those verses work their way into the subconscious and the heart, and connections are gradually made that are beyond our immediate consciousness. I was quietly chanting the Beatitudes using a prayer rope, trying to remember their sequence without consulting my Bible, when it suddenly occurred that the Beatitudes, as they are embedded in the narrative of Matthew and understood with the aid of the Psalms and Isaiah, are Twelve Steps on the Way of discipleship of Jesus. They are keys in enduring and persisting on the Way to the Kingdom of Mercy despite the seemingly invincible power of evil and suffering in the world and discouragement at the delay of the coming of the Kingdom.

What follows is a way to justify and unpack that insight. My purpose in writing this book is, hopefully, to help those Christians who feel called to continue the mission of Jesus depicted in Matthew's Gospel, to feed the hungry and give water to the thirsty, to heal the sick and clothe the naked, to welcome the alien and visit the prisoner (Matt 25:31–46). The mission to minister to suffering men, women, and children "who sit in darkness . . . in the region and shadow of death" (Matt 4:16).

This book is at least for all those teachers in inner city neighborhoods; doctors and nurses who care for poor people with gunshot wounds, rat bites, and chronically untreated conditions in county hospital emergency rooms; police officers who try to maintain calm and peace in settings of poverty, addiction, gangs, anger, and despair; volunteers who mentor, tutor, protect, feed, clothe, and encourage poor, suffering children in the inner city through nonprofit ministries and organizations; parents and grandparents who try to teach and model compassion, self-respect, faith, and hope to their children, grandchildren, and great-grandchildren in conditions of poverty; people who go on missions to impoverished people in other nations and in our own; people who participate in prison ministries; persons who welcome and advocate for the homeless on our streets and who do the same for the refugees on our southern border who have gotten over the buoys and through the concertina wire; people who have the thankless task of administering underfunded and understaffed government programs to help the poor; family court judges; and on and on. This book is for all those who attempt to follow Jesus in trying to fulfill God's promises of rescue to the suffering and the victimized, but who sometimes despair that God just doesn't seem to be helping enough . . . yet.

First Step

Matthew 4:18–22

¹⁸ As he walked by the Sea of Galilee, he saw two brothers, Simon, who is called Peter, and Andrew his brother, casting a net into the sea—for they were fishermen. ¹⁹ And he said to them, "Follow me and I will make you fish for people." ²⁰ Immediately they left their nets and followed him. ²¹ As he went from there, he saw two other brothers, James son of Zebedee and his brother John, in the boat with their father Zebedee, mending their nets, and he called them. ²² Immediately they left the boat and their father, and followed him.

The silences in this story of the call of these first four followers of Jesus are what fascinate. Why would these men "immediately" leave their lives to follow him? Did they know him personally before these encounters? Had they talked to him or heard him speak? Had they even heard of him? Matthew says of Jesus in the verses just before these encounters that Jesus was "a great light" "seen" in the "darkness" of "the region and shadow of death" of Galilee (Matt 4:15–16). But all Matthew tells us of Jesus' activity before the call and immediate response of these men is: "From that time [the arrest of John], Jesus began to proclaim 'Repent, for the kingdom of heaven has come near'" (Matt 4:17). There is no account of any healings *before* the men "immediately" left their lives to follow Jesus. Was it simply that the Spirit of God was so evidently with Jesus that his charisma possessed them?

First Step: Matthew 4:18-22

The answers to these questions affect whether the response of Andrew, Peter, James, and John should serve as a model for our own responses to Jesus' call to follow him.

Did they have family and coworkers who depended upon them and whom they "immediately" abandoned? Did they even say goodbye? Did they make provision for those who loved and needed them? What about poor Zebedee? Did he need his sons to man his fishing boat, but did they leave him without help? Was he too old to sail a boat, and throw and haul nets himself? In fact, did Andrew and Peter or Zebedee, James, and John own their own nets and boats? If so, why would they just abandon them? Or were they all just hired hands, struggling to get by with almost nothing material to lose? We do know from later in Matthew's story that Peter had a house and mother-in-law (Matt 8:14), so we know at least that he was married or a widower, perhaps had children, and was a property owner or renter. If any of these four men were among the working poor themselves, it might be easier to understand why they would drop everything and follow Jesus. Or perhaps it would be easier for us to understand if they had accumulated some wealth and were not leaving their families bereft.

The story of the call to these four fishermen to follow Jesus immediately is much like the story of the call and response of Matthew the tax gatherer later in the narrative (Matt 9:9). Matthew certainly was leaving behind a comfortable life. And the harsh response of Jesus to the potential disciple who wanted to delay his following of Jesus to bury his father (Matt 8:21) suggests that this immediate and abrupt response to Jesus' call, by placing the Kingdom of Mercy and Jesus above family and all other requirements of life, is intended by Matthew to be a model for response to Jesus' call to follow him (Matt 12:46–50).

Were these four men dissatisfied with the kingdom of Rome and the temple authorities? Were they hungering and thirsting for an alternate kingdom? These men lived in one kingdom controlled by a distant emperor and imposed by a conquering army maintained by coerced taxes. Were these men and their families weighed down by taxes? Were they sick of the indignities and cruelties of the Roman armies? Were they steeped in the Hebrew scripture promising the coming of the Kingdom of the LORD?

Despite any comfort they may have enjoyed as fishermen, and the reliable source of food they had in the steady supply of fish, had they been disturbed by the suffering of the poor and the outcast?

Or were they just bored with the routine drudgery of fishing and sick and tired of mending nets, casting and hauling in nets of fish, and cleaning fish guts? And were they at a stage of life when they wanted to give their lives to something exciting and consequential, like following a charismatic, eloquent rabbi who flattered them by choosing them to follow him? What role did they hope to play as close colleagues of Jesus—to sit at his right hand in his Kingdom (Matt 20:20–28)?

The answers to all these questions are to be given by each of us, and those answers will determine what relevance Matthew's stories of calls to follow Jesus will have in our lives and in our individual situations and stages of life.

Where I come down among the explanations for why the four men "immediately" left their families and settled lives to go with Jesus was that they had heard him proclaim the Kingdom was at hand, that they were dissatisfied with the kingdoms of the world in which they felt trapped, and that they followed Jesus with great hope for a new life for everyone. Whatever responsibilities and relationships that would hold them back were not strong enough to keep them from going "immediately."

What might this story be telling us about God's call here and now?

Jews in Jesus' time had lived for hundreds of years since their Babylonian exile waiting for the promised Kingdom to arrive. Like them, we live in a time in which the Kingdom Jesus promised has failed to appear... for two thousand additional years. We still live in a time when the kingdom of the lion, the asp, and the adder very much reign (Isa 11:7–8). Questions about Jesus' call of the fishermen and their response are as relevant to us as they were to them.

Are *we* really receiving the call of God? Is God asking us to serve others in need more than we serve ourselves and our families? Is *now* finally the time for our "yes" response to the call of Jesus within our lives and the lives of those who depend upon us? Is it ever really a convenient time for such a response to God's call, according to the narratives of the kingdoms dominating this world and the commitments we have made within those kingdoms? If our response does not make us fools in the eyes of those who uncritically adhere to these dominant kingdoms, would we be responding to the call of God at all? Responding to this call to follow Jesus on his Way of the Kingdom of Mercy *always* involves unpredictable and inconvenient sacrifice, but is the sacrifice more on those who depend upon us than upon us? And can we better respond to our calls by using the positions and capacities we are already blessed with to advance the Kingdom?

I firmly believe that most of a person's life is preparation. The big question is "for what?" Perhaps our four fishermen had been in preparation for years for the encounter with Jesus and his call. Perhaps our fishermen were supremely primed to respond to the face, the voice, the spirit, and the call of Jesus "immediately."

Having stated the above reactions, I offer the following:

First, the call to follow and our positive response to that call to the courageous Way of Jesus is a matter of *God's* grace. This is grace righteousness, not works righteousness. This is participation in God's Kingdom of Mercy by God's call and power, not by our own.

Second, this call is issued by God in God's freedom and is received in our freedom. As I will discuss below, most of us don't receive the call of the Jesus of Matthew. Some receive it, but most of these are deaf to it. Having received and heard, some respond but most refuse. And very many mistake their own calls of themselves for God's call, when their call is for their own benefit and honor, and God's is for the advancement of the Kingdom of Mercy and the poor. God makes the calls in God's freedom, and God gives us the freedom not to respond, or to wait to respond, or to respond initially and then to abandon the call, or to continue on the Way of discipleship, step by step. This book tries to be about the Twelve Steps of continuing on the Way in our time and place.

Why do so few receive God's call to leave their lives and follow Jesus on the Way of discipleship in the Kingdom of Mercy? Part of the answer is that God wills most people to continue to catch the fish and grow the crops, and feed and nurture the children, and run the power grid, and, yes, administer the markets of commerce—in short to continue the routine work that keeps the human world spinning.

And why do so many who receive God's call to discipleship in the Kingdom of Mercy fail to hear or respond to the call? Parts of the answer are the many impediments put up by the kingdoms of the world to hearing, responding, and then continuing on the Way of Jesus.

This story in Matt 4:18–22 of the call and response of the four fishermen tells us that it is God who chooses whom to call to walk with Jesus on his Way of the Kingdom of Mercy, and that God often calls people who seem unlikely candidates to the rest of us. Who could have seemed more unlikely to receive the call in Jesus' time than men smelling of fish and a hated profiteer and collaborator with the Roman tax system?

Another example in Matthew is the story of the scribe who tries to call himself to follow Jesus. "A scribe then approached and said, 'Teacher, I will follow you wherever you go.' And Jesus said to him, 'Foxes have holes, and birds of the air have nests, but the Son of Man has nowhere to lay his head'" (Matt 8:19–20). I read in this story that Jesus rebuffed the scribe. Jesus did not call him; the scribe tried to call himself. Perhaps Jesus sensed that the scribe could not follow him into service to the poor, homeless, and deprived. Or that the scribe was intending to serve something other than the Kingdom of Mercy.

Perhaps another example of this is the story of the rich young man in Matt 19:

> [16] Then someone came to him and said, "Teacher, what good deed must I do to have eternal life?" [17] And he said to him, "Why do you ask me about what is good? There is only one who is good. If you wish to enter into life, keep the commandments." [18] He said to him, "Which ones?" And Jesus said, "You shall not murder; You shall not commit adultery; You shall not steal; You shall not bear false witness; [19] Honor your father and mother; also, You shall love your neighbor as yourself." [20] The young man said to him, "I have kept all these; what do I still lack?" [21] Jesus said to him, "If you wish to be perfect, go, sell your possessions, and give the money to the poor, and you will have treasure in heaven; then come, follow me." [22] When the young man heard this word, he went away grieving, for he had many possessions.

This young man was motivated to be a disciple of Jesus for his own benefit. "Teacher, what good deed must I do to inherit eternal life?" And he wanted to choose his own role, with Jesus as his "teacher," not his Messiah. The traditional role of the disciple was to be taught, and this seems to be the extent of the relationship he sought with Rabbi Jesus. But Jesus called him to be much more than a student of Torah. He called him to be a follower on the Way of Jesus and the Kingdom of Mercy, a servant primarily for the benefit of the poor and not himself. This young man's response to Jesus' call was the opposite of the responses of four fishermen and the tax gatherer Matthew, even though he spoke to Jesus face-to-face and even though Jesus evidently saw potential in him. The rich young man was free to reject the call to follow. Had he responded to Jesus' call, we might know his name as well as we know the names of Andrew, Peter, James, John, and Matthew! Has anyone in the history of our faith ever refused a greater opportunity to contribute to the growth of the Kingdom of Mercy than this rich young man? For how many contemporary Christians is this rich man's story our story? How many of us are refusing the call to contribute to the coming of the Kingdom of Mercy?

Third, the authentic call of God comes most often through an encounter with a person—in the case of these four fishermen and Matthew with Jesus himself, but in most cases with a person in need. God calls us the loudest and most insistently through the suffering of the other. For me this call came in an encounter with four terrified children at a murder/suicide scene in Washington, DC. I was a federal criminal prosecutor in an investigative unit with two homicide detectives. We were looking for a witness to a murder of a homeless man late one night when we were directed by police radio to the scene of a shooting. Inside a tenement house in an impoverished inner-city neighborhood, we found that a man had murdered his wife with a shotgun and then had shot himself in the head. In the small bedroom where the shootings had occurred we discovered two small children crying so hard at what they had witnessed that they couldn't catch their breaths to make a sound. In the kitchen just below the room where the shootings occurred were two toddlers on a mattress on the floor as blood dripped through the ceiling above and pooled around their bed. The children were screaming because they felt trapped on their mattress by the surrounding blood. The memory of those children and their poverty haunted me in dreams for years until I eventually felt compelled to answer Jesus' call to a ministry to protect children from violence. I responded eventually, not "immediately." A wonderfully caring CRNA friend of mine named Karen heard my story and said to me, "You got picked. Some people get picked, and you are one of them." And I try to provide in my story below a fictional but realistic example of such a call of God to four women through their encounter with a suffering mother and her infant.

Fourth, we may faithfully question the reasoning and realism of these fishermen in leaving their lives "immediately" without knowing what they were getting into (Matt 8:20–22; 10:37–38; 12:47–50; 16:21–26; 17:22–23; 19:27; and 20:17–24). But none of us knows what God has in store for us or our families at the moment we respond to the call to discipleship on the Way of the Kingdom. Our roles are chosen by God through the evolving requirements, joys, and hardships of the Way when we are on it. The initial issues are whether we are truly discerning that we are receiving *God's* call, and how we respond. After responding, we are often and increasingly called, ironically, to choose to give up to Jesus our freedom of choice. The continuing issues are then whether we stay with Jesus on his Way when we are confronted by the unanticipated joys and hardships of the journey, and how much control we give up to God over our lives. We cannot calculate and appreciate the hardships and benefits we will in fact experience in responding initially to Jesus' call to follow, just as our four fishermen did not appreciate those hardships and benefits when they embarked on the Way. The blessings we will likely receive will be very different than the blessings we expect, just as the hardships will be different and more difficult. But still we are called to follow.

Fifth, the kingdoms of the world will always have plenty of reasons that are prudent within their universe of values *not* to respond to Jesus' call to discipleship on the Way of the Kingdom. In the view of these kingdoms of the world, we are indeed acting like fools when we respond to a call to discipleship in the Kingdom of Mercy.

The First Step of the Way of the disciple is to be blessed to take the first step of following Jesus after receiving the call from God.

***

What could answering Jesus' call to follow him on the Way of the disciple of the Kingdom of Mercy look like now?

Dr. Felix Cotswald, the senior pastor of First Kingdom of God Church of Metroplex, Texas, the largest independent church in the city of more than two million souls, stood on the floor of the sanctuary in front of the full pews and asked for quiet.

Behind and above him, looming over the pulpit platform and the choir loft, was a stained glass window depicting part of the story from Matt 14:28–33 of Peter stepping out of a boat to walk on the water in response to Jesus' command to him to "come." The actual scene was of Jesus rescuing Peter when he became scared and began to sink. Etched in the glass at the bottom of the window was "O ye of little faith, why did you doubt?"

"Let us begin with a prayer," said the pastor. "Bill, will you speak to the Lord for us?"

Bill Anderson, the chair of the church board of trustees, seventy-five years old, six foot three and lean with combed back, steel silver hair, stood imperiously, cleared his throat, waited impatiently for silence, and then spoke in a stentorian voice, "Lord Jesus, inspire us to make the decision you would have us make at this difficult crossroads for our church. Help us to listen and deliberate with respect. Most of all, inspire us to make the responsible decision for the future of this church. Amen." He verbally punched the word *"responsible."*

The pastor spoke again. "Brothers and sisters in Christ, next Sunday, in accordance with our Book of Governance, we will hold a meeting for all members of the church who choose to attend to determine the future of our mission building and ministries. The meeting will start just after our 11 a.m. worship service. A vote of those members present will be held, and the future of the mission will be determined by majority of those attending. The vote will be a simple yes or no on the recommendation of the trustees to close the mission and cease its operations. In order to avoid more disharmony than is necessary, only three people will be allowed to speak for each side at the meeting, with each person restricted to no more than three minutes. The resolution has already been published on the church website, but the Book of Governance requires that it be read in this meeting. Bill, if you please?"

Anderson stood again, took out two typed pages and read:

> Whereas, the mission building and mission ministries of this church have been open and in operation for more than twenty years, providing free clothing, food, infant formula, counseling and prayer to the poor in the downtown neighborhood of the church, and
>
> Whereas the mission operations generate no income and are an increasing drain on the finances of the church, and
>
> Whereas, a flood of illegal aliens have invaded our country through our southern border and have swollen the homeless population of our city, and
>
> Whereas, the aid and support of these illegal aliens by our mission staff has been publicly criticized by the sheriff of this county, a columnist of our local newspaper, and the coalition of downtown businesses, and has caused pledged donors of this church to withhold their contributions until this aid and support of illegals ceases, and
>
> Whereas, our church mission and its ministries should not be encouraging and enabling illegal activity and exposing our church to criticism, criminal prosecution, and civil litigation, and
>
> Whereas, there has been a rise in vandalism and break-ins of our church property and all downtown businesses by illegals

> seeking a place to sleep and relieve themselves and an influx of illegal drugs including fentanyl, and
>
> Whereas, the trustees have determined that the aging mission building and surrounding parking lot can be sold for enough money to re-carpet the entire main church buildings, to make long needed repairs to the exteriors, and to replace the old sanctuary organ, and
>
> Whereas, the professional staff of our mission has already resigned in protest of this recommendation of the trustees and our orders that they not serve illegals,
>
> The Board of Trustees, after prayerful deliberation, unanimously recommends to the church that the mission ministries cease operations immediately, that the mission building be closed and sold to a buyer or buyers vetted and approved by the trustees, and that the money realized from the sale be used to make our church building and facilities more attractive and welcoming to new members and donors.

What started as a murmur became an angry din as arguments broke out among members of the congregation. Dozens of hands were raised.

Dr. Cotswald stood again and raised both his hands asking for silence. He remained still and smiling until the congregation quieted.

> Beloved, this is not the meeting for discussion. As I said, next Sunday will be that time. Then we will vote. Nothing is to be gained by delaying resolution of this issue longer than one week. A decision needs to be made up or down on this recommendation by the trustees. I am afraid that some on the side that loses will leave the church. So let me leave you with these teachings of our Lord:
>
> "Blessed are the poor in spirit, for theirs is the kingdom of heaven."
>
> "Blessed are the meek, for they will inherit the earth."
>
> "Blessed are the peacemakers, for they shall be called children of God."
>
> And let me leave you also with a statement of Paul: "Love does not insist on its own way." Let us all strive to be humble peacemakers and loving children of God throughout this process.

Among the church members in the sanctuary that Sunday were sisters named Sarah Bigelow and Anne Barnes. Both women were in their mid-forties, two years apart in age. They each had two children. Both of Sarah's children had graduated from college and moved to other states. Both of Anne's children were in graduate schools in Florida.

Sarah's husband Craig Bigelow was an investment banker. Anne's husband George Barnes owned a highway paving company. The two sisters and their husbands lived a few blocks apart from one another in a rich, gated community adjacent to their country club. Neither of their husbands ever attended their church, instead playing golf on Sunday mornings. Anne and Sarah went to church regularly on Sunday mornings to see friends in their long-time Sunday school class. That particular class rarely engaged in Bible study. They mostly talked about current events and college football before going to the worship service. Since their children had moved away, the sisters always went to lunch together after the service.

The church mission building was at the far end of the extensive church property from the rest of the church buildings. It had been built that far away to discourage the poor whom the mission served from panhandling church members as they were walking from the church parking lots to the sanctuary to worship on Sundays. The only times Sarah and Anne had been at the church mission building was when their Sunday school class painted the mission interior as a project on a Saturday, and when they dropped their old clothes at the free clothing bank there. They had seen the crowds of homeless and poor lining up to get into the mission building when they drove by on weekdays, but had avoided being in the mission when it was serving its clients. Sarah and Anne only attended the meeting that Sunday about the trustees' recommendation to close the mission at the urging of members of their Sunday school class because the "aliens are invading our city." Sarah's husband was so upset over the "invasion" of "illegals" that he almost attended the trustee meeting himself instead of playing golf.

Sarah and Anne's father owned a string of dry cleaning stores. Their mother had died of cancer four years before. Both their husbands were wealthy from their work, so neither sister needed to be employed for more income. But each of them helped their dad two days per week in his dry cleaning stores. Sarah helped with inventory and restocking supplies, and Anne helped with payroll for the employees, most of whom were Hispanic. It amounted to part-time work for both. Neither accepted any pay from their dad, which bothered both their husbands because the father had become wealthy from his business, although not as wealthy as the husbands.

Two other sisters were present in the sanctuary for the meeting. Their names were Janine Bodine and Jazmine Bodine. They were both retired school teachers in their late sixties. Janine had never married. Jazmine married when she was in her twenties, but quickly divorced. Neither had given birth to a child. Both had taught for decades in a private college prep academy favored by the wealthy of the city. Janine taught Spanish and Jazmine history. The sisters lived together in a two-bedroom home in a quiet neighborhood filled with retirees. Janine and Jazmine volunteered at the mission at least twice a week. They each enjoyed seeing and helping the poor women with small children. Janine used her Spanish to help translate the needs of the many Spanish-speaking families, and Jazmine worked in the infant formula ministry. Both sisters were extremely upset at the closing of the mission. And they were disappointed that the paid director of the mission operations and the three other full-time employees had quit over the trustees' order to stop helping families without documents. The employees' protest resignations made it easier for the trustees to recommend closing and selling the mission property.

The next Sunday, the Sunday of the vote on the mission, Janine and Jazmine were walking toward the church sanctuary around 10 a.m. They saw a knot of people outside the side door. Three uniformed and armed private security guards hired by the church were detaining a young girl and a baby there. The girl was dirty, and her clothes were ragged. She was barefoot and her feet were filthy. She was holding tight to her baby, who looked to be not more than six months old. The girl was weeping and pleading with the guards in Spanish to let her and her baby leave. None of the guards or the church members passing by could understand or speak to her.

Janine spoke to the girl in Spanish, while Jazmine questioned the guards. One of the security guards tried to interfere with Janine's conversation with the girl, but Jazmine backed him down with a veteran schoolteacher's look. The head of church security explained that the girl and her baby had been found sleeping in an outside stairwell leading down from the sidewalk to an entrance door to the church basement. They had called city police to come take them away.

"Had any damage been done," asked Jazmine.

"No," replied the guard.

"Then why are you having her arrested? What's going to happen to this baby if mom is put in jail?"

"That's not our call, ma'am."

"Whose call is it?"

"My boss."

"Who's your boss?"

"Mr. Anderson. The board of trustees. They run the property."

The girl told Janine that she was from El Salvador. Her husband, baby, and she had taken buses, trains, and used their feet from El Salvador through Guatemala and Mexico to the US–Mexico border. They had fled El Salvador to escape the gangs, violence, and the poverty in their homeland. One gang had threatened to kill her husband if he didn't help sell their drugs. But if he sold one gang's drugs, he would be a target of the rival gangs. There was no noncriminal work to be found there. So they left for the hope of a better, safer life in the US. They had to pay a "coyote" to get them across the border into Arizona and had made their way here.

"What is your name, young lady?" Janine asked her in Spanish.

"Please don't make me tell you."

"I won't make you do anything you don't want to. Where is the father of your baby?"

"In jail, I think. He got arrested last week for panhandling. He has no papers. Maybe they sent him south to Mexico."

"How old are you, dear?"

"Eighteen."

Janine smiled at the girl. "How old are you really?"

"Sixteen."

"How old is your baby?"

"Thirteen months."

"Boy or girl?"

"Girl."

"What's her name?"

"Maria Esmeralda."

"That's a really pretty name.... She seems small for thirteen months."

"I haven't been able to get enough to eat, and my milk has dried up."

"Where have you been getting food since you have been here?"

"At the mission, but they stopped serving people like us."

"People like us?"

"People without papers."

"*Hija*, why didn't you stay overnight at the homeless shelter?"

"That place is scary. We went there once. But the men there were looking at me and saying things I didn't understand.... I couldn't sleep. The baby kept crying and waking everyone up, and men got angry."

"Do you have family or friends here?"

"No."

"Why did you sleep down here last night?"

"I thought we'd be safer next to the church."

Janine looked down the stairway to the spot outside the basement door where the mother and her baby must have slept. "What did you sleep on? There's no mattress or sleeping bag."

"On the concrete."

"Without any padding?"

"Yes."

"What did your baby sleep on?"

"On me. I lay on my back, and she slept on my chest."

"Aren't you sore from sleeping on concrete?"

"Yes."

"The men in that shelter must have really scared you."

Two city police officers arrived. Church members were streaming by into the church building, slowing down a little to look as if it were a traffic accident on the other side of the highway. The head of church security talked to the police. One officer asked the young mother in Spanish if she had papers. The girl began to cry again. The police radioed for a female officer to come to the scene and had the girl sit on the sidewalk with her baby while they waited. Jazmine asked if they could take the girl and her baby inside while they waited. The head security guard said the trustees had forbidden that.

When the female officer arrived, she tried to take the baby from the mother. The mother screamed and grasped the baby to her chest. The baby cried. The two male officers pulled the mother's arms away from the baby and handcuffed her. The female officer started to walk with the baby to her own patrol car.

Tears were streaming down Janine's and Jazmine's faces. The mother was screaming and wailing and pleading for Janine to take her baby, to keep the police from taking her. Jazmine ran after the woman officer, stepping between her and her police car.

"Step away, ma'am," the officer said to Jazmine.

"What will happen to this child?" Jazmine asked.

"Child Protective Services will try to find a family member."

"What if she has no family here?"

"Then the child will have to go into foster care."

"When will the baby and the mom be reunited?"

"I have no idea. Over my pay grade."

First Step: Matthew 4:18–22

The mother was screaming louder, begging Janine again to take her baby, saying, "She's a good baby," over and over. "*Ella es una buena bebe! Ella es una buena bebe!*"

Janine ran over to the officer. "I'll take the baby. My sister and I will take the baby."

"You related?"

"No. Of course not."

"Then you'll have to apply with CPS to foster her."

"How do we do that?"

"I don't know."

"Where are you taking the baby right now?"

"I can't tell you that. I'm not going to tell you again to step away from me, lady. You are interfering with police operations."

The officer selected from one of many child seats in the trunk of the cruiser, secured the seat, placed the crying baby in the seat and drove away.

Jazmine tried to keep up with the cruiser, yelling, "The baby hasn't eaten. And the mother has been nursing her. What will she be fed?"

The mother was being driven away at the same time, twisting her body in the back seat of the police cruiser to try to see where her baby was being taken.

Sarah and Anne had been watching from the edge of the small collection of church members who had stayed to watch. Anne was crying, dabbing at her eye make-up with her handkerchief. Sarah's face was red with anger.

Sarah stepped out of the crowd to confront the head of church security.

"You didn't have to call the police. You just caused this baby to be separated from its mother. God knows for how long."

"I have to follow orders, ma'am. It isn't up to me. We are ordered to protect this property just like it was any downtown property."

"Protect the property?! From what? Protect from whom? A teen-aged mother and a tiny baby who have nowhere else to go?"

"I'm sorry, ma'am. It didn't seem right to me either. But we have to do what we are ordered."

The guards walked away.

So much time had passed since the sisters had first walked up to the church that the 11 a.m. worship service was about to finish.

The four sisters came together and introduced themselves. The four women were shattered. They stood in silence for a time until Sarah spoke to Janine, asking her to repeat what the mother had said to her in Spanish. Janine told Sarah and Anne that they volunteered at the mission and had seen some young mothers and their children there.

"We admire you so much for what you tried to do," Sarah said to Jazmine and Janine. "Does the mission help lots of women like that? Are there lots of people without documents here?"

Jazmine said, "I think so. I hope so. We just try to help whoever the staff at the door let inside. It is only recently that we heard that the trustees were requiring the mission staff to turn some folks away because they have no papers."

"How many people does the mission help a day?" asked Sarah.

"Between three and four hundred walk-ins, depending upon the weather and the season," said Janine. "The best part of the ministry to me is the free infant formula we provide to mothers. Jazmine works in that ministry."

Jazmine said, "That's free formula for maybe three hundred fifty children a month."

"Where do the mothers come from?"

"All over the city. The mission is on a major bus line."

"Who pays for the formula?"

"Donors. Maybe a few charitable foundations. We get a discount on purchases from a supplier."

"How long have you two volunteered there?" asked Sarah.

"About three years," said Jazmine. "Since we retired."

"Isn't it depressing?"

"Sometimes. It surely can be. But mostly it's a blessing to be able to help. The children are beautiful. All children are beautiful."

It was time for the meeting on the future of the mission to begin.

"I don't think I can sit through this meeting," said Anne.

"I think we need to," said Sarah. "People need to know what just happened. And I'm starting to get pissed at this whole thing."

The four women sat together in the middle of the sanctuary.

Some church members who had passed by the arrest of the mother came up to the sisters to ask what had happened. Sarah spoke for all four.

"The church security guards found a homeless mother and her baby sleeping in an outside stairwell and had them arrested. Police separated the mother and her child."

"What will happen to them?"

"God knows."

The meeting began. Dr. Cotswald opened with a prayer.

Bill Anderson, the head of the trustees and an investment banker who knew Sarah's husband well, read the resolution in its entirety again. Then Dr. Cotswald announced that three people had been selected to speak for and three against the measure for no more than three minutes for each speaker.

A member of the trustees spoke first by reading a column from the local newspaper decrying the number of "homeless, infected, drug addicted, fentanyl carrying, and illegal aliens" who were "infesting our city's downtown streets and bringing drugs into our hometown." The columnist blamed First Kingdom of God Church and its downtown mission building for attracting them. The speaker finished by saying that the church was losing needed donations from large and small donors alike in protest of the mission activities. The church has a two million dollar annual budget and is in grave danger of falling short of its fundraising for the first time since the recession in 2008.

A member of the board of directors for the mission spoke next, reporting the numbers of people who had been served by the mission so far that year—the number of bags of groceries, the number of sack lunches, the number of families given used clothing, the number of babies provided infant formula, the number of counseling sessions and job referrals. "Where will these people go if the mission closes?" she asked.

An angry man stood. "You people have brought this on yourselves! You didn't have to serve the illegals! You could have screened them out and kept doing what you have always done! All you had to do was demand that everyone show a driver's license before they got anything! You have put this church in a position of aiding and abetting law breaking! If this resolution doesn't pass, my wife and I are leaving this church and never looking back. And we've been members here for more than forty years."

A volunteer stood and yelled.

"And if it does pass, me and dozens of others who have been volunteering at the mission for years are leaving."

"And good riddance!" the first angry man yelled. "I say we take the vote right now. We've talked enough." Cries of agreement came from some in the crowd.

The senior pastor stood.

"Let's have peace, please. Peace . . . Peace." He waited. "Peace. Now, Ralph. Let's not jump the gun. We are going to do this according to the Book of Governance. It will only be a few more moments before we vote. Then we will take a vote. This church has survived controversy in the past. With God's help it will survive this one. Let's get this meeting back on track."

Another member of the trustees gave details of the improvements needed on the church buildings and the sanctuary organ, and the money that could be realized from sale of the mission property and surrounding parking lot.

A mission volunteer then told a story of a poor family that had been helped by the mission ministries. "Where will families like that one go if the mission closes?" The speaker pointed out that the cost of the mission's ministries, paid staff, and building upkeep constituted less than 3 percent of the church's annual budget because so much of the goods provided were funded by grants.

Then the chair of the security subcommittee of the board of trustees reported the number of vandalisms and break-ins in the main church building in the last year compared with previous years. He said that most of the increase is attributable to the increase of illegal aliens who have made their way here from the border and who are attracted to the food given out by our mission. "Just this morning," said the speaker, "our security stopped a woman from breaking into the church to steal God knows what."

Sarah stood bolt upright. She raised and waived her hand.

"Pastor! Pastor!"

"Yes?"

"That statement is . . . incorrect. That woman is a teenaged mother with a tiny baby. She didn't try to break in. She and the baby were sleeping in the stairwell to be safe from predators in the streets. And because the trustees have instructed our security guards to call the police, that young mother was arrested and separated from her baby. She came to the church for safety, and instead we had her arrested."

"And she is illegal," said the speaker. "She shouldn't be here anyway. That's on her. We can't let people sleep on our church property. She had defecated in the stairwell."

"*If* it was her, and we don't know that, it was probably because she had no toilet to use."

The senior pastor interrupted.

"Ma'am. Thank you for that clarification. But it's getting late and we have some older people in need of lunch here. So let's move on toward the vote. We now have our last speaker in opposition to the recommendation."

An elderly lady stood in her place in the congregation. She took a Bible from the pew rack in front of her and opened it. She looked to her right and her left. Six more members then stood up with Bibles in hand.

"Pastor, you said earlier that we needed to do this according to the Book of Governance," said the first woman. "We think we need to do this according to this book," holding up the Bible.

All seven standing members began to read in unison from Matt 25:31–46.

> When the Son of Man comes in his glory, and all the angels with him, then he will sit on the throne of his glory. All the nations will be gathered before him, and he will separate people one from another as a shepherd separates the sheep from the goats, and he will put the sheep at his right hand and the goats at the left. Then the king will say to those at his right hand, "Come, you that are blessed by my Father, inherit the kingdom prepared for you from the foundation of the world; for I was hungry and you gave me food, I was thirsty and you gave me something to drink, I was a stranger and you welcomed me, I was naked and you gave me clothing, I was sick and you took care of me, I was in prison and you visited me." Then the righteous will answer him, "Lord, when was it that we saw you hungry and gave you food, or thirsty and gave you something to drink? And when was it that we saw you a stranger and welcomed you, or naked and gave you clothing? And when was it that we saw you sick or in prison and visited you?" And the king will answer them, "Truly I tell you, just as you did it to one of the least of these who are members of my family, you did it to me." Then he will say to those at his left hand, "You that are accursed, depart from me into the eternal fire prepared for the devil and his angels; for I was hungry and you gave me no food, I was thirsty and you gave me nothing to drink, I was a stranger and you did not welcome me, naked and you did not give me clothing, sick and in prison and you did not visit me." Then they also will answer, "Lord, when was it that we saw you hungry or thirsty or a stranger or naked or sick or in prison, and did not take care of you?" Then he will answer them, "Truly I tell you, just as you did not do it to one of the least of these, you did not do it to me." And these will go away into eternal punishment, but the righteous into eternal life.

When they read the verse "Truly I tell you, just as you did not do it to one of the least of these, you did not do it to me," they raised their voices to a cry. When they had read the scripture through once, they started over again without a pause. And then again. It became evident that the readers intended to continue reading to stop the vote. Still more members of the congregation stood spontaneously, took out their pew Bibles, and read the passage with them. Sarah, Jazmine, and Janine stood and joined in the reading . . . after they were able to find the right Gospel, chapter, and verses. Anne sat quietly trembling in her pew.

Angry voices tried to interrupt, calling the readers to sit down and for the senior pastor and the head of trustees to regain control over the meeting. Members rose and walked out. Soon, a quarter of those originally there had left.

The senior pastor and the trustees gathered in the front of the sanctuary as the reading continued. The pastor approached the woman who started the reading and spoke quietly to her. She stopped reading and waved to her fellow readers. The reading slowly ceased.

"Brothers and sisters, under these circumstances, the board of trustees has voted to withdraw their recommendation . . . for now."

The woman replied, "We want to vote now."

The head of trustees responded that the resolution is withdrawn for now. "There is nothing to vote on."

Another man stood. "So the mission operations continue? At least for now? There are so many poor families and homeless still in need. We have volunteers who still want to help."

The head of trustees said that the mission professional staff has resigned. The director has already taken another job in another town. "There is no one to run operations at the mission to keep it open," said Anderson.

"There must be someone who can run it until all this is sorted out?" said the woman.

"But who?" asked the senior pastor. "It's a huge, demanding job. There is no one who can handle the funding and purchases and manage the volunteers. They'd have to be able to speak Spanish, and solicit donations, and keep track of supplies and deal with all those needy people. It wouldn't be fair to ask that of a nonprofessional. We can't afford to pay anyone to do all that now. We can't ask anyone to drop what they are doing and take this on. They wouldn't know what they were getting themselves into. Again, we couldn't pay them anything."

Sarah and Anne immediately looked at one another. Jazmine and Janine saw what was in their eyes and nodded at one another. Sarah quickly stood and slid in front of the people sitting in her pew to the center aisle. She looked back at the other three women. Anne stood, and then Jazmine and Janine. They joined Sarah in the aisle. All four walked together to the front of the sanctuary where the senior pastor was standing.

"We'll do it," said Sarah. "Together, we have most of those skills."

Anne up looked at the words etched in the stained glass window over the choir loft: "*O ye of little faith, why did you doubt?*"

SECOND STEP

Matthew 4:23–25

²³ Jesus went throughout Galilee, teaching in their synagogues and proclaiming the good news of the kingdom and curing every disease and every sickness among the people. ²⁴ So his fame spread throughout all Syria, and they brought to him all the sick, those who were afflicted with various diseases and pains, demoniacs, epileptics, and paralytics, and he cured them. ²⁵ And great crowds followed him from Galilee, the Decapolis, Jerusalem, Judea, and from beyond the Jordan.

What did the four fishermen believe they were following Jesus to do? What did they think it meant to "fish for people"? The Scripture doesn't tell us. All the narrative reveals is that Jesus was demanding repentance and proclaiming that the Kingdom of heaven had "come near" before he called the men and they responded "immediately." The narrative discloses no description by Jesus of the arriving Kingdom before the call of these four. We do not find out anything about the brothers' expectations and ambitions until later in the story (Matt 16:21–28; 17:22–23; 20:20–23). Would they have left their boats and followed Jesus if they had known what the Way was to demand of them?

As I fill in the gaps in their story, and you should do the same for yourself, the four men took the first step of discipleship by responding enthusiastically and optimistically to the call to be an important part of Jesus' Kingdom. They believed they were going to be his right-hand men within the orbit of his power and importance. They were to receive his honor vicariously. But Jesus quickly showed these men about the demands of their roles in the Kingdom of Mercy. They were not to become the right- and left-hand men in the inner circle of any kingdom they had ever conceived. Their status was not to be enhanced because of their proximity and access to a new ruler. They were not to live in comfort and power in a palace or a safe sanctuary, screening supplicants and dignitaries to the presence of the king. Jesus was not to become like any king they had ever imagined. They quickly were exposed to the mission of the One they had been called to follow. They learned soon after leaving their fishing nets and boats that they had not been chosen to raise themselves above the crowd's "suffering." Instead, they had been called to go with Jesus into the "darkness" in the "region of the shadow of death" (Matt 4:16) by immersing themselves in the suffering.

At the outset of this discussion, I need to emphasize, and I mean *emphasize*, that ministering to and living with the suffering poor and outcast was and is central to discipleship in Jesus' Kingdom of Mercy. I expand on this step by step in this book. But many liberal Christians want to downplay the stories of Jesus' healing of the sick, blind, deaf, mute, maimed, crippled, leprous, and possessed as anachronistic myth or symbolic metaphor. To them, these healings are symbolic signs of Jesus' status as Son of God rather than signposts on our own Way of discipleship. They want to focus instead on God as our divine friend who wants us to feel fulfilled in our material comfort. And many fundamentalist Christians want to downplay these stories of what Jesus did for the poor, the suffering, and the outcast to emphasize instead believing the correct things about Jesus and casting judgments on false belief and sinful sexual practices. But the call to discipleship of Matthew's Jesus was above all a singular and *repeated* call to touch and be touched by the wretched of the earth, and to be immersed mercifully in their suffering (Matt 4:23–25; 8:1–4, 14–17, 28–34; 9:2–8, 18–26, 27–31, 32–33, 35–36; 10:5–8; 11:2–6; 12:9–14; 14:13–21, 34–36; 15:29–38; 17:14–18; 20:29–34; 25:31–46). *We of course need to take Jesus at his word. But we need to take Jesus at his actions even more.*

The fishermen must have been shocked at what they saw and experienced as described in Matt 4:23–25. We do not know how much these four men had been previously exposed to desperate people suffering from sickness, disease, pain, demonic possession, epilepsy, and paralysis (Matt 4:24). But we may be sure that they had never been exposed to these numbers of sufferers. Every sufferer had their own story of despair and pain. Every sufferer had their own face and voice of pain. These four fishermen could surely see and hear the pain, exhaustion, and hopelessness in their faces and voices.

Jesus and the four men traveled "throughout Galilee." Word went out about Jesus' power to "cure" terrible suffering. It is unsurprising that his "fame spread," and that "all" the sick, disabled, and mentally ill people were brought to him by family and friends from all of Galilee, from Jerusalem in Judea, and from lands east of the Sea of Galilee and the Jordan, including the ten gentile cities of the Decapolis. The verses describe people without hope of cure who suddenly had heard a rumor of hope. Given the time it must have taken for these disabled and sick people to be brought to Jesus from so far away, the period of Jesus' ministry described in Matt 4:23–25 had to have lasted many weeks.

We may also be sure that the desperate demands of these suffering people did not allow Jesus and these four men to rest. The empowering spirit of God was clearly with Jesus, but Jesus, Andrew, Simon, James, and John must still have been overwhelmed by trying to manage the crush of these frantic, miserable people and their advocates hour by hour and day by day. I picture the brothers having a thankless and almost impossible task of creating a buffer around Jesus, and of prioritizing and organizing people whose pain and need would not be managed. As some were cured, their cries and tears of joy must have burst forth, causing waiting people still sick and disabled to become more frantic and to push harder to reach Jesus, threatening to trample others in their paths. And as some of the cured left, more and more sick and disabled people were arriving. It must have felt like trying to hold back the ocean tide. Stress and fatigue must have overcome the awe of the four fishermen at the cures Jesus was working.

There must have been another element in this experience. We will confront this if we truly give ourselves to this narrative. Surely none of these four fishermen or the crowd had ever witnessed a power like Jesus' to cure illness and suffering. Their initial reaction must have included relief, wonder, and sheer joy. But for some it must also have included fear. They must have sensed they were in the presence of the numinous—of a power that was wholly other and beyond comprehension. Perhaps it was like the experience a truly devout Jew could have in the Temple in proximity to the Holy of holies where the glory of YHWH dwelled. Perhaps there were Jews in the crowd who were familiar with the descriptions in

Hebrew scripture of dangerous human encounters with the numinous (Exod 3:5–6; 20:18–19; Isa 6:1–8; and Ezek 1:28c). Matthew later expands on the numinous presence with and in Jesus in the story of the transfiguration (17:1–8). Perhaps some in the crowd were so frightened of Jesus and his power that they fled. An example of such a reaction is when Jesus was "begged" by scared townspeople "to leave their neighborhood" after he had cured a demoniac (Matt 8:34).

Some of us have had experiences of the numinous. Perhaps in awe-inspiring places in nature that seem saturated with the holy power of our creator God. Perhaps in a vision that seemed eerily real during a period of meditation. Perhaps in a dream. Perhaps in an experience of the presence of one who has died. Perhaps in a place or during a service of worship. Perhaps in an unexpected cure that could not be adequately explained by the doctor. Perhaps when two angry, hurt people surprisingly reconcile and embrace. Perhaps when you looked for the first time at your newborn. Perhaps in the presence of someone of great charisma of the type that was present in Jesus. Surely none of our contemporary experiences of the numinous could compare to what the fishermen and the crowd were experiencing in the presence and power of Jesus. Perhaps the four fishermen endured the burden of ministering with Jesus to the suffering masses because of their awe at his power.

A few years ago, I was fortunate to accompany a medical mission team of physicians and nurses to Zambia in Africa to treat people who had almost no access to health care. We started the mission in the capital city of Lusaka in a shanty town or *komboni* called the Misisi, a closed area of about 10,000 people. The overwhelming majority of people who lived in the Misisi were children orphaned by AIDS. Some of these children were suffering themselves in the last stages of the virus. We drove into the slum in old yellow school buses. As we entered the *komboni* and neared the stone-block Anglican church where we would set up our free clinic, scores of beautiful but emaciated African children ran alongside our bus, laughing, calling to us, tumbling over one another, and reaching up through the open bus windows to touch us. When we arrived at the church, we saw dozens of children lying on the packed dirt of the plaza in front of the church, some on pallets and some on the bare dirt, too ill to rise. All of us had been told what to expect when we arrived, and many of us were veterans of medical missions to poor folk in Africa and Haiti. But the sight of all these beautiful, suffering children caused many of us to remain weeping in the buses until we could compose ourselves and set up the clinic.

During our days there, each of us on the team were given the chance to ladle a hot, fortified, thick cream of wheat into the bowls of hundreds of children, the only meal most of them would receive that day. As we did so, each of the children made a point of touching our hands in gratitude. When my turn came to ladle out the meal and as the children touched my hands, I was overwhelmed with an experience of the numinous far deeper than the joy in being able to help. I sensed a glow surrounding the children and myself. That is the only way I can describe it.

But this mysterious sense of the numinous is rarely present in the courageous Way of discipleship in Jesus' Kingdom of Mercy. I doubt that the four fishermen felt it during much of their times immersed in the suffering of the crowd, even in their proximity to Jesus. Discipleship rarely comes with this kind of high.

For instance, at the end of our days in Lusaka and in the village of Choma in southcentral Zambia, we set up our clinic in a ramshackle community center in Livingstone, a few kilometers north of the Zambezi River. It was our last day of the mission. We were tired, some of us were ill, and, worse, we were running out of medicines. The center had an elevated porch that ran the length of the rectangular building, and the tables with the medicine staffed by two of our nurses were on that porch. There was a huge crowd of people, mostly adults, waiting in the yard below the porch. When it became clear to us that we were close to running out of medicines, two of us with the team walked through the crowd of people, selecting the sickest ones to jump the line to be treated before we had to shut down. People realized what we were doing and became desperate and angry. A few charged into the center, surrounding the doctors and nurses in the treatment area. Our greatest fear in the melee was that desperate people would scoop medicines from the tables on the porch, run away, and ingest them later without instructions. We finally got control of the situation by singling out the three men who had been the loudest in complaining about the prospect of being left out of treatment. We put them in charge of calming things down. We didn't experience the numinous in that situation. Most discipleship in the Kingdom of Mercy is hard and discouraging. We are mistaken if we believe we will often sense the numinous in the midst of the suffering.

As the three weeks of the mission wore on, a number of the team had crying breakdowns. All of us suffered some periods close to despair.

Almost all of us had to take a day of rest. The number of sick, infected, and disabled people in need and pain, people whom we couldn't cure, broke us down. It was rare that we could actually heal anybody. The most useful treatments we provided were the anti-worming pills for the children and antibiotics for people with infections. Sick people in pain are stressed and not at their best. There were multiple incidents daily of patients in need being angry, selfish, demanding, ungrateful, and verbally abusive. These were a tiny percentage of the total people we treated, but it was hurtful. No sense of the numinous in that either.

In the Methodist Justice Ministry where I have worked since 2006, we receive twenty-five to thirty requests each week for legal, counseling, and financial help from indigent women, relatives, and friends to help them protect and provide for abused children. The numbers of abused children needing our help over more than eighteen years have been overwhelming. Most often the persons making the requests are grateful and focused on the children. But some are angry, insulting, and entitled. And the behavior of the abusers is terrible. And the impact of the abuse on the children, which is often sexual, is worse than terrible. The sheer number of cases have been overwhelming at times. We have hired lawyers over the eighteen-plus years of our ministry who have left us quickly because the emotional pain was too much for them. It's courageous, hard work even as we believe we are on the Way of Jesus. Never have we had an experience of the numinous in this work. But we have believed we were on the Way of the Kingdom of Mercy.

During Jesus' teaching, proclaiming, and healing time in Galilee described in Matt 4:23–25, Andrew, Peter, James, and John must have gone through something like what we in the justice ministry and on the mission to Zambia went through, but with more intensity. That flood of people in Galilee needed to be directed, ordered, comforted, and fed. It couldn't just have been a free for all, people rushing helter-skelter at Jesus and demanding his touch. And there must have been some people not at their best who were angry, selfish, demanding, ungrateful, and abusive. Their sheer numbers alone must have been daunting. To stay within the parameters of Matthew's story, it surely must have been wonderfully energizing that Jesus was able to cure them. But the weight on the brothers must have been more than they could bear at times.

I ask again that you give yourself to this narrative in which Jesus is endowed with extraordinary power. Did any of the brothers wonder why Jesus was obsessed with the pain of the crowd, and didn't use his power for his and the brothers' benefit? Did any of them consider slipping away to return to their families and their fish to get away from the suffering? Did any think they had followed Jesus long enough? Did any wonder why God allowed this much pain, disease, paralysis, epilepsy, and possession to continue when God had the power to cure all these through Jesus? For all the good that Jesus was doing, did any of the fishermen wonder at the power and goodness of God, who had allowed so much suffering to continue for so long before the coming of this anointed One? At the God who continued to allow the suffering for the millions who had not heard of Jesus and had not been able to reach his touch?

And did any of the four brothers wonder if this Kingdom which Jesus taught and proclaimed would include fulfilling the description of the coming Kingdom of God in Isa 9:4–5 and 11:6–9 by disarming the military? Since Jesus had the power to cure demonic possession, why not the power to "cure" Israel of its possession by the demonic Roman army of occupation? Is this what the four fishermen were hoping for when they left everything to follow Jesus?

Jesus originally called the two sets of brothers to follow him. They had done so, although probably not to what and whom they expected. The crowd is also described in Matt 4:25 to have followed Jesus. We may be certain that there were many members of this crowd who were there selflessly, bringing to Jesus helpless family members or friends from far away. Were the fishermen any different than those crowds who followed him? Did the brothers wonder if there was any benefit or blessing for them because they followed when they were not in need of physical cure? Were they with Jesus because they wished for a personal blessing, much as the crowd did?

Matthew's narrative does not separate Jesus' teachings, proclaiming the good news of the Kingdom, and his merciful acts for those in desperate need. In fact, the narrative emphasizes teaching and proclaiming the arrival of the Kingdom *through* Jesus' many merciful acts. Bearing the Kingdom of Mercy necessarily includes all three. Matthew's Jesus does indeed call the disciples of the Kingdom of Mercy, *then and now*, to the Way of teaching, proclaiming the good news and, *most of all*, acting out that good news by acts of mercy to the suffering. This is the discipleship of Matthew's Jesus.

The Second Step in the Way of the disciple is to be blessed to follow Jesus on his mission to minister to those who suffer.

Second Step: Matthew 4:23–25

***

The afternoon of the Sunday meeting when Sarah, Anne, Janine, and Jazmine stepped forward to offer to keep the mission operating until the trustees and the church could decide the mission's future, the four women met with some veteran mission volunteers about what was needed. After the excitement and drama of stepping forward before the congregation to offer to run the mission, all four of the sisters were having doubts about what they had taken on. Anne in particular was feeling panic.

"What have we gotten ourselves into?" Anne whispered to Sarah. "Is it too late to back out? How could we know how much this was going to require of us? What will your husband and my husband say?"

As Anne was worrying, Sarah was listening to the veteran volunteers and making a list of what needed to be done to keep the mission running. The volunteers were all elderly and retired. Many had chronic health issues and family plans that would render their participation intermittent. None of them had the energy to help the sisters, other than to volunteer as they could and to provide collective information about how the mission operated. The former paid staff members were gone and not coming back.

Janine and Jazmine were familiar with how the infant formula and used clothing bank operated, but no one at the meeting of volunteers had an overall grasp of what it would take to keep all the programs of the mission running—what were the sources of the infant formula, the food for the grocery bags and the sack lunches, and the used clothing? How would all these be paid and accounted for, delivered to the mission, organized and sorted for storage and distribution? Who would do all this? How would eligibility of the recipients be determined? What records must be kept and how and where? Who were the veteran volunteers and how were they to be contacted and organized? Would the volunteers be able to come on the days needed? What were the stations and roles of the volunteers? What and when did utility bills need to be paid? What accounting had to be done to any foundations that provided grants? Heck, who had the keys to the mission building?

Janine and Jazmine agreed to recruit, manage, and assign the volunteers to various tasks. Sarah and Anne were the only ones with any experience running a business, but Anne acted as if she was looking for the door. Sarah realized that the overall management was on her alone. She had made a public commitment, and she had to live up to it. The experience with the young mother and the baby that morning was the motivation she required. And the reading of Matt 25 in the meeting still moved her. "Truly I tell you, just as you did not do it to one of the least of these, you did not do it to me" echoed in her mind.

Sarah learned that the mission was open for its clients from 10 a.m. to 2 p.m. on Monday, Tuesday, and Thursday of every week. On those days, mothers with nursing age children were given a week's supply of free infant formula. One large bag of grocery staples, including milk, was handed out to all who could prove with rent or utility bills that they had a residence where they could keep and prepare the food. Up-to-date records had to be kept of who received the formula and the groceries. The used clothing bank was open, and people were allowed into that separate room to rummage through the clothes. Free sack lunches of sandwiches, chips, fruit, and bottled water were given to all who appeared, mostly the downtown homeless who lived and slept on the streets or under bridges. Toilets, showers, and washers and dryers were made available. People with children who could prove that their water or electric were about to be cut off because of no or low income could receive temporary monetary help. Some people asked for a prayer partner, and would be accompanied by a church volunteer into the mission's small chapel. Some clients wanted help trying to locate and contact relatives in another city. Some needed a bus pass to get to a job opportunity in the city or bus fare to return to a distant family home. Some needed an address where their mail could be sent and that they could put on a job application. Some wanted information about night shelters or a government program that might help them. Some needed immediate transportation to a clinic. Some just needed a friend to treat them like a child of God and give them a good listening. Many just needed to get out of the weather.

The mission needed to be cleaned after each day of operation. Groceries, lunch bag supplies, clothing, and infant formula needed to be received, restocked, and accounted for. The grocery and lunch bags had to be prepared.

Sarah was staggered by the requirements of the operation. She was able to have a brief phone conversation with the old mission director who was now working for a nonprofit in a distant city. But she was still feeling her way in the dark. The organization of the mission operations was going to be a seven-day-a-week job for her. She already had a commitment to help with her dad's dry cleaning business. She arrived at the mission at 7 a.m. or earlier on Wednesdays, Fridays, and Saturdays, worked until

3 p.m. and then went to her father's business to account for employee hours, do payroll, and manage the ordering and receipt of supplies of dry cleaning fluid, hangers, and plastic wrap. On the days the mission was open to its clients, she arrived at 7 a.m. and stayed all day, even helping to sweep the floors and clean the bathrooms before heading home exhausted. Sarah hadn't cleaned her own house for years. But she was cleaning the mission, sometimes by herself, three days a week.

What indeed had she gotten herself into when she answered the call and walked down to the front of the sanctuary!

Anne, Janine, and Jazmine came to the mission only when it was serving people. Janine was the only volunteer who spoke Spanish, although her Spanish was Castilian, a bit different than the dialect of many of the clients whose families hailed from Mexico or Central America. So Janine spent her hours in the mission hustling from station to station, translating and finding bilingual clients who could help. Anne and Jazmine stood at the door and tried to let clients in a few at a time, explaining to first timers what services were available and where in the building the services could be found, asking Janine for help with Spanish speakers. People waiting outside at the door often tried to cut in line and push their way inside, saying they needed to use the toilet. Mothers with children often begged to get inside immediately, afraid of others in line. Once inside, many people refused to leave even after they had been served. Anne was far too small and soft spoken to be effective at persuading people to go here or there. Having been a school teacher, Jazmine was marginally better at getting people to mind her. As every mission day wore on, the interior was packed with far more people than the fire department's occupancy limit permitted.

Every day the mission served the neediest and toughest of crowds. Some were among the working poor who just did not make enough money, or who were in a temporary crisis and could not make ends meet. The majority of the crowd was homeless for as many reasons as there were individuals. Some suffered from untreated mental illness, or had just been released from jail and had no family who would take them in, or were addicted to drugs or alcohol, or were victims of family violence and were living in their cars or on the street to escape their abusers, or were undocumented refugees, or had been injured and lost their jobs and their apartments. Almost half the homeless were periodically employed, but could not make enough to afford an apartment.

The people served by the mission, as many as four hundred each day, were mostly ragged and unwashed. They were tired, scared, anxious, crying, and angry—sometimes all emotions at once. There were children whose appearance and circumstance were heartbreaking and alarming. There were adults who clearly needed urgent medical attention, but who ran away if an ambulance was called because they were afraid they would be arrested on an outstanding warrant for trespassing or petty theft, or civilly committed for mental illness. Life was dangerous on the street, and arguments and fights broke out almost daily outside and inside the mission. Many had learned to lie as a survival skill. Almost everyone had a story to tell to try to get more than their allotted share of what the mission had to give.

Weeks of these operations went by without the church trustees reaching a consensus on keeping or closing the mission. The trustees were counting on the failure of Sarah, Anne, Janine, Jazmine, and the volunteers to keep the mission running. When, not if, they failed, the decision to close would be easier. The trustee leadership even instructed the church security force not to help maintain order at the mission, as they had done before the paid director and staff resigned.

As the operations continued, Sarah was close to exhaustion from the hours and pressure of the work and the worry that she didn't know what she didn't know. Sarah and Anne had never before been exposed to so many people suffering with these needs and problems. Anne felt increasingly scared and depressed when she was there. She was reporting everything she saw and experienced to her husband, who insisted that she quit. Anne's husband repeated to his brother, Sarah's husband, what Anne was telling him. Sarah's husband kept criticizing "those people" to Sarah, blaming them for their own poverty. He tried to order Sarah to quit as well, only to be angrily cut off by her.

Janine and Jazmine had volunteered at the mission before, but had each worked at only one mission station, and had never before been exposed to the numbers and the depth of suffering and need of the clients. Jazmine was beginning to have health issues related to her emotional exhaustion. All four women were having trouble sleeping, unable to put the images of some of the clients out of their minds. Sarah and Janine talked about whether the mission's services were accomplishing any more than putting a Band-Aid on the chronic wounds of the people in need. So what was the point of all this sacrifice and anguish?

Third Step

Matthew 5:1

[1] When Jesus saw the crowds, he went up the mountain; and after he sat down, his disciples came to him.

This is the very first use in Matthew of the word "disciple"! Andrew, Simon, James, and John were not called "disciples" when they immediately left their old lives and first followed Jesus. They were not called disciples even when they joined with Jesus in proclaiming and acting out the arriving Kingdom of Mercy in ministering to the suffering crowd. And the crowds are not called disciples when they also "followed" Jesus (Matt 4:25). Here these four men are for the first time called disciples, but only after they had left their boats, witnessed the miseries of the "crowd," experienced the hardship and selflessness of Jesus' ministry to the suffering, and *resisted the temptation to abandon the Way to return home.*

But why are not the members of the suffering crowd, and the friends and family who were helping them reach Jesus, also called "disciples" in this narrative? As will be seen throughout the book, the discipleship described by the Jesus of Matthew's Gospel involves repentance of mind, heart, and life by leaving the disciple's "boat" to follow Jesus into the world of the suffering poor and outcast. The typical disciple described in this Gospel's narrative is called to leave a life of some comfort and means, like the fishermen with their boats and nets (Matt 4:18–22), and the tax collector with his tax booth (Matt 9:9), and the rich young man who refuses Jesus' call (Matt 19:16–22). But the poor and the outcast have no boats. They are already drowning in their suffering. They would gladly leave their old lives behind. But they cannot leave because of their disabling conditions, the relentless struggle to provide basic necessities for themselves and all who depend upon them, and the lack of welcome offered them into a more comfortable world. In my experience, many of the poor and the outcast exhibit all the blessings of discipleship described in these Beatitudes below: broken hearts and crushed spirits because of their pain; mourning for the suffering of others and the evil in the world; enduring trust in God despite the suffering; righteousness; mercifulness; awareness of God's presence in and with the suffering; peacemaking; and persecution. I have consistently seen much greater sacrificial behavior among the economically poor than I have ever seen among the comfortable. For instance, we in the justice ministry have helped hundreds of grandparents and great-grandparents obtain legal custody of their grandchildren and great-grandchildren to protect them from drug addiction, violence, and abuse in a parent's home. We have even helped neighbors unrelated by blood obtain custody of children to protect and provide for them. All of our clients are economically poor or they wouldn't be eligible for our *pro bono* services. By taking the responsibility to provide for these vulnerable children in their homes, these grandparents, great-grandparents, and neighbors make themselves even poorer materially than they already are. Yet they do so without hesitation, almost always out of their faith in Jesus as well as their love and empathy for the children. These blessed people are the greatest disciples of the Kingdom of Mercy I have encountered. But their discipleship is different than the discipleship described in Matthew. Their discipleship takes place in the suffering world they already inhabit, not one they enter from another, comfortable world.

Instead of slipping away, like the rich young man slipped away in Matt 19:22, these fishermen still "came to him" by climbing up the mountain after him (Matt 5:1). With Jesus they looked out over the suffering crowd. In *staying with Jesus* after experiencing and sharing the hardships of his mission, they *became* disciples of Matthew's narrative. The Way of the discipleship is not just responding initially and enthusiastically to Jesus' call to join him in the Kingdom of Mercy. It is not just leaving old lives and taking the First Step of following him into a new life of sacrificial mercy. Discipleship is *continuing* on the Way after first encountering the hardships of sacrificial and selfless mercy and the pain of others. Each Step in discipleship thereafter involves enduring on the Way despite hardship, fatigue, and doubt.

I am proposing that "disciple" is not so much a noun as a verb. Discipleship is not so much what we are as it is what we continue to do. We are not so much disciples, as we are "discipling." Once we stop following Jesus into the darkness of the suffering, we cease being disciples because we have ceased "discipling." You may argue with this, but I humbly submit that then you are arguing with Matthew's Jesus.

After their initial exposure to discipling, these men must have been tempted to leave Jesus and return to the comfort of their old routines. They could have justified to themselves and to family and friends that they had done their share. How many people over the Christian centuries have answered the call to serve Jesus and the needy only to abandon their commitment when it proved to be too long, too hard, and too different than they hoped? How many have taken the first two Steps on the Way of discipleship only to turn back when discipling proved too demanding and selfless?

This Third Step on the Way will not be taken unless God blesses the potential disciple with a deep empathy that will not allow them to leave the Way at this early stage. Many people who are first exposed to mass suffering have an existential repulsion. They are so shocked to see the terrible plight of so many people that they have doubts about the fundamental goodness of life and of life's Creator. Rather than wrestle with this shock and doubt, many blame the sufferers for their own plights and leave the Way. Or they simply decide to again put the sufferers out of mind and sight.

Many lay volunteers in church ministries today are in it primarily to feel good about themselves, but fall away when they find that it is about selfless service to the other in need. I have a friend who retired from the practice of law and decided to volunteer in his church's Room in the Inn. This is a ministry in which churches set up bedding and provide food in their buildings for their homeless neighbors one night a week. My friend was asked to help set up pallets for women and children who were escaping family violence so they could sleep on the floor of his church's gymnasium until housing could be found for them. And he was asked occasionally to spend the night on a pallet in the gym with them to look out for their needs. He quit the ministry after a few overnights because he found he was too anonymous and too uncomfortable relating to people in such need. He was disturbed by their obvious pain. He took the first two Steps on the discipleship Way but then turned aside. In my experience this is a very common occurrence.

Jesus addressed this phenomenon in his parable of the sower at Matt 13:

> ³ Listen! A sower went out to sow. ⁴ And as he sowed, some seeds fell on the path, and the birds came and ate them up. ⁵ Other seeds fell on rocky ground, where they did not have much soil, and they sprang up quickly, since they had no depth of soil. ⁶ But when the sun rose, they were scorched; and since they had no root, they withered away. ⁷ Other seeds fell among thorns, and the thorns grew up and choked them. ⁸ Other seeds fell on good soil and brought forth grain, some a hundred fold, some sixty, some thirty.

Within Matthew's narrative, this parable is about the call to discipleship. The sower is Jesus and the seed is his call to follow him. The first people called do not respond at all. The seed does not germinate because of how deeply they are attached to their present lives and their fears of responding to the call (Matt 13:4). Two other sets of seeds sprout, but then wither or are choked (Matt 13:5–7). These are people who take the First Steps of following, but then leave the Way of discipleship because their commitment was shallow (v. 6) or because the hardships of discipleship ("thorns," v. 7) are too great.

It was only after his potential disciples, Andrew, Simon, James, and John had been initiated into his ministry that they were ready to be taught the truths of the Sermon on the Mount. In this sermon and in the remainder of Matthew, they were shown by Jesus repeatedly that discipleship requires "following" Jesus' teachings, his example of merciful service to the poor and his own suffering (Matt 5:10–12; 16:24–25; 19:21, 27). Discipleship in Matthew is not spreading words of doctrine and belief about Jesus. It is "making disciples" of others by "teaching [them] . . . to obey everything [Jesus] has commanded" by word and deed (Matt 28:19–20).

What Matthew's Jesus is telling us is that God will make the Kingdom of Mercy come, now and whenever the final culmination will be, by using a relatively small number of people who faithfully incarnate Jesus. Jesus teaches that God will make those few mustard seeds grow throughout the huge field (Matt 13:31–32) and this small bit of leaven fill the large loaf (Matt 13:33). In these two parables, mustard doesn't become the entire field, pushing all the other plants out, and leaven doesn't constitute the entire loaf.

Experience shows that only some follow Jesus into his mission of rescuing the suffering from their darkness. Only a few sustain that following for a significant period of their lives. And what this book attempts to be about are the Steps in *that* discipleship of following Jesus into that darkness. Those who are called to discipleship and want to follow the call must leave behind their boats, their settled ways, their gated communities (if they live in one), their comfortable circle of friends, their private clubs or gatherings (if they have them), their growing collection of possessions, and their insulated, isolated churches. The hurting *are* all around us. *And churches need to quit proclaiming that it is easy for members to be disciples while remaining in their boats.*

This is not a gradation of superior Christians from the inferior crowd, which could be inferred by some from Matt 5:1 ("Jesus saw the crowds . . . his disciples came to him"). This is definitely not a distinction between professional religious and lay people. Surely there were those in the crowd in Matt 4:23–25 who were courageous and who were caring mercifully for the suffering. There were those whose responsibilities to family and community prevented them from leaving their "boats" longer than this episode in their lives of bringing their suffering relative or friend to Jesus. These were "discipling" during this labor of mercy and love. But not everyone is "picked" to be a disciple within the sense of Matthew's narrative. That does not mean that they have no place in the Kingdom of Mercy. Indeed, the Kingdom is for everyone's benefit. Jesus proclaimed that God the Father loves the people whom his disciples are called to suffer for and with—and everyone else (Matt 5:45).

What if the Kingdom will only come through God's use of a small number of mustard seeds and small amount of leaven? Isn't that the most that can realistically be hoped? Not everyone *can* leave their boat. Many must care for their families and many have to catch the fish. Some have to grow the grain, fix the refrigerators, maintain the roads, run the financial markets, found and lead businesses that employ people and provide needed goods and services, administer the government, even collect taxes like Matthew in his former life. Some of us can respond to Jesus' call at some stage of our lives but not at others. How can a poor, single, working mother, a working class father, a grandmother with custody of her grandchildren, middle-class parents saving to put their children through college—how can any of these leave their boat without regard for whom and what they leave behind? Only a few get called, and they get called at particular times in their lives.

There is of course a loud note in the melody of Jesus' teachings in Matthew that the Kingdom is already arrived and growing, even in the midst of the strong opposition of the kingdoms of the world. The salt of the Kingdom of Mercy is already in the earth (Matt 5:13). The lights of the Kingdom's mercy are already shining in the darkness (Matt 5:14–16). Seeds of the Kingdom are already planted and growing (Matt 13:1–9, 31–32). The leaven of the Kingdom is already in the flour (Matt 13:33). Some fruits of the mercy of the Kingdom tree are already ripe (Matt 7:17; 12:33). The Kingdom of Mercy's foundation of rock is already underfoot, if only we would build upon it (Matt 7:24–27).

But there are just not yet enough salt, light, growing seeds, leavened and rising loaves, ripe fruits, and houses on sound foundations. There aren't enough disciples on the Way of the Kingdom of Mercy. There are too many disciples of the kingdoms of the world. With the Psalmists we ask, "O Lord—how long?" until the Kingdom of Mercy finally comes (Pss 6:3; 13:1–2; 35:17; 74:10; 79:5; 80:4; 89:46; 90:13; 119:84). But when we ask this, we are called anew to follow Jesus on the Way of mercy. If we are not following Jesus, do we have any standing at all to ask "how long?"

The Third Step on the Way of the disciple is the blessing of the will to persist in following Jesus after the initial experience of the suffering of the crowd and the hard demands of the Way.

***

Sarah called Anne, Janine, and Jazmine on Sunday afternoon, asking if they could meet her at 4 p.m. the next day at the mission when the building would be closed for the rest of the day. She told them that she had been approached by Dr. Cotswald that Sunday morning to invite the four of them to a meeting in his office in a month. He and a number of the trustees would be there and wanted to discuss the mission operations and its future. He previewed to Sarah that the trustees were concerned by reports from a mission volunteer that undocumented aliens were still being served at the mission. Sarah asked Cotswald why a month would pass before the meeting was held. The pastor said the passage of time was to give the four women a fair chance to experience what they had gotten themselves into.

"Then why are you telling us about this meeting now?" she asked.

"Because I thought it was only fair to tell you what to expect ... and that you have someone among the volunteers who is reporting on you to the trustees," he replied.

"Which volunteer is it?"

"I can't tell you that, Sarah."

"Can't or won't?"

Cotswald made no response.

"They think we will cut and run by then, don't they?"

"I'm sure that's not it, Sarah."

"I think you are sure that is it," replied Sarah.

The four women gathered in Sarah's tiny mission office for privacy. Sarah repeated what the senior pastor had told her.

"How are we supposed to tell if people are undocumented? Ask everyone who speaks only Spanish to show us their driver's license? There are plenty of American citizens we have served for a long time who don't have one. We'd be refusing to help people in need who are eligible according to the trustee's own rules." Janine paused to get control of her frustration. "If people are hungry, why should we care where they were born or why they are here? Documents aren't hungry. People are."

"And what about hungry children?" added Jazmine. "It's not their fault if their parents brought then here without documents. We are supposed to refuse food to a child ... or infant formula to a hungry baby?"

"The way I see it, we have two alternatives," offered Sarah. "We can just deny that we are serving undocumented people and claim that we are requiring driver's licenses before we serve anyone."

"But that would be lying, and the volunteer who is the snitch would tell the trustees," interrupted Janine.

"Or we could just admit we are not screening for driver's licenses, and invite them to send church security down to do it," said Sarah.

"But if security is here, it will scare off people in need who are eligible," said Jazmine. "The third alternative is to be honest that we are not screening and that we will not screen."

"This is all so ugly. And un-Christian," said Anne. "Is the senior pastor going to fight the trustees with us on this?"

"I don't think this is a hill he is willing to die on," said Sarah.

"There isn't a hill in the world he is willing to die on," replied Janine.

"Not even Golgotha," said Sarah. "My concern is that no matter what we say, the trustees will use it as an excuse to shut the mission down. So we are back to square one. We can agree not to serve all people in need so that we can continue to serve some. Or we can stand for what we know is right . . . and Christian, and challenge the power of the trustees to close this ministry without a vote of approval by the whole church. . . . Anne, you haven't told us what you think we should do."

Anne sat with her face looking down at her hands in her lap. She paused a long time before answering. "How much longer can the church ask us to keep the mission open without hiring a new director and giving us some professional help?"

"Anne, I am afraid that they won't do that. They want us to give up so they can add that to their justifications for selling this place," said Jazmine.

"So it's all on us? . . . That's not fair."

"Of course it's not fair. And nothing about life is fair for anyone who comes to this mission," said Sarah.

Jazmine said, "I am afraid it is all on us . . . for now."

"Isn't it someone else's turn?" said Anne.

The three other women sat in silence.

Tears welled up in Anne's eyes, and her voice cracked. "I just can't do this anymore. It's so . . . depressing. I can't stop shaking when I leave here. I had no idea there were so many people going through this, so dirty and hungry and alone. I am ashamed to say this . . . but I have to drop out."

"Anne," said Sarah. "Won't you come with us to the trustee meeting anyway? You don't have to say anything. I don't want them to guess that any of us are giving up."

"I think my husband already told the pastor I am stopping. . . . I have to go now. I am so sorry. But I just cannot look at the faces of these children anymore."

The three remaining women sat quiet for a long time.

"How much longer?" asked Janine.

"No idea," said Sarah.

"I meant, how much longer can each of us keep up this pace?"

"Until Jesus returns, I guess," said Jazmine with a thin smile.

"Aren't we *all* depressed and discouraged? And tired? Anne isn't alone in that. Why *is* this so hard? Why does God let this go on? This poverty and suffering? And these hearts of stone in this church? If God won't step in, how can we change things?"

"I've never heard you talk about God like that, Jazmine."

"This entire experience makes me feel closer to God. And further away."

Fourth Step

Matthew 5:2–3

² Then he began to speak, and taught them, saying: ³ "Blessed are you who are the poor in spirit, for yours is the kingdom of heaven."

As we begin to consider the first Beatitude, we should consider whether this and all of the Beatitudes are goals for which we should strive (becoming "poor in spirit," "mourners," "meek," "pure in heart," "children of God," "persecuted") or descriptions of what happens to us by the grace of God as we are empowered to persist on the Way of discipleship with Jesus.

Because the Kingdom of Mercy described in Matthew, the Hebrew scripture, and the book of Revelation has still not come as promised, and because kingdoms of darkness have continued to reign on earth for so long, the Beatitudes have been spiritualized and interiorized. Indeed, I find two basic strains of Christianity in scripture and in history—one emphasizing the *rescue* and another emphasizing the *presence*. The rescue is variously from slavery, oppression, poverty, injustice, sin, heresy, illness, mortality, or death. The presence is the experience of God in being lifted out or in the midst of the suffering and mercilessness of this world. The presence is experienced in worship, sacred music and art, the communion body and blood, the beauty of nature, love, solitude, meditation, prayer, and respite from the struggle.

But in the incarnation, reflected in these Beatitudes, the *presence* of God brings *rescue*. Presence and rescue are inseparable. Jesus is "Emmanuel," God with us (Matt 1:23), and he brings the presence of God in the rescue of the Kingdom of Mercy from suffering and injustice (Matt 4:23–25; 8:1–4, 14–17, 28–34; 9:2–8, 18–26, 27–31, 32–33, 35–36; 10:5–8; 11:2–6; 12:9–14; 14:13–21, 34–36; 15:29–38; 17:14–18; 20:29–34; 25:31–46).

Many view the values of the Kingdom as paradoxical. "So the last shall be first, and the first shall be last" (Matt 20:16; 19:30). "For those who want to save their live will lose it" (Matt 16:25). "The greatest among you will be your servant" (Matt 23:11).

But these values are not so much paradoxical as they are in conflict with the values of the kingdoms of the world. Perhaps the first challenge of trying to live a Christian life in the midst of the kingdoms of the world is gaining insight into how deeply our values and desires, and the values and desires of our children, are shaped by the pervasiveness of these kingdoms' values.

Many will say that the values of Jesus' Kingdom of Mercy are unrealistic and even naïve, given that we must live in the midst of the sinful kingdoms of the world. This world, they say, is not a covenantal community created by God, but an *agon*—Greek for "struggle"—a pitched competition for limited resources, power, and honor. And these many say that the values of the Kingdom of Mercy are unrealistic and naïve because of the innate and irredeemable human will to power, anger, violence, selfishness, greed, and fear of people in groups different than our own who stand in the way of what we demand of the scarcity.

But humans also have an innate capacity for mercy, empathy, generosity, and sacrifice for all those in need and for the common good. The kingdoms of the world maintain their existence and power, and their self-serving and destructive values, by belittling and resisting the values and ethics of the Kingdom of Mercy. But the survival of humanity, and given the increasing human power to despoil the environment and destroy other species, the survival of the creation as we know it, depend upon the human community making the values and ethics of the Kingdom of Mercy respected, supported, and thus realistic.

Jesus started this growth of God's Kingdom with the work of his disciples. Disciples are called with Jesus to be suffering servants with him (Isa 53:2–9; Matt 5:10–12; 10:16–18, 24–25; 16:24–25; 20:24–28; 24:9). All of us suffer unwillingly in our mortality. As much as we may deny it, to be human is to suffer. Some of us want to be so insulated from pain that we never let the suffering of others get into our hearts and under our skins. But Matthew's narrative affirms that a disciple of Jesus is called to serve *and* to suffer with and for those who are served. This selfless, suffering, sacrificial life is foolish and unrealistic within the kingdoms of the world. But it is the sunlight and oxygen, and the bread and butter, the seed, the salt and the leaven, the foundation of rock and the fruit of the Kingdom of Mercy.

As an aside that may offend some readers, and I apologize if I do so offend, I was a US Marine infantryman. In the Corps the highest value is placed on the willingness of every Marine to sacrifice their life for their fellow Marine. This is not merely an aspiration within this "service." This is a powerful ethos, very much at odds with the self-centeredness of the other kingdoms of the world. I am *not at all equating* the Marine Corps with the Kingdom of Mercy. The Corps is very much a part of the violence of the kingdoms of the world. It claims to be a necessary response to the violent threat from those foreign kingdoms. Some will say that the Corps itself is such a threat. I am merely saying that communities of real "disciples" of a kingdom whose values are at odds with the selfishness of the kingdoms of the world have been and can be created. There are better examples than the Corps for self-sacrifice and sacrificial love. The first is a good family in which people regularly sacrifice and would literally die for one another. Others are monasteries and convents, Roman Catholic and Protestant religious and laity who stay faithful to their values of humble service; servants to communities of want in the US and throughout the world; underpaid employees of nonprofits serving the poor; nurses in emergency rooms and in clinics in poor neighborhoods; physicians with Doctors Without Borders; men and women who risked their safety and their lives in the American civil rights movement; teachers in inner-city schools; and on and on. The mustard seeds are everywhere. The kingdoms of personal profit, materialism, and fear are supremely effective at creating their own disciples who see gratification of every selfish desire as their highest priority. Every business department in every university in America proselytizes the "goodness" of capitalism, profit, materialism, and militant consumerism. In contrast, Jesus teaches that his disciples should proselytize and spread the compassion, generosity, justice, and selflessness of the Kingdom of Mercy with our words and deeds of service and sacrifice (Matt 5:16).

These first four disciples likely left their nets and boats with naïve enthusiasm, followed Jesus by leaping into an ocean of suffering, felt themselves drowning, but resisted the temptation to save themselves by returning home. So, as reported in Matt 5:1, they climbed the mountain with Jesus and looked out with him over the suffering crowd. Imagine their fatigue, despair, and doubt! How random the suffering is! How unjust! How cruel! How long must this suffering go on? They are beginning to recognize that what they are seeing is a tiny fraction of the suffering and random injustice in all of God's creation. And perhaps they are wondering where God is in all this, and why God allows the innocent to suffer while the indifferent and the wicked prosper. Jesus would soon teach them to pray, "Your kingdom come. Your will be done, on earth as it is in heaven" (Matt 6:10). So, they may have wondered why this Kingdom has not already come. If this suffering isn't God's will, as Jesus' ministry was proving, why was there so much of it? After what they have seen and experienced since they left their nets and boats, they can no longer be indifferent. Perhaps they feel cursed with their empathy for these sufferers. Maybe they stayed with Jesus and came up the mountain with him to hear his answers to this suffering. Maybe they were giving him one last chance.

And what does Jesus say to them? "You are blessed to be here and feeling what you are feeling!" Blessed!

"Blessed?" Blessed as in "happy"? As in "fortunate"? As in "graced by God"?

Speaking of a mountain, mountains of words have been written about the meaning of "blessed" in these Beatitudes. A challenge to understanding what Jesus meant by this word is that he was probably speaking in Aramaic to men who knew their scripture in Hebrew. His teachings were later translated into the Greek of the Gospels, a Greek which of course has a separate set of words that could express the meaning of what Jesus said. And from the *koine* Greek, the word Jesus used is translated into the English "blessed" in our Bibles.

Even "beatitude" is something of a misnomer and the result of the challenge of translations. "Beatitude" comes from the Latin word for "blessed"—*beati*. The word translated into the English "blessed" from the Greek manuscripts of Matt 5:3–11 is *makarioi*, which can mean "blessed," "fortunate," or "happy."

In the context of Matthew's narrative, the most applicable sense of Jesus' meaning of "blessed" for me is "fortunate." "Fortunate" because God's presence is with you in and through the suffering you are experiencing on the Way of discipleship. "Fortunate" because of what you will receive as part of God's presence on the Way. "Fortunate" because you are giving your life for the pearl of the greatest value (Matt 13:45–46).

And what are the disciples experiencing as expressed by Jesus in Matt 5:3 in the Greek of the original manuscript? They are experiencing "poverty of spirit." Many offer that Matthew's Jesus combined "poor" with "spirit" to commend the blessedness of humble meekness. But that is the message of the Beatitude of Matt 5:4 ("Blessed are the meek"). Why would Jesus repeat? In the context of Matthew's narrative about what these disciples had just been through, I sense that "meekness" as the meaning of "poor in spirit" misses the main point.

Consider the Hebrew *ruach*, which is generally translated "spirit" in our English scripture, but can also mean "breath." In Gen 6:17, God threatens to "bring a flood of waters on the earth, to destroy from under heaven all flesh in which is the breath (*ruach*) of life." In Isa 61:3, one is "of a faint spirit (*ruach*)" when they are mourning their captivity with broken hearts. So a person who is "poor in spirit" would be one in whom the breath or spirit of their life—their life force—was weak because of life's injustice and evil. The "poor in spirit" are about to give up. This would describe not only the disciples after they were immersed in the crowd's suffering. It would also describe the desperate members of the crowd.

So for the meaning of "poor in spirit" of these four disciples within Matthew's narrative, Ps 34 speaks to me deeply:

> [4] I sought the LORD, and he answered me,
> and delivered me from all my fears.
> [5] Look to him, and be radiant;
> so your faces shall never be ashamed.
> [6] This poor soul cried, and was heard by the LORD,
> and was saved from every trouble. . . .
>
> [8] O taste and see that the LORD is good;
> happy are those who take refuge in him. . . .
>
> [15] The eyes of the LORD are on the righteous,
> and his ears are open to their cry.
> [16] The face of the LORD is against evildoers,
> to cut off the remembrance of them from the earth.
> [17] When the righteous cry for help, the LORD hears,
> and rescues them from all their troubles.

> [18] The LORD is near to *the brokenhearted*,
> and saves *the crushed in spirit*.
> [19] Many are the afflictions of the righteous,
> but the LORD rescues them from them all. (Emphasis added)

The narrative lying behind Ps 34 has much in common with the narrative of the four first disciples in Matthew. This psalmist is "brokenhearted" and "crushed in spirit" (v. 18) because he and the innocent are afflicted in this world. But the psalmist maintains his trust and hope in the LORD, who rescues him (vv. 4–6) from all his fears and afflictions. The day of the LORD will come when all who continue to trust in the LORD by following the LORD's way will be rescued (vv. 15–19). The happiness or blessing (v. 8) of the afflicted includes that the LORD is "near" them even in their affliction (v. 18).

The psalmist speaks out of the experience of having been rescued from his suffering: "I sought the LORD and the LORD answered me" (v. 4). But while he was suffering the "afflictions of the righteous" (v. 19) we may be sure that he was despairing and fighting disillusionment. The version of the world he had relied upon—one in which the righteous are rewarded and protected by God and the wicked are punished—was proving *not* to be the actual world. That was the cause of his broken heart and crushed spirit (v. 18).

The first four disciples in Matthew's narrative were surely suffering the same kind of despair and disorientation. The goodness of the kingdoms of the world in which they had found relative comfort as fishermen was shown by the suffering of the crowds to be a façade. The lives they had lived had been proved by the afflictions of the crowd to be an escape from reality. They were indeed *brokenhearted* and *crushed in spirit*. Their choices were to flee back into their old life, re-embracing those kingdoms' illusions, or to continue to repent and follow on the Way to a new Kingdom of Mercy. They chose to continue to follow Jesus up the mountain.

Why would Jesus call the disciples "fortunate"? Because they have now given up on the kingdoms of the world, and are ready for complete commitment to the Kingdom of Mercy in its community of rescuing, healing, feeding, and mutual support.

Within this narrative of Matthew, I hear the first Beatitude, which Jesus gives to these four men to begin their orientation into his new Kingdom, as "Fortunate are you who are brokenhearted and crushed in spirit, for the Kingdom of Mercy is now yours." "Brokenhearted" and "crushed in spirit" seem to me to be the same as "poor in spirit" in this context. Why are you fortunate? Because God has called you here and is near you in your suffering. Fortunate why? Because now you are learning through our mission of healing and hope that this pervasive, random suffering is against the will of God. Because you are being offered a role in God's great rescue mission from this pain and injustice. Because broken hearts and crushed spirits are necessary for you to leave behind the kingdoms of darkness and embrace the Kingdom of Mercy. You are fortunate that you are now prepared to commit to this Way because you now see the evil and suffering as God sees it. This vision is God's gift to you. In seeing as God sees, you experience God's presence.

The Kingdom of Mercy is the counter to the kingdoms of the world. It is a gracious gift and the Way to follow. It begins with repenting from all the other failing kingdoms that are based upon fear, violence, exclusion, and selfishness. The Kingdom of Mercy is both a last resort and the first choice when the only other responses to the failing kingdoms are hopelessness, resignation, and nihilism. It is the last and final kingdom that arrives when people are ready in their desolation. The Kingdom of Mercy is a force, a movement, and a community, a counter-culture and counter-narrative, a faith, a trust, a grace, a blessing, and *the* Way.

Only when the other kingdoms and the sad worlds they create have broken your heart and crushed your spirit, only when the state of the world seems hopeless and Godless—with endless wars, ubiquity of fear, widespread homelessness, hunger, illness, oppression of the poor and demonization of the stranger, the fouling of our planet, the prevalence of lies and the eagerness of citizens of democracies to embrace these lies, the skepticism about the power of mercy—only then does the Kingdom of Mercy open its true possibility and necessity to us.

The Fourth Step on the Way of the disciple is receiving the blessing of our experience of broken hearts and crushed spirits over the random suffering in the world, but still to persevere on the Way.

***

After their meeting with Sarah and Anne on Monday, Jazmine and Janine drove together and parked on a back street overlooking the fields and overpasses where many of the mission's homeless clients slept in tents or in the open on bedrolls. They sat there in silence for almost an hour, studying the crowd.

"God, this is heart breaking," said Janine. "Why aren't there more shelters in this city?"

"Even if there were," said Jazmine, "there are a lot of homeless who prefer sleeping outside, because of their mental illness and their fear of some of the men who sleep in the shelters."

"But there are bathrooms and food for them there. There is a roof over their heads."

"Hard to say what I would choose if I were in that situation. You know that older woman with the bald patch? Makayla is her name."

"Yes. She's a sweetie."

"Makayla says there is a feeling of family among the people in these fields. People look out for one another here. And she says no one judges anybody else. Everybody here has a story, but no one presses anyone if they don't want to share it."

"It is still so difficult for me to see this. People ought to have a roof, and heat and air conditioning, and a toilet and a refrigerator and a stove, a place to put their stuff, and a door they can lock. It can't be healthy here long term. . . . I had no idea that so many people lived like this."

"Oh my God," cried Janine. "Look over there underneath the bridge next to the barricade."

"What is it?"

"See the police? It looks like they are checking for IDs."

"Those aren't city police. Those are sheriff's deputies. Our compassionate county sheriff was elected on a promise that he would order his deputies to help the immigration police detain people without papers."

"But those people aren't bothering anyone."

"Ohhh! Remember that young mother who was sleeping in the outside stairwell at the church? The one with the little baby; the one church security had arrested?"

"How could I forget? That was terrible."

"Isn't that her being questioned by the deputies?"

"I think you're right. But where is the baby?"

"I've got to get down there to her," said Janine.

"Do you think that's wise?"

"Nothing we've been doing is wise."

Jazmine drove the car back down the street and turned right into a paved apron next to the field. The two of them walked through the

Fourth Step: Matthew 5:2–3

clumps of tents and bedrolls to the underpass where the teenaged mom and the deputies were talking. The girl was crying. Her baby was nowhere in sight. The two deputies were becoming increasingly frustrated. It was clear that neither deputy spoke fluent Spanish.

"Deputy, may we help?" asked Janine.

"Who the hell are you?"

"We are friends of this young lady," said Janine, putting her arm around the girl. The girl looked up and seemed to recognize Janine.

"*Ellos estan tratando de arrestarme de nuevo* (They are trying to arrest me again)," she said.

"Where is your baby?" asked Janine.

"No one will tell me." She began to cry again.

"You have no idea where she is?"

"No."

"How long were you in jail?"

"Two nights. They gave me a ticket for trespassing and told me I could pay a hundred dollar fine and go free. I had no money so they gave me a piece of paper and told me to come to court."

"Did you give them your name?"

"I gave them my mother's name."

"When are you supposed to be in court?"

"I don't know. My backpack was stolen, and I had the paper in there."

"Why are these men questioning you?"

"I don't know. I asked them where my baby is but they don't understand."

Janine turned to the deputies, "Can I help you, deputies?"

"We were checking people for outstanding arrest warrants and lack of documents when this girl stopped us. She keeps asking about her baby. She won't tell us her name and won't show us a driver's license. I'm asking you ladies again, who are you?"

"We are retired school teachers. We work at the church mission of First Kingdom of God Church downtown."

"Is that how you know this girl?"

Janine and Jazmine looked at one another. "No," Janine said. "Maria was in my class the year before I retired."

"In your class? How is it she speaks no English?"

The lie was quickly unravelling.

"It was a special class for children who had just arrived in the US."

"So she is illegal."

"Oh, no. Her father is a worker with some kind of special skill who had a work visa and got to bring his family."

"She was in your class and can't speak a lick of English?"

"Deputy, I don't want to embarrass her, but she was in a special education class. She has an audial impairment."

"You are lying to us, ma'am."

"I am most certainly not lying to you! I am a school teacher and a Christian!"

"Okay, calm down, lady. Then what is she doing out here? And why does she look like that?"

"I told you, deputy. She has an intellectual impairment. She has run away from home before, and she was found here. Her father asked us to help him look."

"Then why does she keep asking about her baby?"

"She has a baby at her father's house."

Jazmine joined the conversation. "Deputy, just let us take her home."

"Give us a minute." The two deputies went to their car and used the radio. They came back. "What's her name?"

Janine didn't hesitate. "Maria Hernandez."

"Yeah, 'Maria Hernandez.' Just like a hundred other Mexican girls out here.... I think you are selling me a load of bullshit.... Just get her out of here. We don't want to see her here again."

"Thank you, deputy. Right away."

Jazmine and Janine walked Maria to their car. The girl was in a daze. "Where are we going?" she asked.

"To our home."

"Oh, no. I couldn't do that to you. And I need to find my baby."

"You can't find her tonight. You can't stay out here. Please just come home with us for now. You need a hot meal, a shower, some clean clothes, and a safe bed to sleep in. At least for one night."

When they got to the sisters' home, Jazmine went into the kitchen and started preparing some chicken, beans, and rice. Janine took the girl, who revealed her true name to be Estrella Espinoza-Sanchez, into their spare bedroom and helped her undress and into the shower. Janine came into the kitchen carrying Estrella's dirty clothes. She looked shaken.

"Janine, what's wrong?"

"She has bruises on her upper thighs inside her legs. And she has what look like cigarette burns on her lower stomach."

"What? Whatever from?"

"She wouldn't tell me much, but I think she was assaulted by a group of men under the bridge. They wanted to give her drugs for sex and when she refused, they assaulted her. I told her we had to get her to an emergency room in case she is injured or pregnant . . . or infected. She started pleading with me not to make her go. She is afraid she will be arrested and deported and never find her baby. So I told her I wouldn't take her. . . . I am worried she is going to run away from us tonight after we go to sleep." Janine began to cry. "Jazmine, we just can't let her go back to the street. We have to promise her we will help her find her baby."

Jazmine went to her sister and hugged her. They cried in each other's arms.

"God put her in our path," said Jazmine. "We'll keep her safe here for as long as she will stay with us. But we can't force her."

"Oh thank you, thank you, thank you. It would have crushed us both to put her back out on the street." Janine leaned back and looked into Jazmine's face. "But what about all the other Estrellas?"

"God will just have to put them in someone else's path."

"I wish God would hurry the hell up. There are so may Estrellas."

Fifth Step

Matthew 5:4

[4] Blessed are you who mourn, for you will be comforted.

What did this Beatitude mean for the ones who heard it from Jesus' lips? And what does it mean for us now? That those of us who mourn the death of someone we love can be comforted by the promise of their resurrection? I have heard this preached more than a dozen times, and I believe it is true. But I do not believe that this is what Jesus was telling his disciples in *this* saying in the context of *this* narrative.

He *is* saying that these disciples were fortunate to be mourning! He is saying that we are fortunate to be mourning in the context of our own "discipling."

How false is this claim by Jesus within the values of the kingdoms of the world in which insulation and escape from sadness are among the greatest priorities! But how is the saying true within the values of discipleship in the Kingdom of Mercy? How is mourning an early step on the Way of discipleship within this narrative of Matthew?

When we are brokenhearted, crushed in spirit, and tempted to abandon the Way, we are focused on our own pain, even when the source of that pain is the suffering of others. It is *our* heart that is broken and *our* spirit that is crushed. But when we are in the mourning process, we focus more on the other whose plight we are mourning—the other's life cut short or wasted, the other trapped in graves of poverty, homelessness, illness, injury, addiction, cruelty, and exclusion. The Fourth Step of crushed spirits and broken hearts came from the four disciples' shock and despair upon seeing and feeling the pain of the "crowd" (Matt 4:25—5:1). This Fifth Step, intimately connected to the Fourth, was taken when the disciples' mourning was caused more by the pain of others than by the disciples' own suffering at being immersed in the pain. With this Step, they began to mourn others and the world first and themselves second. They mourned the power of evil over the innocent. These first four disciples must have mourned the hopelessness of those who were not fortunate enough to come to Jesus to be healed. They mourned the loss of their illusion that the world is fair and that those who were righteous would be protected by God. And they mourned the loss of their own trust in God to fix the entire world. How could they sustain such trust in the God of Exodus, Second and Third Isaiah, and so many of the psalms—a God who *could* use God's power to rescue the righteous from their misery—when God had failed to use that power and had let the world sink so deep into its grave with so many innocents buried with it? In a sense, they were mourning the death of the God they had once believed in, even as they were actually witnessing God's power exercised in Jesus' healing of those relative few who were able to come to him. Why did God not exercise that good power for all the righteous afflicted? Why did only Jesus have the goodness and power to bind up the broken hearts in the world?

Just as we are tempted to abandon the Way of discipleship when we suffer our own broken hearts and crushed spirits at the depth and breadth of suffering in the world, perhaps we are tempted to abandon our mourning for others by returning to our old lives. But this Fifth Step of mourning for the world requires us to persist in our new Way. We can't retreat back into material comfort and denial to escape our own brokenheartedness, when the world's heart continues to be broken. Once we have seen the unjust misery, we can no longer deceive ourselves that the world isn't in darkness, even if we hide from the darkness in lives of light and warmth—not if we have moved through our own broken hearts and crushed spirits into real empathy and mourning for the other.

This Fifth Step of mourning the world is one from which we can never completely retreat. If we are able to stay on the Way, it is because we have sensed Jesus moving our focus from our pain to the pain of the others. A disciple cannot avoid her own pain by quitting the Way, because she cannot unsee what Jesus has shown her. She cannot eliminate the suffering of others simply by putting it out of her own sight. The suffering goes on and on, in the world and in her heart, even if she tries to avert her eyes. But if her primary focus is not moved from her own heartbreak and crushed spirit to mourning for the pain and plight of others, she cannot stay on the Way. If her focus is moved from self to others, she will remain on the Way *in her heart*, even if she tries to return to her old life.

I am privileged to know a woman who had taken a position leading a shelter for indigent and abused women and children. Ironically, she had led a sheltered life personally. She was recruited because she had been a huge success as CEO of a profit corporation. She decided she had made enough money to last her more than a lifetime, and wanted to give back to her community. But when she started her new job, and was exposed for the first time to the suffering and hardship of the poor, she became depressed and exhausted. She thought she was a person of deep faith, but praying to God during her sleepless nights wasn't helping to defeat her despair. She quit eating and lost her ability to concentrate and innovate. She was about to resign her new position. But on advice of a woman who had helped hundreds of abused women and children in the shelter for years, the CEO began to pray at night for the women and children instead of for herself. Eventually she found herself praying for the abusers, too. The switch of her main focus from her pain to the pain of the people she was trying to help energized and enabled her to continue her service, where she remains to this day. She has come to consider herself blessed to be entrusted by God with the safety and welfare of these vulnerable woman and children. She lost herself in her mourning for others rather than in her own broken heart and crushed spirit.

Most American Christians run from heartbreak, crushed spirit, and mourning over the state of the world. Instead we desire things that won't truly benefit us and fear things that won't truly harm us. We drink too much alcohol and eat too much expensive food and purchase too many luxuries as anesthesia. We seek escape from the suffering in the world through trivial diversions. We root passionately for local sports teams, as if the successes or failures of overpaid adults playing children's games warrant any passion. We live vicariously through the lives of celebrities who are no happier than we are. Most of us are desperate to escape exposure to the suffering of the vulnerable. Ironically, we want to be blind to the lack of light in the world. We live like the rich fool in Jesus' parable (Luke 12:16–21) or the rich man in Jesus' parable about Lazarus (Luke 16:19–31) or the priest and the Levite who passed by the suffering man in Jesus' parable of the Good Samaritan (Luke 10:29–37). We use the values of the kingdoms of the world to condemn those who suffer in poverty and exclusion in order to justify our flight from them.

In this Beatitude, Jesus senses the temptation of these four disciples to hide from the pain of the world by abandoning the Way. He tells them to embrace their mourning for the world's victims. He tells them they are fortunate to be in mourning. Why? Because they "will be comforted." "*Will* be." He doesn't offer them some immediate elimination of their pain, like a helicopter parent tries to shield his child from any hardship or failure. And he also doesn't say, "... because the reasons for your mourning will be eliminated." He says only that the disciples "will be comforted" while still in their pain of mourning.

I wish we could hear the conversation among the disciples as they were trying to understand Jesus' assurance of comfort.

"He said we are fortunate because we will be comforted. But following him was what led to this pain of mourning. So would we be as fortunate if we had not followed and never mourned like this? Or if we left him now?" asked Andrew.

"*How* will we be comforted?" asked Peter.

"*When* will we be comforted? I am ready for comfort," said James.

"Ready? We all *need* the comfort," said John. "The entire world needs it. Now!"

So we ask God now, with these disciples, how and when are we to be comforted if we don't abandon our mourning?

To my eye and mind, the roots of this Beatitude are in Isa 40–55 and Isa 56–66. These writings can open for us a deeper understanding of what mourning Jesus was speaking of and how the comfort was to come. First Isaiah (Isa 1–39) was written by a prophet of that name before the Babylonian conquest of Israel, the destruction of the Jerusalem Temple, and the taking of Israel's leaders into exile in Babylon. Second Isaiah (Isa 40–55) is thought to be the words of another unnamed prophet written during the Babylonian captivity and who was speaking about the return of the Jews from exile. Third Isaiah (Isa 56–66) is thought to be the words of still another prophet written after the people of Israel had been returned to their homeland.

We know that Second Isaiah was important to the discipleship call narrative of the Jesus of Matthew's Gospel because of Matt 3:3, which quotes Isa 40:3: "The voice of one crying out in the wilderness, Prepare the way of the LORD, make his paths straight." Matthew 3:17 references

Isa 42:1: "in whom my soul delights." And Matt 4:16 refers to Isa 42:7: "those who sit in darkness."

For this Beatitude, "Blessed are you who mourn, for you will be comforted," Jesus was likely drawing from Third Isaiah:

> ¹ The spirit of the Lord God is upon me,
> because the Lord has anointed me;
> He has sent me to bring good news to the oppressed,
> to bind up the brokenhearted,
> to proclaim liberty to the captives,
> and release to the prisoners,
> ² to proclaim the year of the Lord's favor,
> and the day of vengeance of our God;
> *to comfort all who mourn;*
> ³ *to provide for those who mourn in Zion—*
> to give them a garland instead of ashes,
> the oil of gladness *instead of mourning,*
> the mantle of praise instead of a faint spirit. . . .
> ⁴ They shall build up the ancient ruins,
> they shall raise up the former devastations:
> they shall repair the ruined cities,
> the devastations of many generations. (Isa 61; emphasis added)

Who were the ones who had been mourning in this passage? The oppressed, the brokenhearted, the faint of spirit, the former captives of the Babylonian exile, and the imprisoned debtors. Those whose world had been destroyed but was now being restored by their God. Those who had believed their God had abandoned them forever as punishment for their unfaithfulness. The entire people of God had been mourning for one another and for the world, and were now being comforted by God's rescue.

The assurance of comfort runs through Second and Third Isaiah. Second Isaiah begins at 40:1–2: "Comfort, O comfort my people, says your God." The people were comforted that they were being forgiven by God, freed from suffering, oppression and captivity, restored to their land, forgiven their debts, healed in their hearts, and strengthened in their spirits.

> ¹³ Sing for joy, O heavens, and exult, O earth;
> break forth, O mountains, into singing!
> *For the Lord has comforted his people,*
> and will have compassion on his suffering ones. (Isa 49; emphasis added)

Fifth Step: Matthew 5:4

¹ Listen to me, you that pursue righteousness,
you that seek the Lord.
Look to the rock from which you were hewn,
and to the quarry from which you were dug.
² Look to Abraham your father
and to Sarah who bore you;
for he was but one when I called him,
but I blessed him and made him many.
³ *For the Lord will comfort Zion.* . . .

⁷ Listen to me, you who know righteousness,
you people who have my teaching in your hearts;
do not fear the reproach of others,
and do not be dismayed when they revile you. . . .
¹² *I, I am he who comforts you.* (Isa 51; emphasis added)

⁷ How beautiful upon the mountains
are the feet of the messenger who announces peace,
who brings good news,
who announces salvation,
who says to Zion, "Your God reigns."
⁸ Listen! Your sentinels lift up their voices,
together they sing for joy;
for in plain sight they see the return of the Lord to Zion.
⁹ Break forth together into singing, you ruins of Jerusalem;
for the Lord has comforted his people,
he has redeemed Jerusalem. (Isa 52; emphasis added)

¹⁴ It shall be said, "Build up, build up, prepare the way,
remove every obstruction from my people's way."
¹⁵ For thus says the high and lofty one
who inhabits eternity, whose name is Holy:
I dwell in the high and holy place,
and also with those who are contrite and humble in spirit,
to revive the spirit of the humble, and to revive the heart of the contrite.
¹⁶ For I will not continually accuse,
nor will I always be angry;
for then the spirits would grow faint before me,
even the souls that I have made.
¹⁷ Because of their wicked covetousness I was angry;
I struck them, I hid and was angry;
but they kept turning back to their own ways.

> [18] I have seen their ways, but I will heal them;
> *I will lead them and repay them with comfort,*
> *creating for their mourners the fruit of the lips.* (Isa 57; emphasis added)

> [20] Your sun shall no more go down,
> or your moon withdraw itself;
> for the LORD will be your everlasting light,
> and *your days of mourning shall be ended.* (Isa 60; emphasis added)

The mourning in Second and Third Isaiah was for the loss of the presence of God and God's power to make the world right. And the great comfort proclaimed was that God was present again, intervening in their lives and rescuing them from their sufferings.

Perhaps Andrew, Simon, James, and John wondered why a good and powerful God would have allowed the terrible suffering of the crowds to go on for so long. Was it because God had been turned away because of the people's sins? As the disciples were experiencing Jesus' astounding power to heal suffering, surely they were appreciating the extent of the suffering in the world and the extent of God's potential power to heal it. The comfort that Jesus promised to the disciples was the present and coming rescue by God of the sufferers through the present and coming Kingdom of Mercy. The comfort which the disciples would have heard and understood in this Beatitude would have been the world's promised liberation from the old kingdoms of darkness and death into Jesus' present and still coming Kingdom of Mercy. These disciples would have been truly fortunate if they felt that the healings they were seeing and the community of mercy being formed around Jesus were just the beginning of an inexorable tide of God's comfort sweeping over creation.

But disciples today still mourn deeply that the kingdoms of darkness, death, and suffering still predominate, and that the promised comfort still has not fully come. Jesus is not still with us using his numinous power to cure paralytics and the blind. How do we then endure our broken hearts, crushed spirits, and mourning souls to persist in the next Steps on the Way?

The Fifth Step on the Way of the disciple is to receive the blessing of mourning more deeply for the pain of others than for our own pain, and to persist on the Way.

Fifth Step: Matthew 5:4

***

Anne had coped with depression and anxiety most of her adult life. Her symptoms became more severe when her two children stopped living at home, and she could no longer cook and care for them and live as vicariously through them as she once had. Her work at her father's dry cleaning business was routine and not really needed by her father. Most days she sat alone at home watching television. She went to lunch with a steady group of friends as often as she could. Her husband was away from home at the work sites of his paving business at least three nights per week. She sank into depression, often staying in bed until 11 a.m. When the opportunity to work at the church mission presented itself, she swallowed her fears and joined her more assertive sister there. She hoped that this work would get her out of her house, provide a source of energy, and add some purpose to her life. But the opposition of her husband to her involvement at the mission and the tragedies she witnessed there only increased her depression and brought on anxiety. After she quit the mission, the anxiety subsided but her depression deepened. She could not stop thinking about one family that came to the mission once per week for groceries and sack lunches.

Their last name was Parker. The family consisted of a father, a mother, and three children aged eight, nine, and ten. The mother and children lived in a government housing project close to downtown across an interstate highway. The parents were both in their early thirties. Anne quickly learned that the father, Obadiah, had recently been paroled from prison after serving seven years for armed robbery, and that he was of course having a difficult time finding steady work paying a living wage. The housing project management forbade people with felony records from living there, so the father was sleeping in a homeless camp most nights each week. When he could avoid discovery, he snuck into the family home after midnight. But the family could not afford to be evicted, and eviction would happen if he was caught sleeping there. The mother, Eileen, suffered from lupus, which caused her to be bedridden when her symptoms worsened unpredictably. Then the three young children became more out of control. Eileen and the children lived on her disability payments and food stamps, and on what income Obadiah could produce doing manual labor through the local labor pool. Eileen was unemployable. Their reduced rent was only $75 a month for their two-bedroom apartment, and they couldn't afford to pay more somewhere else.

Addy, the ten-year-old girl, had been diagnosed by a physician at the local pediatric hospital with autism, ADHD, a speech impediment, anxiety, and emotional disturbance. Barnabus, the nine-year-old boy, had been diagnosed with autism, ADHD, intellectual disability, mixed receptive-expressive language disorder (speech disabled), lack of impulse control, oppositional defiant disorder (ODD) with sensory triggers, tendency to violent outbursts, and chronic diarrhea from his medication. Caleb, the eight-year-old boy, had been diagnosed with ADHD, global delay, specific speech delay, and tendency to violent outbursts. Anne knew these specific diagnoses because the former mission director, a social worker, had obtained their diagnostic records from the mother, and the records were in the family's mission file.

The two boys were frequently suspended from their schools. Caleb had attacked a teacher with scissors. They had frequent violent outbursts against one another at home. Barnabus was caught stealing Addy's panties from her dresser drawer. These children would have been too much for a healthy mother to control and direct. This home really needed the father, but the family could not risk eviction if he were to be caught there. They had no family or friends to shelter them.

When Eileen and the children came to the mission on the bus, the two boys often fought with one another and other boys. When Jazmine asked the mother why she brought her children with her, the mother said she could not leave them at home unattended, that their father was at work, and that she needed the children's help to carry the groceries home on the bus.

Anne was so moved by the family's troubles that she drove them home from the mission in her Lexus three weeks in a row. She was shocked to see the conditions they lived in—the cockroaches and mice, the leaking air conditioner, the old malfunctioning space heaters, the cracked dry wall, the mildew and mold. But Anne's husband George discovered that the back seat of the Lexus was streaked with feces and demanded to know why. When Anne tried to describe the nine-year-old's diarrhea and the extent of this family's problems, her husband exploded and forbade her to let this family into the car again. He said it was dangerous for her to drive into that housing project. She might be robbed and the car stolen. And he increased his pressure on her to quit her mission work. Even after she quit, Anne could not stop wondering and worrying how this family was doing.

Anne, George, and two other couples were having drinks and dinner together at their country club on a Saturday night. Anne was not drinking alcohol because of the anti-depressant she was taking. One of the male friends, Robert, asked if she had become so religious that she had "taken the pledge."

"No," Anne said. "Just on a diet."

"Tell us about what you do at the church mission," asked the friend named Doris. "We all admire you and your sister so much."

George broke in. "Anne had to stop. It was just too dangerous. And help doesn't do those people any good. It was a waste of her time."

"Oh," said Doris, pausing awkwardly. "Well, it was so good of you to try."

"It wasn't a waste of my time. It was just too hard. I had no idea that so many people in this community are so poor."

"It's their own damn fault," said their friend Robert, sipping his third scotch. He nodded knowingly at George and the other male friend.

"How do you know that, dear?" asked Doris, Robert's wife. "Why don't we let Anne speak? She was there and we weren't."

Robert was undeterred. "Anyone who is poor in this city is just too damned lazy. Have you seen the latest jobs report? There are thousands of jobs in this city going unfilled. If they are poor, it is because they would rather suck on the government's teat than work."

Anne summoned courage to speak she had never felt before. Her worry about the family poured out in anger. "What about if their mom has lupus and can't work? What about if they have children who are autistic with developmental delays, a nine-year-old child who can't even speak? Are *those* people poor because they are lazy?"

Robert replied angrily, "Then why did they keep having children? We taxpayers are supposed to subsidize their stupidity?"

George broke in. "Anne, let's change the subject."

"These families I saw down at that mission can't change the subject."

Robert interrupted, "I hear that your mission is serving illegal aliens. Aliens who are bringing drugs like fentanyl and disease into our city."

"We *do* serve people without documents there. People who have endured incredible hardships to get here. People who are running from gangs and drugs and poverty in their own countries. We are proud to serve them. They get hungry just like we do. So do their children. More hungry than we do. They just can't get into a club like this . . . unless they are cleaning the floor."

"We?" asked George. He looked away from his wife and toward the others. "It's no longer 'we.' I made her quit."

"Well, I just un-quit. How about that, George? I was thinking too much about my own troubles and not enough about theirs." She turned to the two women. "If any of you want to help, give me a call. It will open your eyes. And maybe your hearts . . . once you get over the shock. It did mine." Anne excused herself and walked the two blocks home from the club.

George joined her at home an hour later. He stormed into the kitchen where Anne was making herself a sandwich.

Anne turned to George and said preemptively, "Don't you ever speak to me like that in public again. Or in private."

"All right. You'll learn how pointless what you are doing is. But you can't use my car anymore."

"That's my car, too."

"That shows how ignorant you are. That car belongs to my company."

"Which belongs to us both."

"Only my company is on the title. And I am going to start driving it."

Anne stepped into a bathroom and took out her cell phone. She called Sarah.

"Sarah, this is Anne. I want to come back to working at the mission. I'll need a ride from you every day."

Sixth Step

Matthew 5:5

⁵ Blessed are you who are meek, for you will inherit the earth.

In Matthew's narrative the first four disciples enthusiastically and optimistically left everything they previously relied upon to follow Jesus. They went with him into a tidal wave of human suffering. They stayed with him despite the desire to cut and run for home and their old lives. They became personally heartbroken and crushed in spirit from their intimate exposure to the suffering. And they sank into mourning for the wickedness in the world and the seeming absence of God. But still they stayed with Jesus, climbing the mountain behind him to look out over the afflicted crowds. There he told them that they were fortunate to be heartbroken and spirit-crushed, because now they could free themselves from their attachment and allegiance to the kingdoms of the world and commit fully to the Kingdom of Mercy. And he told them they were fortunate to be in mourning for the suffering of those in the crowd, because God was present with them in their mourning and they would be comforted in the present and coming Kingdom.

Next he told them they were fortunate to be "meek"! Why meek?

We are really deeply into the values of the Kingdom of Mercy now and the conflict of Kingdom's values with the values of the world's kingdoms. Meekness is not valued in the dominant kingdoms in our world. It certainly wasn't in the dominant kingdoms of Jesus' time. Alpha males were and are valued. Omega males weren't and aren't. Type A personalities were and are valued, not Type Z. The kingdoms of our world reward self-made people, take charge people, people who impose their will on others, "damn the torpedoes and full speed ahead" people, "my way or the highway" people, "nothing is going to stop me now" people.

In the Methodist Justice Ministry, we have helped hundreds of women who have been abused into meekness. With legal, counseling, and material help, we have tried to help them and their children make new lives free of fear and abuse. As a part of this we have tried to empower them to be the opposite of meek—confident, assertive, independent, and intolerant of abuse of themselves and their children. Men who abuse their female partners are generally guilty of repeated, almost uniform patterns of conduct. They tell the women that they deserve the physical abuse. They belittle the women with demeaning names yelled at them in the presence of their children. They tell the women that they are lucky to be living with their abusers because no one else would want them. They tell them that no one would help them if they tried to leave, and that they are not capable of making it on their own. They separate the women from other family and friends. They control all the spending in the household. They do not even allow the women to go shopping for groceries without them. They close the blinds when they leave home and punish the women if they discover they have opened the blinds while they were gone. And when a woman is momentarily fed up with the abuse, very often the abuser quotes Scripture that she must forgive him seventy times seven (Matt 18:21–22).

Our first task in the justice ministry after helping the abused woman and her children find a safe place to stay is to help her understand that the abuser is the one who is inadequate and wrong, not her. Hundreds of times in the experience of the justice ministry staff, a woman has finally taken the courageous first step of leaving her abuser because her son was starting to imitate the abusiveness. Some of the most satisfying moments in my more than forty-eight years in courtrooms have come when I stood beside an abused woman before a judge, and she looked at me in wonder that someone would actually try to protect her. Women come to us in the justice ministry who are trying to repent of their meekness. You can see why I have a visceral reaction to a teaching that the meek are fortunate for any reason. There is a lot of ground between being meek and abusive. Why are not those "fortunate" and "blessed" who inhabit that middle ground? No one but an abuser would call them fortunate to be meek. Jesus was not an abuser. So what is Jesus saying?

There are many positive examples in Matthew of a woman who refused to be meek. Consider, for instance, the Canaanite woman in 15:21–28:

> ²¹ Jesus left that place and went away to the district of Tyre and Sidon. ²² Just then a Canaanite woman from that region came out and started shouting, "Have mercy on me, Lord, Son of David; my daughter is tormented by a demon." ²³ But he did not answer her at all. And his disciples came and urged him, saying, "Send her away, for she keeps shouting after us." ²⁴ He answered, "I was sent only to the lost sheep of the house of Israel." ²⁵ But she came and knelt before him, saying, "Lord, help me." ²⁶ He answered, "It is not fair to take the children's food and throw it to the dogs." ²⁷ She said, "Yes, Lord, yet even the dogs eat the crumbs that fall from their masters' table." ²⁸ Then Jesus answered her, "Woman, great is your faith! Let it be done for you as you wish." And her daughter was healed instantly.

This was to me not our Lord's finest hour. If that woman had been meek, she would have been intimidated by the disciples telling Jesus to send her away. If she had been meek, she would have been deterred when Jesus twice said he would not help her child, even calling her and her child "dogs" because they were not Jewish! But this courageous woman persisted and taught the Son of God a lesson about faith, persistence, and inclusion. Was this Canaanite woman the model for Jesus' parable about the unjust judge and the woman who would not be denied justice at Luke 18:1–8? We should all say our own Beatitude, "Blessed is the woman who overcomes repeated refusals to help her child and herself, for she will not be trapped in the kingdom of meekness."

At Jesus' crucifixion, when all the male disciples had run away in fear, "many women were also there, looking in from a distance; they had followed him from Galilee and provided for him. Among them were Mary Magdalene, Mary the mother of James and John, and the mother of the sons of Zebedee" (Matt 27:55–56). Matthew is identifying these women as disciples, by saying that they "followed" Jesus into the darkness and then did not abandon him. And it was Mary Magdalene and the other Mary who followed Jesus' body to the tomb (27:61) and who were the first to return to the tomb for the gruesome task of anointing his dead, mangled body (28:1).

Other women who refuse to be meek are presented positively in Luke's Gospel. "A woman of the city and a great sinner" burst into a meal at a Pharisee's home where Jesus was being dishonored to wash his feet with her tears and anoint him with precious oil (Luke 7:36–38). A woman named Mary, sister of Martha, insisted on sitting at Jesus' feet and learning from him rather than performing "woman's work" (Luke 10:38–42). And, as stated above, Jesus lauds a widow who hounds an unjust judge for justice (Luke 18:1–8).

None of these women were "meek," and all are presented as role models.

I have heard a number of sermons in which the preacher proclaimed that the Beatitudes are descriptions of Jesus himself, including Jesus' "meekness."

Growing up, we often sang in my church a hymn written by Charles Wesley:

> Gentle Jesus, meek and mild,
> Look upon a little child;
> Pity my simplicity,
> Suffer me to come to Thee.
>
> Lamb of God, I look to Thee;
> Thou shalt my example be:
> Thou art gentle, meek and mild;
> Thou wast once a little child.
>
> Fain I would be as Thou art;
> Give me Thine obedient heart:
> Thou art pitiful and kind;
> Let me have Thy loving mind.
>
> Loving Jesus, gentle Lamb,
> In Thy gracious hands I am;
> Make me, Savior, what Thou art,
> Live Thyself within my heart.

Charles Wesley tells us to sing not only that Jesus was meek but also that disciples are called to be meek just as he was.

But how was Jesus meek? As we have seen, he went into the darkness of the region of the shadow of death, he resisted the devil, he battled and experienced terrible suffering, he made himself homeless, he willingly went to Jerusalem knowing that the cross awaited him, and he confronted the religious authorities of his day who were oppressing the poor with religious rules impossible for them to obey in their poverty. Anyone who claims Jesus was meek hasn't spent any time studying the twenty-third chapter of Matthew!

But here at Matt 5:5, Jesus tells the first disciples they are fortunate to be meek. What in the Kingdom's name could he have meant?

The Cambridge Dictionary Online defines meek as "quiet, gentle, and not willing to argue or express opinions in a forceful way."[21] Merriam-Webster Online defines meek as "enduring injury with patience and without resentment, deficient in spirit and courage, and not strong or violent."[22] Dictionary.com defines meek as "humbly patient or quiet in nature when under provocation from others, and overly submissive and compliant."[23]

On first analysis, these definitions of meekness may seem to fit teachings of Jesus elsewhere in the Sermon on the Mount.

A few verses after 5:5, Jesus will teach these same four disciples at 5:38–42:

> [38] You have heard that it was said, "An eye for an eye and a tooth for a tooth." [39] But I say to you, "Do not resist an evildoer." But if anyone strikes you on the right cheek, turn the other also; [40] and if anyone wants to sue you and take your coat, give your cloak as well; [41] and if anyone forces you to go one mile, go also the second mile. [42] Give to everyone who begs from you, and do not refuse anyone who wants to borrow from you.

These teachings seem to be calling for the meekness defined above of "enduring injury with patience and without resentment, deficient in spirit and courage, and not strong or violent."

But the teaching at 5:39 translated into English in the NRSV as "do not resist an evildoer" in Greek is "*Me anthistemi to ponero*." The Greek *anthistemi* generally means "resist violently," not merely "resist." For me, this teaching is best understood as akin to "do not repay anyone evil for evil," as Paul explained in Rom 12:17.

In the above verse 39b, Jesus teaches the disciples not to run away meekly when someone strikes them "on the right cheek." Instead they should stand their ground and turn their left cheek for their assailant to strike again. The specific reference to the right cheek is the key to understanding this teaching. Picture that the disciple is facing the person who slaps him. The right hand of most people was and is the dominant hand. But to strike the disciple on the right cheek would require a blow with the left hand or a slap with the back of the right hand, both an insult in Jesus' time and place. Use of either hand in this way would be intended to demean a person as inferior to the assailant, not to injure a peer. Jesus advises the disciple to stay and openly expose the other cheek to the insulter, as if to say, "I will not be demeaned by you. I am not afraid of you. You may injure my body but not my will. I will not grovel as if I am inferior to you. You should be ashamed of yourself." This is not meek conduct.

Likewise at verse 40 Jesus teaches the disciple to shame and try to reform the creditor who sues for the debtor disciple's coat by giving them their outer cloak as well. Under Torah, a creditor could not keep the outer cloak of a poor debtor overnight, because the person might need the cloak to sleep in (Deut 24:10–13). For a relatively rich creditor to sue a poor debtor to publicly take his coat would be mostly to demean and embarrass, for how much could a creditor profit by selling the used coat of a poor man? So Jesus teaches the poor disciple to seize the initiative, embarrassing and reforming the creditor by giving the creditor a garment for which the creditor could not legally sue. This also is not meek conduct.

Verse 41 describes a too common event in the Roman Empire. Under Roman law, a Roman soldier could legally treat a subject of the Empire as a beast of burden by forcing him to carry the soldier's armor . . . but for one mile only. Rather than claiming inability, running away, or sullenly carrying the armor one mile and not one step further, Jesus teaches the disciple to carry the armor one mile more. By this the disciple would be insisting on his humanity and trying to reform the soldier. This also is not meek conduct.

In verse 42, Jesus teaches these disciples to give to anyone who begs and lend to anyone who seeks to borrow. But this was not to be in meekness, but in mercy.

Soon after his teaching about meekness in Matt 5:5 Jesus will also teach these disciples at 5:43–45:

> [43] You have heard that it was said, "You shall love your neighbor and hate your enemy." [44] But I say to you, Love your enemies and pray for those who persecute you, [45] so that you may be children of your Father in heaven; for he makes his sun rise on the evil and on the good, and sends rain on the righteous and on the unrighteous.

This is not meek submissiveness. This is aggressive mercy in imitation of our Father (5:48). It takes resolve and courage to actively love an enemy, particularly in the midst of your community's hatred of that enemy.

Jesus also taught: "Do not judge so that you may not be judged" (Matt 7:1). This seems to counsel meekness according to the definition in the Cambridge Dictionary Online of "not willing to argue or express opinions in a forceful way." But Jesus is not calling us to meekness with this teaching, but instead pointing out to us our hypocrisy in judging: "Why do you see the speck in your neighbor's eye but do not notice the log in your own eye?" (7:3). And he is telling us not to use judgment and condemnation as justification for refusing mercy to our neighbors and to our enemies.

So who are the meek whom Jesus taught in this Beatitude will inherit the land? What is the meekness Jesus told the disciples they were blessed and fortunate to receive?

For me, the key to understanding is the psalm that is the likely source of Jesus' Beatitude. Please be patient with me as I quote here the entire Ps 37 because of the importance of its overall message:

> [1] Do not fret because of the wicked;
> do not be envious of wrongdoers,
> [2] for they will soon fade like the grass,
> and wither like the green herb.
>
> [3] Trust in the Lord, and do good;
> *so you will live in the land*, and enjoy security.
> [4] Take delight in the Lord,
> and he will give you the desires of your heart.
>
> [5] Commit your way to the Lord;
> trust in him, and he will act.
> [6] He will make your vindication shine like the light,
> and the justice of your cause like the noonday.
>
> [7] Be still before the Lord,
> and wait patiently for him;
> do not fret over those who prosper in their way,
> over those who carry out evil devices.
>
> [8] Refrain from anger, and forsake wrath.
> Do not fret—it leads only to evil.
> [9] For the wicked shall be cut off,
> but *those who wait for the Lord shall inherit the land.*

¹⁰ Yet a little while, and the wicked will be no more;
though you look diligently for their place, they will not be there.
¹¹ But *the meek shall inherit the land,*
and delight themselves in abundant prosperity.

¹² The wicked plot against the righteous,
and gnash their teeth at them;
¹³ but the Lord *laughs at the wicked,*
for he sees that their day is coming.
¹⁴ The wicked draw the sword and bend their bows
to bring down the poor and needy,
to kill those who walk uprightly;
¹⁵ their sword shall enter their own heart,
and their bows shall be broken.

¹⁶ Better is a little that the righteous person has
than the abundance of many wicked.
¹⁷ For the arms of the wicked shall be broken,
but the Lord *upholds the righteous.*
¹⁸ The Lord knows the days of the blameless,
and their heritage will abide forever;
¹⁹ they are not put to shame in evil times,
in the days of famine they have abundance.

²⁰ But the wicked perish,
and the enemies of the Lord are like the glory of the pastures;
they vanish—like smoke they vanish away.

²¹ The wicked borrow, and do not pay back,
but the righteous are generous and keep giving;
²² for *those blessed by the Lord shall inherit the land,*
but those cursed by him shall be cut off.

²³ Our steps are made firm by the Lord,
when he delights in our way;
²⁴ though we stumble, we shall not fall headlong,
for the Lord *holds us by the hand.*
²⁵ I have been young, and now am old,
yet I have not seen the righteous forsaken
or their children begging bread.
²⁶ They are ever giving liberally and lending,
and their children become a blessing.

²⁷ Depart from evil, and do good;
so you shall abide forever.
²⁸ For the LORD loves justice;
he will not forsake his faithful ones.
The righteous shall be kept safe forever,
but the children of the wicked shall be cut off.
²⁹ *The righteous shall inherit the land,*
and live in it forever.

³⁰ The mouths of the righteous utter wisdom,
and their tongues speak justice.
³¹ The law of their God is in their hearts;
their steps do not slip.
³² The wicked watch for the righteous,
and seek to kill them.
³³ The LORD *will not abandon them to their power,*
or let them be condemned when they are brought to trial.

³⁴ *Wait for the Lord, and keep to his way,*
and he will exalt you to inherit the land;
you will look on the destruction of the wicked.

³⁵ I have seen the wicked oppressing,
and towering like a cedar of Lebanon.
³⁶ Again I passed by, and they were no more;
though I sought them, they could not be found.

³⁷ Mark the blameless, and behold the upright,
for there is posterity for the peaceable.
³⁸ But transgressors shall be altogether destroyed;
the posterity of the wicked shall be cut off.

³⁹ The salvation of the righteous is from the LORD;
he is their refuge in the time of trouble.
⁴⁰ The LORD helps them and rescues them;
he rescues them from the wicked, and saves them,
because they take refuge in him. (Emphasis added)

When Jesus said to these disciples, "Fortunate are you because you are meek, for you will inherit the earth," I hear, particularly within this narrative, that he was referring them to the overall message of Ps 37. He was not taking verse 11 out of its context. He was invoking the entire psalm, which faithful Jews would have known.

The identical Hebrew phrase *"yeru su ares"* is used in verses 9, 11, 22, 29, and 34 of this psalm. The phrase is translated in the NRSV as "inherit the land." The phrase could be equally be translated "inherit the earth," because the Hebrew *ares* may mean earth or land. The promise of God to the Hebrew people is so linked to the promise of the land of Israel that it is fitting that the poet of Ps 37 would have meant "land" rather than "earth." And the universal mission of Christianity also makes it fitting that the teaching of Jesus refers to the more universal "earth" rather than "land."

What was Jesus communicating to his first four disciples when he taught them: "Fortunate are you because you are meek, for you will inherit the earth"? What would these disciples have understood? For this we need to consider what this psalm teaches overall.

Who were the "meek" referred to in Ps 37:11? Consider the descriptions in the psalm of the people who will "inherit the land." Those "who wait for the LORD" (v. 9). The "meek" (v. 11). Those "blessed by the LORD" (v. 22). The righteous "who are generous and keep giving" (vv. 21, 29). Those "who wait for the LORD and keep his way" (v. 34), and who "trust in the LORD and do good" will "live in the land and enjoy security" (v. 3).

The psalmist "frets" (vv. 1, 7, 8) at the "prosperity" (vv. 7, 38) and "evil devices" (vv. 7, 14) of the "wicked" (vv. 1, 10, 12, 13, 16, 17, 20, 21, 28, 32, 34, 35, 38, 40). The psalmist is impatient for their just punishment (vv. 9, 10). But he teaches that we should "be still before the LORD and wait patiently for him" (v. 7), "trust" in the LORD (vv. 3, 5), and "wait" (vv. 7, 9, 10) for the LORD to enact justice by thwarting the wicked and saving the meek from their suffering (vv. 9, 13, 17, 20, 28).

"Be still" in Hebrew is *daman*, which is stillness is the sense of silence but not inaction. So while we are waiting for the LORD, we should refuse to complain, follow his way (vv. 5, 7, 23, 34) by giving generously (v. 21) and doing good (v. 27). Trusting in the LORD does not mean for this psalmist doing nothing and leaving all up to God.

So we should be steady in our trust in God to bring the Kingdom. In the meantime, we should be just, give generously, and do good. Our faith in God's promises should empower us to persist on the Way of the Kingdom of Mercy. An abused mother of three children, for instance, can be "meek" toward God under this Beatitude by trusting God enough that she is empowered to take the risk of leaving her abuser, and thereby giving generously to her children a peaceful, safe home, doing good to herself and her children.

Sixth Step: Matthew 5:5

When Jesus directs the disciples to the message of Ps 37 to continue to wait in trust and faith for God to bring mercy and justice to the suffering world, Jesus is engaging with them in the issue of *theodicy*—the justice of God.

Disciples generally hold in their hearts and minds at once three essential propositions:

1. God is good and therefore merciful and just.
2. God is powerful.
3. Evil and the suffering it causes are real and pervasive.

The burning question of our time is how our God the LORD can be just and good when God doesn't use God's power to end the evil of so much unjust suffering?

When our first four disciples were called by God through Jesus into the crowds of suffering humanity, and witnessed Jesus' good power to cure, all three of these essential propositions seemed to fit together in a faithful whole. Jesus was using God's goodness and power to defeat the evil of suffering. The evil of the suffering of the crowd was clearly real and pervasive. But through Jesus God was good and powerful enough to "cure" them (Matt 4:24).

But even Jesus' powerful goodness could not continue to be enough for these disciples to vindicate the justice of God. Jesus was curing only a fraction of suffering humanity during his time with the disciples. When Jesus was resurrected, his good power of curing the suffering left the world too soon, evidently leaving creation in its former condition. If God had the power to send Jesus to end the unjust suffering within Jesus' sight and touch, why did the good and powerful God not also end the suffering everywhere? Was God's goodness and justice only temporary and arbitrary? Hasn't the rank injustice of the world increased since Jesus was killed and raised? Will the justice and goodness of God be manifested totally and permanently when Jesus returns, the Kingdom comes to full fruition, when "[God] will wipe every tear from their eyes. Death will be no more; mourning and crying and pain will be no more" (Rev 21:4)? Even if Jesus does return to end all suffering, why has God let this suffering go on so long? What if the apocalyptic world view is wrong, and he never returns as predicted in Rev 21?

For us now, at least one of the above three propositions of God's power, God's goodness, and evil's pervasiveness must be modified for us not to give up on the Way. The many ways to make this modification may include singly or together:

- Despite the suffering of the innocents, the goodness of God causes or allows suffering to continue because suffering is the spur and the arena for human mercy and meaning; or
- God's goodness confers freedom and autonomy on humanity and all of creation, at the cost of chaos, bad choices, injustice, and suffering; or
- God delegates to us the entire stewardship of the human community and all creation; or
- God lacks the power to change the essential nature of creation, which includes mortality, sin, impermanence, suffering, and death; or
- God's power is limited by God's essential humility, so God does not impose God's power and justice on creation; or
- Suffering is just and therefore not evil because we have sinned and brought the suffering upon ourselves and creation; or
- The evil of suffering is qualified by its transience and the transience of this world; or
- God will defeat the injustice of evil and random suffering with the final judgment and the bliss of heaven to those who remain righteous through the evil; or
- God's time is not our time; or
- Who are we to question the wisdom of God?

All of these attempts to defend the justice of God pale when I see so very many children who have been sexually abused by their fathers. Or when I read about how white people of this nation, including some of my own ancestors, enslaved Black people. Or how we, in league with many churches, oppressed the First Nations of North America by stealing their land and confining their children in so-called schools in the late nineteenth and early twentieth centuries to "kill the Indian, save the man."[24] Or when I see film clips of children wounded and killed from the bombing during Vietnam, or during Russia's aggression in Ukraine, or during the war upon innocent children by Palestinians and Israelis, or from the bombing of hospitals in the Gaza by Israeli forces, or from the war in Sudan, or from senseless mass school shootings in the US, or when I learn again how we are fouling this precious planet out of our ignorant greed.

And all the above attempts to defend the justice of God surely seemed feeble to Andrew, Simon, James, and John when they experienced the suffering of the crowds, and particularly of children.

But I also believe that Jesus was the Messiah who spoke for God and was God. So I am back to what these Beatitudes say. And back to what keys Ps 37 provides about understanding "blessed are you who are meek."

This psalmist confronts the *theodicy* challenge. He despairs over the injustice and the prosperity of the wicked in a world he hopes will soon be under God's reign. But he does not give up hope. He does not give up the Way of faithfulness to the LORD. He tells us to be still before the LORD and wait patiently for the rescue of God's good justice. He tells us not to fret over those who prosper in their oppression of the poor, because God will soon cut them off. He tells us that we can and should therefore refrain from anger. He says that the meek are those who continue to trust and commit themselves to the Way of the Kingdom of Mercy while waiting patiently for the LORD's mercy and justice to prevail over the evil. He writes that the meek are those who are righteous by mercifully lending and giving, and by doing good while waiting. He assures us that these meek are the ones who will finally prosper by receiving the promise of the land from the LORD. The wicked use violence and force against the poor and the needy. The wicked borrow and do not pay back. The wicked prosper in all their ways. But they will not finally prevail. "Yet a little while, and the wicked will be no more" (v. 10), writes the psalmist. It is the righteous, not the wicked, who will inherit the promise of God.

Evil is pervasive, says Jesus when he quotes a portion of this psalm to his disciples. But God is still to be trusted, because God is still good and powerful. The coming of the mercy and justice of the Kingdom has been delayed, but the arrival is "at hand" (Matt 4:17). Despite your broken heart and crushed spirit, despite your mourning for the wickedness of the world and for all who suffer in it, Jesus says to trust God "meekly" by continuing to follow God's Way. God's Kingdom of Mercy will prove not only to be good but also powerful. The Kingdom of Mercy is here and on its way. The meek *will* inherit the land. We can be sure that Jesus believed this, committed himself to this belief, and died for his commitment. It is as if he said, "The Father's time is not our time," says Jesus. "And the

Father's time to bring the Kingdom and defeat the evil and injustice is finally at hand! So jump out of your boats and follow me!"

The strongest temptation to leave Jesus' Kingdom Way now is that it hasn't been "a little while" (v. 10). Psalm 37 was composed hundreds of years before Jesus arrived. The people of God had been waiting for God to protect the meek and punish the wicked for a long time before this psalm was composed and have been for a long time since.

Jesus gave his disciples and us this Beatitude about hoping in God for the future to sustain us on God's Way in the present. "Fortunate are you meek" (in the present), "for you will inherit the earth" (in the future). All of his teachings and his example were about our Steps on the Way while we are *still* waiting for the Kingdom to arrive finally, steps of mercy that have goodness and power now and help God to bring the Kingdom of Mercy now and finally.

We reach and abide in this Step of meekness, as Jesus taught it, when we realize that we alone cannot defeat the causes of evil. We become meek on the Way of the disciple when we accept that we cannot save the world by defeating the kingdoms of darkness and suffering with their own means and methods. We become meek when we receive the gift of trusting that it is God alone who can *and will* save the world from so much suffering and evil despite the delay, and that we can only serve and bear this salvation by staying on God's Way of Mercy.

Some turn to God and God's Way as a last resort, all other resorts having failed. Some persist in staying on God's Way despite the temptation to abandon it. Some abandon it for a time and then return. Some abandon it forever, because God's rescue has been too long in coming and God's methods seem too slow and weak. The alternative to staying on the Way of discipleship is to give up because of our broken hearts, our crushed spirits, and our mourning—or to turn back to the ways of the kingdoms of darkness or to deny our and the world's pain with distractions and lies. Continuing to "meekly" trust God when we are brokenhearted, crushed in spirit, and mourning at the darkness in the world is a matter of blessing and resolve. It is a gift and decision.

The Sixth Step on the Way of the disciple is to receive the blessing of meekness to trust God's promise of the Kingdom and to continue on Jesus' Way, even as our hearts are broken, our spirits are crushed, and we mourn for so many who suffer.

Sixth Step: Matthew 5:5

***

Sarah asked to meet with Dr. Cotswald before her meeting with the trustees. They sat in his mahogany paneled office in upholstered chairs with a coffee table between them. Commentaries on the books of the Bible lined the shelves on the walls. A huge Bible with gold-leaf–edged pages sat on the coffee table.

After vacuous preliminaries at which Dr. Cotswald excelled, Sarah asked what the trustees wanted to question her about in the coming meeting. The pastor said that they were concerned that she and the volunteer staff continued to serve people in the country illegally.

"Who picks the board of trustees?" Sarah asked him. "How did the church get a board full of trustees who don't care about hungry women and children?"

"Oh I think you are being a little emotional, Sarah. They care."

"They don't care enough for it to impact their decision making. When it comes to issues about property and security, they forget compassion. People are hungry whether or not they have some piece of paper. Why should we care about anything other than their hunger?"

"These are complicated times, Sarah. And this issue is maybe more complicated than you think. People are staying home from church in droves after COVID. We think we have more people attending online than in person. Young people aren't contributing financially as faithfully as their parents and grandparents did. We are running a large deficit in our budget. We have a huge building plant, and it requires a lot of staff and a lot of maintenance. Some of our largest and most faithful donors are all riled up over illegals. If we continue to serve them at the mission, it will be all the excuse many of them need to donate their money elsewhere."

"What of the teaching of Jesus to care for the hungry stranger."

"The mission will continue to serve hungry strangers. Maybe just not all of them. If the choice were between some or all, which would you choose?"

"I think I would choose having a church leadership that changes people's minds and hearts about failing to feed hungry strangers in our midst."

Cotswald flinched and took a moment to sip his hot tea.

"I think you are crediting me with more power of persuasion than I have. People listen to me maybe twenty minutes a week, if they attend worship or watch online. The voices demonizing illegals are many and loud."

"Pastor, won't you come to the mission and meet some of the mothers and children we serve? So you can put faces and names and stories next to your preconceptions? So you can tell their stories in your sermons?"

"I am afraid that would be seen to many as taking sides on this issue."

"Shouldn't a minister of Jesus take the side Jesus took when he was alive?"

Pastor sipped his tea again and made no reply.

"Pastor, you said that the mission would continue to serve some hungry strangers. But the trustees are recommending that the church vote to shut down the mission to sell the building and the parking lot."

"They are concerned about the overall church. They have responsibility to keep the entire church open, not just the mission. . . . Sarah, if you and the volunteers would just stop serving undocumented people, you might, I say might, be able to defeat the trustees' proposal. . . . Please don't quote me on that."

"For how long?"

"What do you mean?"

"How long until they would come up with some other heartless reason to shut down the mission?"

"I can't tell you that."

"I don't know that I have it in me to refuse hungry people food just because they don't have some piece of paper to prove they were born north of a river. We'd lose a lot of volunteers. . . . Jesus! How did the church get an entire board of trustees who don't know any poor people and don't care about what they are going through?"

"May I ask you a question? When did you start caring?"

"I think it was when I watched that young mother get arrested and separated from her baby just because she slept outside of our church. And since I took responsibility for keeping the mission running, I have seen the faces and heard the voices of the people we serve at the mission. That's why I wish you would come to the mission to see and hear them. And for the trustees to do the same."

"Sarah, let's think together about this. The trustees live in a closed world of money and property. It's the only world they've ever known. I don't think they want to know the world of the people the mission serves. And they certainly don't want that world touching theirs."

"So the trustees are people who spend their entire lives, personal and professional, concerned most about money and property."

"Not most. Totally concerned . . . except for their concern for their families. And even that turns into concern about their families having plenty of money and things. We need trustees who know what they are doing in that world of property and money. Trustees deal with property and money for the church. Sarah, like it or not, this church is a business. We must take in at least as much as we pay out, or we close. We need people with business skills to direct how we use our property. Or we will lose it."

"So who picked them?"

"The trustees?"

"Yes."

"There is a committee on nominations."

"And who picks them?"

"I suppose I do, with input from many people."

"What people?"

"People I trust. People who have served the church faithfully. People who contribute consistently to the church budget."

"How long has Bill Anderson been head of the trustees?"

"For many years."

"Is he one of the people who helps you pick the trustees?"

"Of course. He and his family are the contributors of the largest amount of money to the church."

"So the people who contribute consistently to the church budget are the people you trust. And they pick themselves to be trustees and run the property."

Cotswald did not reply.

"Do they own the church?"

"The church is a nonprofit corporation."

"Who owns it?"

"No one. We are independent and independent of any other church organization. We answer only to ourselves."

"Someone has to own a corporation. Who incorporated it?"

"The Board of Trustees at the time."

"Was Bill Anderson on the trustees at the time?"

"No. But his father was."

"Has Jesus ever been listed as an owner? Or a trustee?"

"Now, Sarah."

"Where do you stand on the mission, Dr. Cotswald? Do you support closing the mission to sell the property?"

"I leave that up to the trustees and the vote of the church."

Sarah looked sadly at Cotswald. The silence began to be awkward. "What hill are you willing to die on, pastor?"

He blinked at her and took still another long sip of his tea.

"Sarah, let me be a pastor to you for a moment. How is your marriage?"

"You mean, how is my husband dealing with my commitment to the mission?"

"Exactly."

"I'll just say this. . . . He would fit in well with the trustees."

"Are you willing to sacrifice your marriage for the mission?"

"Pastor, I've seen things I can't unsee. I've heard crying I can't unhear. I want my husband to be open to seeing and hearing the things I am. But he is an investment banker, as you know, and he has his banker's blinders on. He doesn't want to take the blinders off. He won't even admit he is wearing them. The people he is around every day don't want to see and hear anymore than he does. I can't wear those blinders with him anymore. It is pretty much out of my hands. I can't go back to being blind and deaf. And dumb."

"So you understand our trustees more than you were letting on."

"I suppose you are right."

"It's going to break your heart."

"What is?"

"All the need out there and how little you can really do about it."

"You sound like you know what you are talking about."

"I'll tell you something I haven't told anyone else in this church, and I will trust you to keep it to yourself. Can I? Good. I have been ordained for almost forty years. I am about done with ministry. It is too late for me to die on any hill. For the first ten years of my ministry, I was a teacher and the chaplain at a home for children and teens with profound developmental delays and intellectual impairments. Many of them had been physically abused before being abandoned. Some were so impaired that they were unable to perform any activities of daily living for themselves. Many were much more capable than that but so wounded by abuse that they had bouts of uncontrollable rage. All these youngsters were basically confined in that home. It was like a prison.

"After ten years in that place, I was angry and disillusioned. I guess I was what they call now 'burned out.' But more than being burned out I had lost my faith in the presence of God. How could God allow those innocent children to suffer like that? So I took a leave of absence from ministry. I hiked and camped out. I stayed away from church. I took a job as a toll booth operator. But as time went on, and as I thought back on what I had seen in that hellhole, I developed some perspective. My faith came back.

"I did see a lot of undeserved suffering in that place. I saw a lot of employees there who were just going through the motions and who could also be impatient and cruel to the kids. It was a very challenging job. But I saw more acts of kindness than I saw acts of indifference or cruelty. I saw underpaid staff who stayed at that job for years just because they really cared for those kids. I finally reached a point where I realized that it is all in God's hands and we have to trust him. So I came back to ministry to serve as a traditional pastor in traditional churches. I worked my way up the ladder to this church by respecting the demands and challenges of the world in which the members of my churches live. Although the members of this church are generally quite comfortable materially, their lives can still be filled with crises. I have tried to be more of a pastor than a prophet to them."

"So you haven't asked the members of your churches to take on other people's challenges in other worlds—the world of the poor, the world of the suffering," said Sarah.

"Everyone suffers, Sarah. You know that. God put me here. I really believe that. So I am pastor to the people here, not people somewhere else."

"But, Dr. Cotswald, God put you in a downtown church in a city and a neighborhood where homeless and poor people live! They live here, too!"

"Sarah, my hands are filled with the members of the church."

"So if we get the people we serve at the mission to become members of the church, will your hands then be large enough to help them?"

"I can see I have made a mistake being this honest with you."

Sarah would not let up.

"If this weren't bothering your conscience, pastor, you wouldn't have been this honest with me. Because you know we are right about this, and it is bothering you that you are staying off the hill we are about to die on. What about the consciences of the people who are members of this church now? What about their souls ... and their relationships with God? Aren't they called by Jesus to use their resources to help those in need?"

"They are using their resources to help people through the mission. Our mission has been operating for decades."

"And the trustees are trying to close it! And most of the funding for the mission comes from grants from foundations not from the members of this church!"

"Sarah, I appreciate your passion. But we have to be realistic.... Will you pray with me?" He reached out both his hands to her.

"No, I won't pray with you! I won't let you use prayer to keep from facing this!"

Sarah saw that Cotswald's hands were trembling and that he looked clammy. "I'm sorry. If you want to pray, let's pray."

"No," he said. "You are right."

Beads of sweat were appearing on Cotswald's face.

"Do you want me to leave, pastor? Have I gone too far? I realize that you are caught between two sets of responsibilities here. I have been too critical of you."

"No. Stay. I need to step out for a moment. Please stay here." Dr. Cotswald stood, walked shakily out of the room, and closed his office door behind him. Sarah was left in the room alone. A few moments later, Cotswald's secretary knocked gently, opened the door, and looked in.

"Does Dr. Cotswald want me to leave?" Sarah asked the secretary.

"No," she said, "he wants you to stay. I think he went into the little chapel. He has diabetes, and he needed to check his blood sugar on his monitor. He'll be right back. Can I get you some more tea?"

"No, thank you." Sarah sat in uncomfortable silence for more than ten minutes. She stood to leave just as Cotswald returned. They both sat back down.

"Are you okay?" asked Sarah.

"Oh yes, I just needed to attend to something."

"Is it type 1?"

"Type 1 what?"

"Diabetes."

"How did you know that I have diabetes?"

Sarah said nothing. Cotswald turned and stared at the closed office door.

"That's one more thing I will ask you to keep in confidence," he said.

"I promise that I will."

Sixth Step: Matthew 5:5

They sat in silence again.

Sarah spoke first. "As you said a minute ago, everyone suffers."

"Yes, everyone."

"Is this threatening your ability to stay at this job?"

"My diabetes is brittle, as they say. Big swings of blood sugar. Starting to affect my energy and even my eyesight. Stress seems to worsen it."

"This controversy about the mission can't be helping."

"You keep worrying about the mission and its clients. That is your calling now. . . . Sarah, you can only do what you can do. The result is not entirely in your hands. Just like my diabetes and my energy don't seem to be entirely in my hands anymore. The prayer I was going to say with you was the serenity prayer. 'God give me the strength to change the things I can change, the faith to accept the things I can't change, and the wisdom to know the difference.'"

"So are you telling me that I should quit trying to change the trustees, meekly follow their directions, and leave it all in God's hands?"

"No, I am not telling you that. I am saying that if the church votes to close the mission, I hope you don't lose your faith. Or your passion. My point of using the serenity prayer is for you to consider that there is one thing you can change. You can change your policy of serving the undocumented. But then . . . maybe you can't change that because your conscience won't let you. I guess I don't know what I am telling you. Isn't that pathetic? I don't know why I told you so much about myself. I just felt moved by your passion to tell you. . . . But I do know this. There is so much suffering out there that it will break your heart if you dwell in it. Not on it. In it. It will suck the joy of life right out of you. One person—you—can only see a small amount of all the suffering out there, but even seeing that much can ruin life for you. You can only do so much about it. I know I am rambling here, but there is so much suffering that only God can fix it. And God isn't. Or hasn't yet. So how can we? We all hope that God will fix this mess someday. But in the meantime, God is in the joyful places too. And I want this church to be a place of joy, not a place of controversy and meanness. So maybe I would advise you to take your turn helping these poor people who are hurting. But then I would advise that you get back to the happy parts of life where God is too."

"I hear you, pastor. But I am still asking you to come to the mission to see the faces of the people we are helping."

"Thank you, Sarah. But I just can't. I can't look at those faces anymore."

"Dr. Cotswald, why are you trusting me with all this about yourself?"

"I don't know. I shouldn't have made this about me. Maybe because I have been where you are now. And I don't want you to lose the happiness in your life or your trust in God."

Seventh Step

Matthew 5:6

⁶ Blessed are you who hunger and thirst for righteousness, for you will be filled.

Are we fortunate to hunger and thirst to be righteous ourselves, for God to be righteous, or for the arrival of the righteousness of the Kingdom of Mercy? My answer is "all three." They are inseparable.

The four disciples abandoned their boats at the chance to change their lives' purpose by going with Jesus. They must have been excited and inspired by his charisma and his promise that the long-awaited Kingdom was at hand. So, they changed everything—their minds, their hearts, their lives—and went with him. But then they encountered the demands of the Kingdom of Mercy and its discipleship. The depth and breadth of the suffering crushed their spirits. Their hearts were broken, and they mourned deeply for the world and all its afflicted. But then Jesus blessed them with the trust and patience in God of the meek, and they were blessed to be empowered to stay on the Way of the disciple.

This Seventh Step of hungering and thirsting for righteousness is the necessary and natural next Step as we continue on the Way. The four disciples' initial enthusiasm and energy have been wounded by the suffering they witnessed and experienced, but they meekly continued on the Way. The suffering they had seen fueled an even deeper hunger and thirst for the arrival of the righteousness of the Kingdom of Mercy. It's as if they said, "Alright, Father. We will meekly continue to trust you and walk the

Way toward your Kingdom. But . . . where is it? When is it going to save your people from the darkness of their terrible suffering? Whenever it comes will not be soon enough." Their meekness did not turn into complacent acceptance of the evil and suffering in the world. Trusting meekly in God did not lead them to leave all in God's hands or retreat back to their boats. They found a middle ground between believing that everything depended upon them alone and that everything depended upon God alone. Their hope in the coming Kingdom was renewed, inspiring an insistent, greater yearning for its arrival.

Being "still before God" (Ps 37:7) can lead to a deadly passivity. People who put everything in God's hands can abdicate any responsibility to minister to the suffering crowd. "After all, it's all in God's hands. If God doesn't deal with it, why should I? It must be God's will that the crowd suffers while I am so comfortable." It is the hunger and thirst for the righteousness of ourselves, of God, and of the Kingdom, to relieve the suffering that keeps us on the courageous Way.

I have a treasured friend who serves on the board of directors of the Methodist Justice Ministry. Mike Moncrief will always be for me the mayor of my home town of Fort Worth. Mike was raised in a wealthy home, but he has deep passion for helping the poor and particularly the homeless. He and his wife Rosie have used their personal wealth and his positions as the county judge, a Texas state senator, and as mayor to protect and provide for the poor. Mike has a saying, probably not original to him but one he has made his own and is very much to the point of this Beatitude. "When you pray," Mike always tells us, "move your feet."

These four disciples had been rescued from their despair by the promise that the LORD would soon set things right. The Kingdom of Mercy needs disciples with fervor and passion, not ones who are simply going obediently through the motions. The Kingdom needs disciples who will "move their feet" in a run while they pray and trust God with the outcome. The Kingdom needs disciples who will indeed "wait for the LORD" (Ps 37:9), but who will also "mount up with wings, like eagles," who will "run and not be weary," and who will "walk and not faint" while they wait (Isa 40:31).

Poverty of spirit and mourning alone will lead eventually to loss of ardor. Jesus describes in this Beatitude a resurrection of the passion and energy that caused the disciples to leave everything originally to follow him. Jesus says to these men in this Beatitude, "A blessing from God causes you to recover your 'hunger and thirst.' Then you become even more deeply committed."

The Greek word translated hunger in this Beatitude is *peinao*, the sense of which is "to crave ardently" or "to seek with eager desire" (*Strong's Online Greek Concordance*).

"Fortunate are you when you hunger and thirst." Not simply "want and desire." Not just "I could eat." True hunger is visceral and all-consuming. When we are truly hungry, the need takes over our personalities. When we are truly thirsty, the thirst consumes us. One day when we were on a medical mission trip in Zambia, in a village far from clean water, our team too quickly drank all of our bottled water in the intense African heat. We were left without any water for another three hours in 110 degrees Fahrenheit because we drank too quickly and our expected supply bus had broken down. We kept treating patients, but our thirst—our ardent craving—for water was much more than a mere want. It was intense and eventually painful. The village had a source of fetid water. If we drank from it, our puny immune systems would have been quickly overmatched. We were so thirsty it was hard for us to think of anything else. That's the severity of thirst Jesus is speaking of in this Beatitude.... A thirst for righteousness.

Consider the thirst of a deer in a dry forest or an arid plain, one who has been hiding from predators during a hot day, waiting to slip to a stream at night to drink:

> [1] As a deer longs for flowing streams,
> so my soul longs for you, O God.
> [2] *My soul thirsts for God,*
> *for the living God.*
> When shall I come
> and behold the face of God?
> [3] My tears have been my food day and night,
> while people say to me continually,
> "Where is your God?" (Ps 42; emphasis added)

This psalmist thirsts for God like a desperate deer thirsts for water. Both God and water are necessary to sustain life. In this Beatitude, Jesus says how fortunate his disciples are when we thirst desperately for God's and the Kingdom's righteous mercy, and for us to become righteous, merciful, and just people of God's Kingdom.

Imagine the hunger Jesus felt after fasting forty days in the wilderness. But when "offered" bread by the devil, Jesus said that what we truly hunger for is not bread but "every word that comes from the mouth of God" (Matt 4:4 quoting Deut 8:3). Likewise, the "righteousness" referred to in this Beatitude is a "word" of God for which we are blessed to hunger. It is the righteousness—the mercy of the Kingdom—for which the world truly hungers and thirsts. Its prolonged delay in coming has led to a kind of death in life. A world without the Kingdom's mercy is at greater risk of death in life than our mission team was without water.

Consider Ps 107:9: "For he [the Lord] satisfies the thirsty, and the hungry he fills with good things." In this Beatitude, Jesus says that the kingdom's merciful righteousness is the good thing with which the Father satisfies and fills us.

Consider Jesus' teaching a few verses later in Matthew 6:

> [31] Therefore do not worry, saying, "What will we eat?" or "What will we drink?" or "What will we wear?" [32] For it is the Gentiles who strive for all these things; and indeed your heavenly Father knows that you need all these things. [33] But strive first for the kingdom of God and his righteousness, and all these things will be given to you as well.

Striving for the righteousness of the Kingdom is also the hungering and thirsting of this Beatitude. How will food and drink be given to us if we hunger first for the kingdom? Because in the community of the Kingdom of Mercy, we share food and drink with one another, and everyone is assured of the necessities of life.

We truly hunger and thirst for what we cannot live without. Jesus is telling his disciples that the righteous mercy of the Kingdom is what we must have to sustain a life truly worth living. Therefore, we are blessed to hunger and thirst for it. We throw ourselves headlong in our search for it. We "repent" of our old hungers and thirsts, and crave righteous mercy.

The kingdoms of the world view the righteousness of the Kingdom as anything but essential to life. The Kingdom's righteousness is an obstruction to what these kingdoms teach their citizens to crave. These kingdoms hunger and thirst for power, wealth, possessions, comfort, and shallow pleasures. The Kingdom of Mercy's righteousness is like the unwelcome mustard plants that infiltrate the other kingdoms' fields (Matt 13:32).

The Greek word in the manuscripts translated in the NRSV as "righteousness" in this Beatitude is *dikaiosune*, a word meaning justice and righteousness. This Beatitude could properly be translated as "Blessed are those who hunger and thirst for justice," which is how it is translated in a minority of translations. *Dikaiosune* is derived from *dikaios*, which is analogous to the Hebrew word *tsadeq*, which may also be translated properly as "righteous" or "just." Righteousness, justice, and mercy are inseparable in the Kingdom.

Justice generally means "rendering to someone *what they are due*," a definition that raises as many questions as it answers. But it is inspiring to consider the "righteousness" of this Beatitude in the sense of justice.

The seven questions running throughout the Hebrew and Greek scriptures are:

> What is God *due* from me as an individual?
> What is God *due* from us as a community?
> What is the other person *due* from me?
> What is the other person *due* from us?
> What am I *due* from myself?
> What am I *due* from God?
> What are we *due* from God?

These are all questions about justice—of *what is due*—and so are about Kingdom righteousness as well. All of these questions concern the righteous and just relationships between God and me, God and us, within the human community, within the many aspects of my and our beings, and among all of creation.

Critical to answering these questions about justice within the human community is how we view the so-called other. Jesus' parable of the Good Samaritan is a clear example of the Kingdom of Mercy's answer (Luke 10:25–37). "Who is the neighbor we are called to love as we love ourselves under Leviticus 19:18?" asks the lawyer. "Anyone in need whom we find in our path," answers Jesus through this parable. This was and is a question of justice—what is this needy stranger "due" under the Jewish law of Torah? In the Great Sermon, Jesus tells us that even the "other" of the enemy is "due" our love (Matt 5:44). Who could be more "other" than an enemy? Yet Kingdom justice and righteousness call us to be merciful in our love for all in need as we love ourselves.

But focus now on an aspect of the just righteousness, or the righteous justice, of the Kingdom in the relationship between God and humans. What are we due from God? In a real sense, God being God and we being God's creatures, we are in no position initially to contend that we are due anything from God (see Job 38:1–2). God has created us from nothing, an act of pure undeserved grace. We should be grateful for whatever God gives us.

Having said this, among the gifts God has graciously made to us are certain promises.

The promise of God that is at the center of Matthew's Gospel is that the Kingdom of Mercy is both at hand and soon to come (Matt 4:17). By making this promise, God has graciously created a merciful relationship with us based upon justice. Why? Because it is only just and fair that God keep that promise. We are "due" for God to keep this promise. Part of the righteousness and justice for which we are blessed to hunger and thirst in this Beatitude is the righteousness and justice *of God* in keeping God's promise to bring the Kingdom—a Kingdom of Mercy that reorders all the relationships among humans and between God and humans. We ask "How long, O LORD?" until God justly keeps God's promise of the arrival of the Kingdom of Mercy (Ps 13:1).

A critical aspect of the Kingdom's righteousness and justice is thinking and speaking the truth (Matt 5:33–37). Much of what the other is due from me is for me to think and speak the truth about the other as an individual and about the group of which the other is a member. What God is due from me is to think and speak the truth about God. What I am due from myself is to think, face, and tell the truth about myself to myself and to others. All this truth thinking and truth telling is part of God's righteousness and justice. Putting it in simpler words, lying about the other, about God, and about myself should be unjust and unrighteous in any kingdom. It *is* unjust and unrighteous in God's Kingdom (Isa 9:15; 28:5; 59:3–4; Jer 9:5; 13:25; 14:14; 23:14, 25; Ezek 13:8, 19; 21:29; 22:28; Hos 7:13; 10:13; 11:12; Amos 2:4; Mic 6:12; Pss 4:2; 5:6; 7:14; 12:2; 58:3; 59:12; 78:36; 101:7; 119:69; 144:11).

Words can be weapons. Lying can be merciless. A great difference between the kingdoms of the world and the Kingdom of Mercy are the truths each kingdom claims to tell and act out about the other, the self, and God. The essential truths of the Kingdom of Mercy are that the self and all others are children of God who bear the image of God, and that God is powerful mercy. The challenge of the Kingdom is to advocate and sustain those truths despite the behavior of the other and the self, and despite the evil and suffering in the world.

A question for us is not only why people lie, but why people being lied to choose to believe and support those lies.

Seventh Step: Matthew 5:6

I have been a trial lawyer for more than forty-eight years. I have questioned hundreds of parties and witnesses who have promised under oath to tell the truth in criminal, civil, and family depositions, hearings, and trials. Experience has led me to some conclusions about why we lie.

We lie because we value something more than we value the truth and truth telling. We lie because we value avoiding responsibility for our actions more than we value the truth and justice. We lie because we value loyalty to a family member or friend more than loyalty to the truth and justice. We lie because we value an unjust outcome in our favor, even if based upon a lie, more than we value a just outcome against us, even if based upon the truth. We lie because we don't recognize the damage to our character and our soul when we lie. We lie because we hate someone more than we love truth telling. We lie because we believe the other side is lying, so we must lie to keep the other lie from winning and doing an injustice. We lie because we are fed lies by the kingdoms of the world until we lack the discernment to determine what is lie and what is true. We lie because we are afraid to live out the risk and consequences of the truth. We even lie to ourselves because we value our own false self-image over a true one.

We lie so much to get what we want—in money matters and business, in law, in personal matters, in politics, in religion, in social life—that we are becoming a nation of the Lie. This is particularly true in our politics, where supporters of candidates become their little bobblehead dolls, nodding assent to whatever self-serving, disproved, and willfully false lies they tell to obtain or stay in power by stoking the fires of our fears and prejudices.

Why do the kingdoms of the world lie about God and persons? They lie because they do not want to be held accountable by the God of Truth for their idolatry of wealth and things and for treating the other as nothing but a means to the ends they desire. Their lies deny the existence of a God who would hold them accountable for their cruelties. They lie because they do not believe the truth that God is merciful and just, that God will hold merciless people accountable for their actions, and that God is bringing about a more merciful and just world. They lie because they are convinced that they see in others and themselves capacities for fear, condemnation, and force that are more powerful than capacities for mercy, justice, and empathy.

How are disciples called to witness to our truths about the other, God, and ourselves? By *acting* out the truths of the Kingdom of Mercy that the other and the self are children of God bearing the image of God, and that God is mercy. If we do not act out those truths, they are not in fact our truths. If we do not act out these truths, the victims and leaders of the kingdoms of the world will not hear or see our truth.

Jesus models the truth of merciful justice and righteousness to the disciples and to us. Discipleship is leaving our comfort to follow him in this modeling. We proclaim the presence of the Kingdom of Mercy by living into it, by touching, welcoming, and feeding people in need without judgment, and by diving into the river of other people's suffering to help them swim.

For Matthew's Jesus, the Kingdom's merciful righteousness is:

- Protecting the vulnerable and powerless (1:19–24);
- Being with and helping the sick and afflicted (4:23–25);
- Bearing the suffering of others (5:3–6);
- Trusting God while continuing on the Way of the disciple (5:5);
- Hungering and thirsting for the Kingdom's righteous mercy as essential to life (5:6);
- Being merciful to all (5:7, 42, 43–44);
- Making peace (5:9; 10:13);
- Foregoing anger and insult (5:21–22);
- Seeking reconciliation (5:23–24);
- Refusing to treat a woman, or any other person, as an object rather than as a precious child of God (5:28);
- Remaining faithful in marriage and in all relationships (5:32);
- Always speaking the truth when we speak (5:33–37);
- Refusing to return evil for evil (5:38–41);
- Sharing with everyone in need (5:42; 6:2–4; 25:31–46);
- Lending and then turning the debt into a gift (5:42; 6:12; 10:8b; 18:27);
- Loving even our enemies (5:43–48);
- Avoiding shows of self-righteousness (6:2–8, 6–18);
- Refusing to accumulate wealth for personal use (6:19, 24);
- Refusing to worry about possessions (6:25–33);

- Trusting and helping the community of the Kingdom of Mercy to provide for everyone's needs (6:25–34);
- Staying in the present moment by trusting God and the community with the future (6:34);
- Refusing to judge who does and does not deserve our merciful acts (7:1–5; 13:24–30);
- Helping everyone in need with empathy and generosity (8:5–17; 8:28—9:8; 12:9–14; 14:13–21; 15:21–38; 17:14–21; 18:10–14; 20:1–16; 20:29–34; 21:14; 25:31–46);
- Feeding impoverished and hungry people without price (14:13–21; 15:32–38);
- Refusing to reduce our faith to ritual and rules (15:16–20);
- Denying self to bear Jesus' cross of suffering and self-sacrifice (16:24–26);
- Seeking and favoring the lost (18:10–14);
- Forgiving from the heart limitless times (18:21–35);
- Giving up possessions to follow Jesus (19:16–26);
- Seeking to be last not first (20:16);
- Prophetically denouncing the commercialization of our faith (21:12–13);
- Welcoming all into the community of the Kingdom of Mercy (7:1–5; 21:31; 22:14);
- Loving God with all our faculties and being, and our neighbor as we love ourselves (22:34–40);
- Acting as the humble servant of all (23:11–12);
- Practicing justice and mercy as our first priority (23:23);
- Staying always on watch for signs of the coming Kingdom of Mercy (24:42); and
- Feeding the hungry, giving drink to the thirsty, clothing the naked, welcoming the alien, tending the sick, and visiting the prisoner as if they were Jesus himself (25:31–46).

The parable of the goats and sheep at 25:31–46 crystallizes Kingdom righteousness and the Way of the disciple more than any other teaching.

It is what Jesus taught and what Jesus did. See verse 37: "Then the *righteous* will answer him."

The Beatitudes and teachings of Jesus proclaim that God will eventually "make things right" in part through the righteous faithfulness of disciples to the behaviors and practices of the Kingdom. This just righteousness for which disciples are blessed to hunger and thirst is God's Kingdom of Mercy, which will transform the entire human community when it finally and fully arrives. The Kingdom is something disciples must strive for and something they and humanity will be blessed to receive. Disciples are called to be active on the Way while waiting for God to bring the Kingdom. This merciful and just righteousness is something we do and that happens to us as we stay on the Way. That is our mission, our gift, our hope, and our goal.

Honest doubt in the coming of the Kingdom of Mercy is a constant companion on this Way if we truly put ourselves among the suffering and outcast. The doubt that is given voice in Ps 37 persists. Spurred by a doubt overcome by hope, we hunger and thirst for the Kingdom's merciful righteousness.

The Seventh Step on the Way of the disciple is the blessing of even greater hunger and thirst for the Kingdom's righteousness despite our broken hearts, crushed spirits, and mourning, and despite the delay of the Kingdom's culmination.

***

Estrella was inconsolable about the loss of her baby, Esmeralda, and her husband. She spent more hours each day crying than not crying for her infant. Her weeping lasted through most of every night. Janine sat on the edge of Estrella's bed every night, stroking her hair, singing and trying to soothe her to sleep. Soon after she was able to nod off, Estrella often awoke crying from a terrible dream about what she and her family had endured to get here from El Salvador or about something terrible happening to Esmeralda.

Estrella had no appetite. It was a challenge to get her to drink water. Janine felt guilty eating when Estrella could or would not. Both of them, the teenager and the woman in her sixties, were looking haggard.

The sisters were so afraid that Estrella would run away that one of them always kept her with them. They took her to the mission with them. She was a help taking care of other women's babies while the women were sifting through the clothes in the clothing bank. But holding someone else's baby deepened her sadness of the loss of her own.

Janine and Jazmine were only able to persuade Estrella to stay with them by promising her that they were getting closer to finding her child. But they weren't. Estrella could not recall if she had given the police the baby's name once she arrived at the jail. She did recall that while she was awaiting her initial hearing before a magistrate, a Latina woman with a name tag clipped onto her jacket had spoken with her about the baby. She remembered only that the last name on the woman's name tag was Castillo. The woman had wanted information about Estrella and about any other family members in the area who could care for the child. Estrella was too upset and scared to tell her anything, other than a lie that her own name was Maria Serrano. She was sure she had not given the woman her baby's actual name.

The sisters made some phone calls to friends who had taught in public schools in low-income neighborhoods and who had some experience with what was required for CPS to place children in foster care. They were told that this Ms. Castillo was likely a caseworker with Child Protective Services, and that CPS would likely have gone to court to be able to place this child in a foster home. Identifying the lawsuit would be the first step to finding where the child was placed and trying to reunite her with Estrella. But they were also told that the name on the CPS lawsuit would be the name of the child, and Estrella denied that she had told the CPS worker Esmeralda's actual name.

Jazmine was developing a temper. She was getting progressively angry that her church had caused such injustice and suffering to Estrella and Esmeralda. The church security staff had followed the trustees' orders to call the police merely because Estrella was sleeping with her baby on church property. The church should have welcomed both mother and child inside, let them use the bathroom, fed them, and helped them find a safe place to sleep. The worst they should have done was to order Estrella to leave the property. Instead they called police, which led to a baby losing her mother after she had already lost her dad.

In her frustration at not being able to locate the baby and her pain with Estrella's suffering, Jazmine made an uninvited visit to Dr. Cotswald's church office. She was tipped off by the sympathetic secretary that a meeting was happening between Pastor Cotswald, Bill Anderson the chair of the trustees, and two other trustees. Jazmine arrived at the offices as the meeting was starting, barged in, and sat down without being welcomed.

"You need to make right a wrong you did to a defenseless mother and her baby," she said without preliminaries.

Cotswald started to speak, but Jazmine pointed her finger at Anderson and the other two trustees. "I'm talking to them. And I'm not leaving this office until they do the right thing or have me arrested like they had that mother arrested."

"Call security," Anderson said to Cotswald.

"Don't do that. Please. Let's give her a moment," said Joan Donaldson, the owner of a commercial real estate firm bearing her name. "You are one of the ladies who volunteered to keep the mission running while all this gets sorted out. Am I right?"

The pastor said she was right. "This is Jazmine Bodine," he said. Anderson fumed. The other trustee, a man named Rusty Ritter, looked on nervously.

Donaldson pulled her chair closer to Jazmine's chair. "Thank you for all you are doing. But whatever wrong are you talking about, dear? Tell us what we can make right."

Four days later Jazmine Bodine, Janine Bodine, and Estrella Espinoza-Sanchez were sitting in Child Protection Court No. 2 of the county, waiting for a hearing to start. CPS worker Maria Castillo and a certified court interpreter sat with them. Estrella was scared of being arrested and detained, but had overcome her fear in the hope that her baby would be returned to her. Her new lawyer, Jimmie Donaldson, sat up front with the other lawyers in the well of the court. The case, now entitled "In the Interest of Esmeralda Sanchez, a Child," was eighth on the court's docket.

As they all sat there, Dr. Cotswald and Joan Donaldson of the trustees walked into the courtroom and sat in seats two rows behind them.

After Jazmine had unloaded on the three trustees in Cotswald's office about the wrong they needed to right, Donaldson had calmly called her nephew Jimmie Donaldson, an experienced family law attorney in the city and a member of the church. Jazmine explained the situation again to the lawyer. Jimmie said he was close to a CPS supervisor and would try to run down the lawsuit and its status. He was able to do so quickly. CPS caseworker Maria Castillo was quickly dispatched to Jazmine and Janine's home, interviewed Estrella, inspected the home, confirmed that

Esmeralda was indeed Estrella's daughter, conducted a background check on the sisters, and obtained a safety plan signed by Janine, Jazmine, and Estrella that provided that the two sisters would accept temporary custody of Esmeralda and Estrella and keep them at the their home for as long as the CPS lawsuit was still pending.

"There is no way I can pay that lawyer," whispered Estrella to Janine in Spanish.

"He is doing this without charging you."

"Why?"

"Because that lady," Janine pointed to Joan Donaldson, "is paying for it."

Estrella stood quickly from her chair, went to a startled Joan, bent down, and hugged her. "*Gracias, gracias, gracias,*" she said. She stood up and looked into Joan's eyes, which were filled with tears. Estrella's own tears fell on Joan's jacket. "*Muchas, muchas gracias. Dios lo bendiga.*"

"*De nada*, sweetheart," said Ms. Donaldson, patting the girl's arms, then putting one hand gently on Estrella's cheek and wiping away a tear.

As Estrella went back to her seat, Donaldson turned to Dr. Cotswald. "What does '*dios lo* whatever she said' mean?"

"It means 'God bless you.'"

Joan took a tissue out of her purse and dabbed her eyes. "What a sweet, beautiful young girl! And she walked here with her baby all the way from El Salvador? She's so strong! Do you know how many miles she walked? And she's only sixteen! What must she have been running from in her homeland! It makes me feel so good to help her and her baby. . . . I can't wait to see that baby."

After a pause, Ms. Donaldson said to the pastor, "But how will she survive? If she can't find her husband, who will support her? How long are these ladies willing to take care of her? She doesn't seem to speak a bit of English. She has no papers. How will she find work? She ought to be in school . . . but how? . . . Maybe she does need to go back to El Salvador. Maybe I can pay her way back."

"I am afraid that the challenges she faces here are nothing compared to the problems back in her homeland," said Cotswald. "If we were to help her get back to her home, we wouldn't be solving her problems. We'd just be getting her out of our sight."

"We need to keep helping people like her. The church needs to keep helping them," Donaldson replied. "But how?"

She sat lost in thought for a time.

"There will be a lot of pushback from downtown businesses if we keep helping the homeless," said Cotswald.

"Yes," said Joan. "Perhaps if we just allowed women and children to sleep on our property. Not men. Then we would be a kind of haven for the women and children."

"Sleep outside, you mean?" asked the pastor.

"Yes. We can't let them in the buildings, can we." She was making more of a statement than asking a question. She fell back into silence. Cotswald said nothing.

"There are just are so many of them. Why are there so many of them in need?" said Joan.

Cotswald shrugged and took Joan's hand in his.

Then she said, "What a sad world. Whatever we can do for her won't be enough."

"If the judge does what I hope she will today and gives Estrella back her baby, the world won't be as sad for that young mother as it was before you started helping her."

"But she still doesn't know where her husband is. Or what the future holds," replied Joan. "It's overwhelming."

"Small steps and small victories, one at a time, are all we can bring about. Big steps and big victories are in God's hands alone," said Cotswald.

"Hmmm," said Joan. "I know my eyes just got opened to all this. But hurry up, God."

More silence.

"I know of another small step," said Joan. "We need to quit arresting homeless women just for sleeping on our property. That's another wrong we can put right."

"All rise," cried the bailiff.

The judge came in to do the justice she could.

Eighth Step

Matthew 5:7

⁷ Blessed are you who are merciful, for you will receive mercy.

Mercy *is* the righteousness and justice of the Kingdom which we crave. Empathy is the soil in which the seed of mercy grows. Empathy is a feeling. Mercy consists of actions. Having reached the Step in which we disciples hunger and thirst for the Kingdom's justice and righteousness, we receive the blessing of insight that we may *only* participate with God in bringing this justice and righteousness by the actions that are within our power—merciful actions. We receive the blessing of insight that life may not be truly transformed and the Kingdom brought by force that defeats, coerces, kills, and silences those who resist. Instead we receive the trust that life may only be transformed and the Kingdom made present in merciful acts that persuade and inspire.

Disciples share in empathy with the suffering of the crowd and persevere through crushed spirits, broken hearts, and mourning. We are able to continue on the Way only if we receive a capacity to continue meekly in our trust in God's promise of the Kingdom, despite the misery and disappointing delay. But the longer we remain immersed in the suffering of others, in confrontation with the darkness of the world's kingdoms, the more we become dissatisfied. In our dissatisfaction we hunger and thirst more deeply for the arrival of the Kingdom's just and righteous mercy. And as we remain on the Way, immersed longer and longer in the suffering and darkness, we are blessed with the recognition that mercy is our *only* hopeful tactic and response. In ministering to the sufferers as we can, we experience that acts of mercy incarnate the Kingdom's coming.

But when our mortal capacity for mercy is exhausted, some of us are forced to abandon the Way. Perhaps after a rest and merciful support from others, some of us find a renewed capacity for mercy. And we return to minister to the suffering in the darkness.

All of us know people who have been in ministries helping the miserable who must take a break, but are later enabled to return to the Kingdom. I am honored to know a married couple in Zambia, a hospital administrator and a nurse, who helped to run a hospital in a town south of Lusaka. They each suffered repeated bouts of malaria. They fought constant battles to obtain the scarce medications and equipment for the hospital. They recruited and trained nurses from the community. They persevered through threats of closure of the hospital because of low funding. They organized a community campaign against the barbaric practice of clitoral cutting of girls when they reached puberty, and faced bitter opposition and threats of physical violence by elders in the community. Exhausted by the opposition, their illness, and the poverty of the community, they returned to the US. After two years of rest, their spirits were refreshed, they returned to Africa, and they are there still. After a kind of Sabbath, they received renewed capacity for mercy. "Blessed are the merciful, for they will receive an even greater capacity for mercy."

This Beatitude is the Eighth of the Twelve Steps on the Way of the disciple. But it is the fifth of the nine Beatitudes, all of which begin with the Greek "*makaroi*." So this Beatitude is at the center, with four Beatitudes before and four after. This Beatitude of mercy is the apex of the Way. Discipleship is mercy, and mercy is discipleship. Mercy *is* the just righteousness of the Kingdom. The people of the world "sit in darkness . . . in the region and shadow of death" (Matt 4:16) because far, far too little mercy is alive in the world.

Mercy was devalued in the kingdoms of the world before and during Jesus' time on earth.

There is a fascinating discussion of this in Rodney Stark's *The Triumph of Christianity: How the Jesus Movement Became the World's Largest Religion*:

> [I]n the pagan world, and especially among the philosophers, mercy was regarded as a character defect and pity a pathological emotion: because mercy involves providing *unearned* help or relief, it is contrary to justice. . . . [C]lassical philosophers

taught that "mercy indeed is not governed by reason at all" and "humans must learn to curb the impulse"; "the cry of the undeserving for mercy" must go "unanswered." . . . "Pity was a defect of character unworthy of the wise and excusable only in those who have not yet grown-up."[25]

But the truly revolutionary principle was that Christian love and charity must extend beyond the boundaries of family and even those of faith, to all in need.[26]

The kingdoms of the world in our time continue to view mercy as inferior and conflicting with justice. Justice is what is due as a matter of obligation. Mercy is merely optional and no obligation at all. In the legal system of these kingdoms, this obligation to treat another with justice is generally enforceable, one way or another. But there is no enforceable obligation to be merciful. The opposite is true in the Kingdom of Mercy. Disciples of the Kingdom are obliged to be merciful as a matter of justice. Jesus taught in his parables that what all are due as a matter of justice are (1) mercy and (2) to be made merciful. Please see my longer discussion of this in *No Mercy, No Justice: The Dominant Narrative of America versus the Counter-Narrative of Jesus' Parables*. People in misery are particularly "due" this mercy. There is no greater difference between the kingdoms of the world and the Kingdom of Mercy than in this affirmation that mercy is part of justice and justice is part of mercy. The just obligation to be merciful *is* enforced within the Kingdom of Mercy (Matt 7:2; 25:31–46; Luke 16:19–31).

Consider Jesus' parable of the laborers in the vineyard (Matt 20:1–16). According to the kingdoms of the world, each laborer described in the parable was due under the oral contract of employment—a legal matter—the wage that was "right" or "just" (*dikaios* in the Greek, v. 4), surely based upon the number of hours each actually worked. But when it came time to pay the laborers, some of whom had worked the entire day and some only one hour, the vineyard owner paid each the same exact living wage. He did so just to be "generous" (v. 15) to all of the laborers and not for his own credit. In fact, paying all the same living wage to every laborer cost the landowner considerably more than if he had paid strictly by the hour. Within the kingdoms of the world, this equal pay based upon equal need but unequal work was and is manifestly unjust. But within the Kingdom of Mercy, the mercy with which the owner treated all the workers was just and righteous. And by paying first the workers who worked only an hour (v. 8), the owner was modeling mercy to the other workers. Within the Kingdom, justice and mercy are both inseparable aspects of Kingdom righteousness.

Consider also the parable of last judgment (Matt 25:31–46). We will receive the ultimate reward of eternal life for being merciful, and the ultimate punishment of eternal death for failing to be merciful to the hungry, thirsty, stranger, naked, sick, and prisoner. Jesus teaches us in this parable that mercy to the suffering is justice, because the mercy was being done to or withheld from Jesus himself. And what mercy is not due to Jesus as a matter of justice, given all that he has done and does for all of us?

But in this last parable in Matthew, the "righteous" (25:37) were not merciful to obtain a reward. They did not recognize that Jesus was in and with the needy whom the righteous were helping. Their motive for mercy was solely to alleviate suffering. These disciples, for surely they were disciples, ministered to the suffering merely because they had received the blessing of empathy and the will to act mercifully from their exposure to the suffering crowd on the Way. To the suffering and to the disciples, mercy was "due" as a matter of justice because the hungry, thirsty, stranger, naked, sick, and prisoner were children of God made in God's image and in whom Jesus and God were incarnate.

Consider also the parable of the unforgiving servant (Matt 18:23–35). This servant had been mercifully and, in the view of the kingdoms of the world, unjustly forgiven a debt of "ten thousand talents"—the equivalent of more than 150 years of labor! His master mercifully forgave this staggering debt so that the servant, his wife, and his children would not be sold into debt slavery. But this same servant then refused to forgive a much smaller debt owed to him by his own slave and had the slave thrown into prison. When the master learned of the servant's unjust mercilessness, he ordered the servant to be tortured until he repaid his own huge debt—an impossibility evoking the image of eternal damnation. The master said to the servant, "Should you not have had mercy on your fellow slave as I had mercy on you?" In the Kingdom of Mercy, it is unjust to be merciless to anyone bearing the image of God when we have ourselves received so much unjustified mercy from God.

The message of the parable of the unforgiving servant can be interpreted as requiring merciful acts merely so the actor can obtain mercy for herself as a matter of reciprocal justice. This seems much like a verse of our Lord's prayer: "Forgive us our debts, as we have forgiven our debtors" (Matt 6:12). So are we to be merciful selfishly to obtain mercy for ourselves? Or must mercy be motivated completely by the desire to rescue the other and not at all for selfish reasons? Is the message of this central Beatitude that the merciful may be motivated by the mercy we will receive as reward? "Blessed are the merciful, for they will receive mercy."

My experience is that self-centered mercy will have much less positive impact than selfless mercy. People who are merciful for their own benefit "have received their reward," like the giver of alms in Matt 6:1–3. The recipients of such mercy can sense when donors are giving more for their own credit than for the benefit of the recipients. Much of the so-called mercy that is done for honor to the donor isn't truly mercy. Citizens of the world's kingdoms will often donate a fortune for the bricks and mortar of a new chapel or for the purchase of a new sanctuary organ *if* a plaque acknowledging the donor's generosity is displayed prominently. This is not really an act of mercy. The same donor will often not act mercifully by giving anonymously to, for instance, a ministry to feed hungry children. And the actor must be motivated by a deep empathy for the persons in need to persist in sacrificial mercy through despair and discouragement. Otherwise, their mercy will be like the seeds that fall on the well-traveled, public path and that the birds eat before the seeds can sprout (Matt 13:4).

The original Hebrew word for mercy, which Jesus used in this Beatitude, was surely *racham*, derived from the word for a woman's womb. What could be more selflessly and completely giving than the womb of a woman to her unborn baby? Mercy, to be truly merciful, must be motivated by much more than a desire for public credit.

Mercy is its own reward. When we act mercifully we experience mystically our God who causes the sun to shine and the rain to fall mercifully on those who are mercifully righteous and those who are mercilessly unrighteous (Matt 5:45–46). When we experience this God of mercy, the Kingdom of Mercy grows in our souls. No other "reward" is as great or as needed.

How does personal exposure to people's suffering make us empathetic and then merciful? It does so only when we "see" the individual reality of the suffering person, when the person is no longer a mere statistic, a caricature, or "one of them." We all know people who are briefly exposed to the reality of the suffering but who quickly turn their heads and immediately get back into their boats. We have all been this unseeing person at times in our lives. So we don't "see" the individual and don't want to see.

One of the stories about Jesus that speaks to me most deeply is told in Luke 7:36–50. Jesus has been invited to a Pharisee's home for a dinner and a debate. Jesus is being dishonored. He is not welcomed as an honored guest with water to clean his feet, a towel to dry them, and oil to anoint them. Then a shunned "woman of the city who was a sinner" (7:37) sees how Jesus is being dishonored and bursts into the dinner to wash his feet with her tears, wipe them with her hair, and anoint his feet with oil. The Pharisee is critical of Jesus because Jesus did not know "what *kind* of woman this is who is touching him" (7:39; emphasis added). In response, Jesus tells the Pharisee a parable about two sinners, and then asks the Pharisee, "Do you see this woman?" (v. 44). Of course, the Pharisee did not see *her*. He only saw what *kind* of woman he thought she was. Because he did not *see* her individual suffering, he was not moved to empathy and mercy. The foundation of this central Beatitude about mercy is that the more we "see" the suffering, the more our empathy and our capacity for merciful acts grow in us. This Beatitude of the merciful is intimately related to the next Beatitude of those who see. We will discuss this further in the next section.

This is the tragedy of the rich young man in Matt 19:16–22. He was called by Jesus to follow him on the Way to see the suffering and then to receive the blessing of a capacity for mercy. Instead, "he went away grieving, for he had many possessions" (v. 22). If he had just gone with Jesus on the first few Steps on the Way of the disciple, perhaps he would have continued until he became as dedicated to being merciful as he was to preserving and managing his wealth. How many of us might say that about ourselves today? Earlier I wrote that one question raised throughout scripture is "What I am due from myself?" This story of the rich young man's encounter with Jesus re-poses this question. What was this young man due from himself? To let God make him merciful! To abandon himself, his fears of the suffering "other," and his addiction to his possessions to becoming merciful! To free himself from the power of the kingdom of his possessions that opposes the Kingdom of Mercy!

What competing priority for a disciple should there be other than mercy?

Doctrine? Boundary rules? Supporting the institution of the church? Striving for eternal life?

How much harm has been done over the Christian centuries by claims of exclusive possession of doctrinal truths? Religious wars. Conquest and coercion of the First Nations of the western hemisphere.

Inquisitions. Intolerance. Division. Coercion. Hate. All of these without mercy. We can remain in our boats and still be devoted to doctrines that justify our complacency and indifference. Adherence to doctrinal propositions never costs us materially or emotionally as merciful actions do.

How many people have been driven away from Jesus by the self-righteous obsession of some churches with outward obedience to "boundary rules" that determine who is "in" and who is "out"? I refer here to rules like ones excluding women from being clergy or in positions of leadership, excluding persons who have not been baptized in a particular church from taking communion there, excluding remarried persons from receiving any sacrament, excluding any nonheterosexual persons from being clergy or married by the church. Churches attempt to increase solidarity within their congregations by condemning churches who do not abide by these rules. Whole denominations are dividing over whom churches include and whom they exclude. Unlike merciful acts to the poor and the marginalized, churches risk nothing by focusing on these boundary rules. And how gratifying it must be to judge yourself superior and "in" with God because of whom you exclude.

How much harm has been done by prioritizing the wealth, status, authority, and reputation of the church? Denying clergy wrongdoing because admitting it would harm the institution? Silencing and shunning victims? Spending donations that could be used to feed the hungry to make church property more impressive, comfortable to the rich, and forbidding to the poor?

How many suffering people have been denied mercy by our neglecting the "weightier matters" of "justice and mercy and faith" (Matt 23:23)?

The kingdoms of the world insist that mercy is weak and slow compared to violence. But the Kingdom affirms that mercy transforms permanently while force erects temporary, assailable barriers. Mercy encourages while force terrifies. Mercy persuades while force imposes. Mercy unifies while force divides. Mercy inspires cooperation while force causes resentment. Mercy makes friends while force makes enemies. Mercy invites while force threatens. (Whoever heard of the "threat of mercy"?) Mercy sees every person while force is blind to its victims. Mercy brings a lasting, true peace based upon justice and empathy, while force brings a temporary, phony peace based upon cruelty and fear.

Tragically, there is a role for force in this lost world. But the world is in the state it is much because of its worship of force and its idolatry of violence. And *regardless of effectiveness*, the disciple is called in meekness to trust in God by following faithfully the God of Mercy into the darkness.

Many will object that mercy alone to a wrongdoer will simply enable and encourage him to continue his wrongdoing. We in the justice ministry have dealt daily with this issue for almost two decades. We have come to see that holding an abuser or any wrongdoer justly accountable is part of being merciful to him. Merely forgiving a man or woman who repeatedly abuses their child is not merciful to the abuser and certainly not to the abused. Such lack of accountability will not make the abuser more merciful. A child who is mercilessly abused will likely become mercilessly abusive himself. Failing to hold an adult abuser accountable will most often enable the abuser to continue the abuse, which will hurt everyone. The goal is to protect the abused and to encourage the abuser to be the merciful person she or he can be. The goal is to lead the abuser to quit abusing his own soul—to make him a more merciful person in the image of God within. Accountability that forecloses repentance is merciless. Accountability that fosters repentance is merciful to all parties. When there is a conflict between protecting an abused child and being merciful to an abuser, the balance must be struck in favor of the child. The main point is that there are no disposable persons—neither the abused nor the abuser. This idea of the relationship between justice and mercy in the Kingdom is applicable in many settings beyond the scope and space of this particular book.

To the disciple of Jesus, it is mercy—not doctrine, rules, or the institution of the church—that is the light in the darkness (Matt 4:16; 5:14–16,) the salt of the earth (5:13), the mustard seed in the field (13:31–32), the leaven in the loaf (13:33), the treasure hidden in the field (13:44), the pearl of greatest value (13:45), and the net thrown into the sea (13:47).

The Eighth Step on the Way of the disciple is being made more and more merciful, through the suffering we see and experience and the blessing of the spirit of empathy we receive on the Way.

***

Eileen Parker's lupus was becoming symptomatic more often. When the symptoms spiked, she was terribly fatigued and suffered fever, pain in her chest and joints, a rash on her face, depression, and anxiety. She had long waits between her appointments with the rheumatologist who practiced at the local county hospital, and the medication she could obtain through Medicaid was ineffective. She was unable to afford the recommended food like salmon and walnuts to help control the disease, and was unable to exercise regularly with the children suspended from school so often. If Obadiah stayed away from work during the day to care for Eileen, the family lost his small but essential income.

Anne's heart was breaking at the family's plight. She could not visit their home in the projects as often as she wanted because her husband had carried through on his threat to take away her car. Anne's friends were reluctant to give her a ride to the store to buy the family groceries and then into the projects to deliver them because they were afraid of the people who lived there. And the friends' husbands did not want their wives taking sides between Anne and her husband. Her sister Sarah would lend Anne her car whenever she could, but Sarah usually needed her car to be available during her work at the mission.

Sarah and Anne's father, John, was a widower in his sixties and suffered from arthritis. On one occasion when the Parker family was almost out of groceries, Obadiah was at work and Eileen was bedridden, Anne persuaded her father to drive her to the grocery store, shop with her for groceries for the family, and deliver them to the Parker residence in the projects. Anne and Sarah had not told their father the reasons for the tension between Anne and her husband, because John was outspoken in his dislike of the husband. On this occasion, Anne simply told her father that her car was in the shop so she needed his help.

When they arrived with the groceries, Eileen was in bed and looked ghastly. The two boys were home on suspension from school and were running wild. Eileen could not control them. Just rolling over in bed was too painful. The living area, kitchen, and two bedrooms were littered with dirty dishes, scattered and broken toys, and mice droppings.

John was aghast at the conditions. He tried to get the boys to calm down but they ignored him. As Anne was restocking the cupboards and the refrigerator and starting to prepare the family some lunch, her father came into the tiny kitchen area.

"Why is the mother in bed?" he asked.

"She has lupus, Dad."

"Ooh. Terrible disease. And she's so young. How often is she down with it?"

"More and more often."

"Is she on steroids?" he asked.

"She is supposed to be, but the side effects are terrible."

He asked how she met this family. She told him about her encounters with them through the mission and her attempts to help them. He asked why the father wasn't making enough money "to get them out of this dump." Anne explained that as well. She told him about the father's criminal record that prevented him from living with his family or getting a decent paying job. And she told him about the diagnoses for all three children and that Medicaid wouldn't pay for the all of the medications they needed.

"How does your husband feel about your helping these people?"

"How do you think he feels, Dad?"

"That why you needed a ride here?"

Anne just looked at him.

"That asshole treats you like hell. . . . I'm proud of you for standing up to him. And for taking this family on."

Anne stood up from putting pieces of bread in the oven to toast. "You are?"

"Yes, of course I am. . . . You looked surprised."

"Given the way you talk about your employees, I am surprised you feel any empathy toward this family."

"Well, I don't excuse the dad committing armed robberies. I'm tired of liberals using poverty as an excuse for crime. And I doubt dad is doing what you say he is to earn money for his family. But that woman in there is obviously sick as hell. My mom's sister had lupus when I was growing up, and that is one badass disease. And these boys . . ."

Anne held her breath.

". . . who could blame them?"

"Dad, have you ever been in the home of one of your dry cleaning employees? Seen what their lives are like?"

"Can't recall it if I have. Had no cause to."

As Anne and her father were driving away, John asked what more Anne knew about Eileen's treatment for her lupus.

"You say that she has to wait months and months to get to see her rheumatologist, even when she has a flare-up like this?"

"That's what she tells me."

"Benjamin Ross is my rheumatologist for my arthritis. Do you think your friend would object to my setting up an appointment with him? Kind of a second opinion?"

Eighth Step: Matthew 5:7

Anne looked again at her father in surprise. "Dad . . . that is very sweet. But she can't afford Dr. Ross if he doesn't take Medicaid."

"Let me see what I can do."

John wasn't able to schedule an appointment for Eileen with Dr. Ross. But he was able to wrangle one with a Dr. Champion, the junior physician in the rheumatology group.

Eileen weighed over 250 pounds and was in the throes of fatigue and terrible pain in her knees. Anne and John needed Obadiah's help transporting Eileen from their home into the doctor's office. John and Obadiah sat next to one another in the waiting area while Anne helped Eileen fill out the pages of paperwork before being seen by Dr. Champion.

John asked Obadiah about how he got work and how much he made each week.

"It's too damn hit and miss. I go to the labor pool building and sign in as early as it opens, usually by 5 a.m. Then I stand around outside with the other men until someone comes by in a truck looking for laborers. If they come by. Ain't no reservations."

"Labor on what kind of job?"

"Lately, it has been tearing down houses on lots where they are going to rebuild a bigger, fancier house. Lots of sledgehammer swinging, lots of shoveling debris, lots of carrying broken wood and concrete blocks."

"Paid by the hour?"

"Yes, sir."

"How much an hour?"

"Maybe $10 if I'm lucky?"

"Why so little?"

"More men wanting to work than there is work. Lots of men in my situation with felonies on their record who can't work anywhere else."

"But why do you accept work for so little money?"

"Low pay work damn sure better than no work."

"Any of these jobs last more than a day?"

"Only if I can get my own transportation to the work site the next day."

"You got a car?"

"Got an old pick-up that doesn't run more than it runs."

"How much you take home a week?"

"Lucky if I get $250. Lots of days I wait around at the pool for hours and don't get picked."

"Can you read?"

"'Course I can read. Got my GED in prison."

"Why were you in prison?"

"Armed robberies."

"How many?"

"Three. Pled out to one."

"Why'd you commit armed robberies?"

"Don't matter. No excuses."

"Anything else on your record?"

"No sir. . . . If you don't mind my asking, why the hell you asking me all this?"

John ignored the question. "What are your goals in life?"

"My goals?"

"Yes, your goals. Why are you smiling?"

"This conversation is turning kind of rich."

"Is there a problem?"

"No sir. We are just grateful for your help. Don't want to offend you."

"Then what did you mean by 'conversation turning rich'?"

"Rich people talk 'goals.'" Obadiah made quotation marks in the air with his fingers. "Black folks . . . brown folks . . . poor folks . . . we don't think about 'goals.' We think about surviving. You got to be sure where your next meal and your next pay day and your next month's rent are coming from before you can start thinking about 'goals.'"

"Obadiah, are you a thief?"

"What did you just ask me?"

"If your family needed food and rent and medicine, you had the chance to take money without being seen from a cash register where you worked, would you help yourself?"

"Never worked around no cash register."

"If you did?"

Obadiah smiled at John. "Don't believe I would."

"Really? Why not?"

"They'd put me back in prison, that's why not. As bad as it is out here, it's not as bad as it is in there. I don't get to see my wife and children in the joint."

"What if they couldn't prove you did it?"

"Like I said, Mr. John, I'm not rich. Proving is for rich folks. Blaming is for the rest of us . . . particularly the rest of us with armed robbery on our sheet. They'd blame me whether they could prove it or not. Then they'd fire me. . . . Let me ask you one thing about your question. Am I being paid enough for honest work in that job with the cash register that I wouldn't have to steal for food and rent money?"

John pursed his lips and narrowed his eyes. "You ask a good question there. You make a good point. You are not dumb."

"You act surprised."

"I apologize for that."

"What job you asking me about, Mr. John?"

"None. Just talking out loud. Passing the time."

A nurse called for Eileen. Obadiah pushed Eileen in a wheelchair through the door to the exam rooms in the back. Anne and her father remained in the waiting room. John had to pay $175 for Eileen's visit. This rheumatologist didn't accept Medicaid because it pays too little. Thirty-five minutes passed. Then Obadiah pushed Eileen back out to the waiting room where Anne and her dad sat. Eileen was crying. Obadiah was downcast.

"What's wrong? What did the doctor say?" asked Anne.

Obadiah said, "The doctor was nice. She seems to know what she is talking about. Spent more time talking with us than any doctor I ever seen. She said Eileen needed a drug she hadn't been getting before, and that if she took this drug regular it would help her and reduce the amount of steroids that she had to take when her symptoms get worse."

"Then what's the problem?" asked John. "Why the tears, sweetheart?"

"This drug," Eileen took out a piece of paper and read, "Saphnelo. Saphnelo it's called. It's not approved by Medicaid because this doctor is not enrolled with Medicaid. She told me that nothing she prescribes will be paid for by Medicaid. Just like this office visit with this doctor won't be paid for by Medicaid."

"We can't even afford this visit, Mr. John," said Obadiah. "Much less this medicine."

"I took care of the visit. Don't worry about that," said John.

"But the medicine. We can't let you pay for that, too. The doctor said you have to stay on this medicine once you start it. No starting and stopping."

Eileen was weeping. "I'm just so tired. I got my hopes up. . . . What was the point?"

John said, "So why can't you get your regular doctor at the county hospital to prescribe this medicine? Then Medicaid will pay. Isn't that what this doctor said?"

Eileen shook her head. "I can't get in to see my regular rheumatologist for another six months. . . . I think I just need to learn to live with this. . . . I just hurt so bad."

Anne looked at her father, begging him with her eyes. Anne and her father stepped outside.

"Daddy, if you pay half, I'll pay half."

"Why do you think your husband will stand for that?"

"I won't tell him."

"Honey, we don't even know how much a prescription of this stuff will cost. It will probably be higher than if it was covered on a private insurance plan."

"Daddy, she is in so much pain. It breaks my heart." She began to cry.

"Anne, baby, we have to be realistic. The needs of this one family are bottomless. Once we start to help, where do we draw the line? Do we start paying for the children's care, too? And why just this family? I am starting to realize how many families out there must be going through this kind of shit. Why do we help this family and not all the rest?"

"Because God has put *this* family in our way, Daddy."

John stared at his daughter. *Where did this faith come from*, he thought. "You really believe that, don't you?" he said to her.

"Can't we just take this one step at a time?"

"This is important to you, isn't it, Anne?"

"It's given me a reason to want to get up in the morning. It makes me feel so good to help them. Good for the first time in a long time. I feel useful and needed again."

John was well aware of his daughter's history with depression and that she was in an unsatisfying marriage. So he hugged her like he did when she was five. He wished he could turn back the clock to those days. He realized long ago that he had been too stern with her growing up. He had spent too much time on his businesses and not enough time with her. His marriage with Anne's mom had become loveless, and he worried that Anne had jumped too soon into a marriage with another cold man just to escape the home she was raised in. The tension between Anne's husband and John had added to the emotional distance between John and Anne. Maybe helping this poor family together would invigorate their emotional relationship and give them something to share. Maybe they could provide one another with some of the warmth they both needed and lacked. Maybe worrying about a family with more problems than they had would get them out of themselves.

"That is wonderful, Anne. How can I say 'no' to you, when you say something like that? If we come to regret this, we will regret it together. Why don't you leave that husband of yours out of this altogether?" He saw the happiness drain from her face. "None of my business. Forget I said that."

"Let me worry about my husband."

"You be the one to tell the Parkers that we want to help with the prescription until they can get it covered by Medicaid," said John.

When Anne and her father went back into the room where Eileen and Obadiah were waiting, he found them in an argument. The receptionist behind the help desk was looking anxiously their way. Obadiah was pressing Eileen not to give up. Eileen was saying she had lost all hope, and that he wasn't listening to her.

Anne took the prescriptions from Eileen. One was for the same anti-depressant Anne took. *Good*, she thought.

"Dad and I want to fill these for you, assuming they won't break the bank."

Eileen started to object, but Obadiah spoke first. "We are drowning here. Any boat you can push our way will be . . ." Then his voice caught and he couldn't speak.

Eileen looked at her husband wide eyed. "I haven't seen you cry since before you went to prison." She took his hand in both of hers as she sat in the wheelchair.

"We would be very grateful," Eileen said to Anne and John. "You are a godsend. I didn't know people like you existed."

The prescriptions were very expensive to fill but not prohibitive for John. The young rheumatologist had written for a ninety-day supply of the Saphnelo, and that cost more than the antidepressant.

John and Anne took Eileen and Obadiah back to their apartment. John helped Obadiah support Eileen back into their home while Anne waited in the SUV. Anne saw a neighbor woman who had been babysitting take the three Parker children into the home. John was in the apartment for so long that Anne started to go in herself. Then John came out and got into his vehicle.

"What took you so long, Daddy? Was there a problem?"

"Those children! They are out of control. And they don't seem to be able to control themselves. Too much for the healthiest of parents. Who could ever solve that problem?"

"What problem can we solve?"

"One, maybe. I offered Obadiah a job in one of my stores."

"You did not!"

"I did."

"Did he accept?"

"Not at first. I had to talk him into it."

"How much can you pay him?"

"$16.50 an hour to start."

"Health insurance?"

"Come on, Anne. Don't ruin this for me. You know we can't afford to offer health insurance on employees. Certainly not on their dependents."

"Is $16.50 an hour going to knock the family out of Medicaid?"

"I called my tax and estate people about that while I was in there. It won't, given that she and the three children are all classified as disabled."

"I can't believe you offered him a job!"

"It won't pay that much, but it will be steady. And it'll be indoors. Won't be nearly as likely to injure himself. Or to get sick from the cold and the heat. I'll bet those employers of his don't even carry workers' comp insurance to cover him if he gets injured. Working in one of my stores will be better than he's had, for sure."

"Daddy, I am so proud of you. . . . How do you feel about it?"

"Best I've felt in a long, long time. . . . We'll see how it goes. They still have so many . . . he's still not supposed to sleep in that apartment because of his felony record. What's going to happen to them if he is discovered and they throw them out? Their rent is only $75 a month! And those kids!"

"How will he get to work?"

"We'll have to get that truck of his fixed. I can at least do that much."

"Daddy, what's happened to you?"

"Damned if I know. You did, I guess. Or that family did. Anyway, something has happened to me. Let's see how I feel about all this when I wake up tomorrow. . . . There is just so much wrong. . . . I wonder how many of my employees are having the same kind of issues."

NINTH STEP

Matthew 5:8

⁸ Blessed are you who are pure in heart, for you will see God.

Of the nine Beatitudes, this would be the most challenging for me to understand independent of its location in Matthew's Gospel.

To unpack this Beatitude, I am going to go at it back to front.

"... for you will see God."

See God?

How could any human, with the all the limitations of the mortal mind and perception, ever hope to "see God"? How could any Jew in particular claim that any human in any condition or situation could ever aspire to "see" the ineffable, holy, unsearchable, other, mysterious God? YHWH, the "I Am Who I Am" God? YHWH, the "I Will Be Who I Will Be" God? YHWH, whose very name thus denotes mystery. "YHWH" whose name was only pronounced once a year on Yom Kippur by the high priest as he alone entered the dwelling of the glory of YHWH in the Holy of holies in the Temple? YHWH, whose name was spoken in respect and awe as "adonai" ("the Lord") or "haShem" ("the Name") whenever a Jew encountered "YHWH" in scripture?

The writers of the Hebrew scripture express in poetry that YHWH cannot be "seen" by a human. And when the chosen few are allowed to see YHWH's glory, as opposed to YHWH's actual being, even this glory is beyond adequate description.

Moses "sees" YHWH only in the fire of a burning bush. YHWH hides in a humble object within Moses' capacity to perceive (Exod 3:2). The experience was bewildering and frightening for Moses. At first he perceived that it was "the angel of YHWH" appearing in the flame, but then he thought that he heard the actual voice of YHWH, telling him to remove his sandals because "the place on which [he was] standing is holy ground" (Exod 3:5). So "Moses hid his face, for he was afraid to look at God" (Exod 3:6).

After YHWH had used Moses to bring the people to Sinai to receive Torah and enter the covenant, Moses was still not able to "see" YHWH:

> [18] Moses said, "Show me your glory, I pray" [19] And he said, "I will make all my goodness pass before you, and will proclaim before you the name 'YHWH'; and I will be gracious to whom I will be gracious, and show mercy on whom I will show mercy. [20] But," he said, "you cannot see my face; for no one shall see me and live." [21] And YHWH continued, "See, there is a place by me where you shall stand on the rock; [22] and while my glory passes by I will put you in a cleft of the rock, and I will cover you with my hand until I have passed by; [23] then I will take away my hand, and you shall see my back; but my face shall not be seen." (Exod 33)

The story of the prophet Elijah's encounter with God on Mount Sinai (called "Horeb" in 1 Kings) recounts the same danger and inability to "see" YHWH.

> [11] He said, "Go out and stand on the mountain before YHWH, for YHWH is about to pass by." Now there was a great wind, so strong that it was splitting mountains and breaking rocks in pieces before YHWH, but YHWH was not in the wind; and after the wind, an earthquake, but YHWH was not in the earthquake; [12] and after the earthquake, a fire, but YHWH was not in the fire; and after the fire a sound of sheer silence. (1 Kgs 19)

The prophet Isaiah's great vision of God was limited to "seeing" God's "glory." His vision was of God's throne "high and lofty" and "the hem of God's robe" "filling the temple." And Isaiah heard "the voice of YHWH saying, 'Whom shall I send and who will go for us?'" But Isaiah could not "see" God (Isa 6:1–8).

The prophet Ezekiel's "visions of God" were uncanny and unsettling. The prophet "saw" God as stormy wind, and clouds flashing fire and amber, and as four creatures with wings, calf's feet, and human hands. Each of these creatures had the faces of a human, a lion, an eagle, and an ox, within four wheels with rims full of eyes. And there was a dome shining like crystal over the four creatures, and the sounds of mighty waters, "the thunder of the Almighty," and "tumult like an army." Ezekiel saw above the dome "something like a throne, in appearance like sapphire," and seated above the likeness of a throne was "something that seemed like a human form." Upward from the loins of this human form was "something like gleaming amber" with "fire all around," and downward from the loins was "something like fire." Ezekiel concludes his vision with: "This was the appearance of the likeness of the glory of YHWH" (Ezek 1:1–28). Ezekiel could not "see" God.

Yet Jesus, who surely knew the above scriptures, tells his disciples that those who are "pure in heart . . . will see God" (Matt 5:8).

Many read this "seeing" as a reference to standing in the Temple and feeling the presence of God there, linked prominently with Ps 24:3–4:

> [3] Who shall ascend the hill of the LORD?
> And who shall stand in his holy place?
> [4] Those who have clean hands and *pure hearts*,
> who do not lift up their souls to what is false,
> and do not swear deceitfully. (Emphasis added)

But during his ministry Jesus does not emphasize the Temple, its ritual, and its sacrificial system. Matthew reports that Jesus was at the Temple only once, and then overturned the tables of the money changers there and called it a "den of robbers" (Matt 21:12–13). What Jesus did emphasize throughout his ministry was the presence of God in the suffering poor and in merciful acts to them. So does it make sense that Jesus was referring to the blessing of "seeing" God in the Temple in this Beatitude?

Moreover, Ps 24 says nothing about actually "seeing" God. A number of psalmists do write of "seeing" or "beholding" God's "face" in the temple: Pss 11:7 ("the upright shall behold his face"); 17:15 ("As for me, I shall behold your face in righteousness; when I awake, I shall be satisfied, beholding your likeness"); 27:4 ("to behold the beauty of the LORD and to inquire in his temple"); 27:8 ("'Come,' my heart says, 'seek his face!' Your face, LORD, do I seek. Do not hide your face from me"); 42:2 ("My soul thirsts for God, for the living God. When shall I come and behold the face of God?"). But this "seeing" of God's "face," "beauty," or "likeness" in the Temple is entirely metaphorical.

All of us have heard sermons explaining this Beatitude: "Blessed are the pure in heart, for they shall see God," as a reference to seeing God in heaven after living a righteous or believing life. But nowhere in scripture is there any claim that our limitations on "seeing" the ineffable, mysterious, holy God would be eliminated in heaven. And the following passage from Matthew brings us back to "seeing" in this life and this earth.

> [31] When the Son of Man comes in his glory and all the angels with him, then he will sit on the throne of his glory.... [34] Then the king shall say to those at his right hand, "Come, you that are blessed by my Father, inherit the kingdom prepared for you from the foundation of the world; [35] for I was hungry and you gave me food, I was thirsty and you gave me something to drink, I was a stranger and you welcomed me, [36] I was naked and you gave me clothing, I was sick and you took care of me, I was in prison and you visited me." [37] Then the righteous shall answer him, "Lord, when did we *see you* hungry and gave you food, or thirsty and gave you something to drink? [38] And when did we *see you* a stranger and welcomed you, or naked and gave you clothing? [39] And when did we *see you* sick or imprisoned and visited you?" [40] And the king will answer them, "Truly I tell you just as you did it to the least of these my brothers, you did it to me." [41] Then he will say to those at his left hand, "You that are accursed, depart from me into the eternal fire prepared for the devil and his angels; [42] for I was hungry and you gave me no food."... [44] And then they will answer, "Lord, when did we *see you* hungry or thirsty or a stranger or naked or sick and in prison, and did not care for you?" [45] Then he will answer them, "Truly I tell you, just as you did not do it to one of the least of these, you did not do it to me." [46] And these will go away into eternal punishment but the righteous into eternal life. (Matt 25; emphasis added)

This teaching is about seeing the God incarnate in Jesus on this earth during the earthly life of disciples, not in heaven. This teaching is a key to understanding Matthew's Jesus. It is the last teaching of Jesus in gospel. As a trial attorney, I hear this parable as something like Jesus' closing argument to his disciples and to us.

The Beatitude at Matt 5:8 ends "for you will see God." While some may have difficulty accepting that the historical Jesus referred to himself as "God," I am considering here the Jesus of Matthew's narrative. In Matthew, there is an intimacy and near identification of Jesus with God. Jesus is presented in Matthew from the beginning as "'Emmanuel,' which

The Greek word translated "perfect" at verse 48 is *teleios*. *Strong's Online Analytical Concordance* defines *teleios* as "having reached its end, complete, or perfect." Within this narrative of Matthew, what Jesus is teaching in 5:43–48 is for the disciple to become "complete" in her mercy, even to enemies—the same as "purity of heart" is the complete willing and intention of mercy of this Beatitude. Consider also Jesus' teaching recorded in Luke 6:36 as: "Be merciful, just as your Father is merciful."

Returning to Matt 25:31–46, consider all the competing commitments and justifications that we give for not acting mercifully to the hungry, thirsty, naked, sick, stranger, and prisoner. Yet Jesus calls us not just to give priority to mercy, but to give a *pure* and *complete* commitment to it.

So for me, "Blessed are the pure in heart, for they will see God" means that those disciples who have received in their hearts the blessing of a pure and complete commitment to the mercy of Jesus above all other commitments will see Jesus and God in the suffering of those in need.

I wrote earlier in the section concerning the Second Step about a medical mission trip to Zambia, and specifically our time in the Misisi in Lusaka, one of the poorest slums on earth. We were in the Misisi for a week. We tried to help hundreds of ill children and adults every day, dawn to dark. At the end of each day we went back to our inn and collapsed, sometimes too tired to eat. There was a still a line of untreated people waiting for God's mercy at the end of every day, and a longer line was there when we returned at dawn the next day. We cared for scores of children with full-blown AIDS, only able to help each of them temporarily with their external sores and their digestive issues. Their infections were out of control because of their compromised immune systems and malnutrition. One quiet angel of a child, five years of age, seemed to our physicians to be in her last days. She was emaciated and running a high fever. She had an excruciating eye infection and oozing, infected sores on her scalp. Her older sister carried her to the clinic for us to try to ease her pain. Their parents had already died of AIDS. We put antibiotic ointment in her eye and gave her sister oral antibiotics and some Ibuprofen to give to her. We cleaned and treated the sores with topical antibiotics. It was a necessarily painful process to debride so many infected wounds on her scalp, but she made not a sound and barely drew back. In retrospect, I thought of Isa 53:7 ("he was afflicted, but did not open his mouth"). The other children shunned this little girl, as they did everyone with such sores. After our woefully inadequate treatment, we watched as her sister means, 'God is with us'" (1:23). At Jesus' baptism and his transfiguration, God's voice from heaven and from a "bright cloud" calls Jesus "my Son, the Beloved" (3:17; 17:5). Peter identifies Jesus as "the Messiah, the Son of the Living God," and Jesus approves Peter's words (16:16–17). The concept of the Trinity—the one God of three persons—begins to emerge in 28:19 ("in the name of the Father and of the Son and of the Holy Spirit.") And in Matt 11:27, Jesus says, "All things have been handed over to me by my Father; and no one knows the Son except the Father, and no one knows the Father except the Son and anyone to whom the Son chooses to reveal him." So in Matthew, the nature and person of God are seen in the words and actions of Jesus, much as this is expressed in "for you will see God" in this Beatitude. And according to the above parable of the Last Judgment (25:31–46), Jesus, and therefore God, are seen in the suffering and service of the hungry, thirsty, naked, sick, stranger, and imprisoned.

Who "will see God" in Jesus? The "pure in heart" (5:8). Understanding the message of this Beatitude through this parable of the Last Judgment, who are the "pure in heart"? They are the "righteous" (25:37). And who are the "righteous"? They are those who are merciful to the hungry, the thirsty, the naked, the sick, the stranger, and the prisoner without "seeing" at the time (25:44) that they are being merciful to God in Jesus.

The "pure in heart" in this Beatitude is the only use of this Greek phrase *katharoi te kardia* and the only use of *katharoi* in the Gospels. The Greek *kardia* or heart was an expression for the seat of the will and the intention (Matt 5:28; 6:21). Given the identification of mercy and righteousness in Jesus' teachings, I hear in this Beatitude that God's blessing of "purity of heart" means complete and unadulterated, and thus "pure," willingness and intention to be merciful. It links to the teaching of Jesus at Matt 5:43–48:

> ⁴³ You have heard that it was said, "You shall love your neighbor and hate your enemy." ⁴⁴ But I say to you, Love your enemies and pray for those who persecute you, ⁴⁵ so that you may be children of your Father in heaven; for he makes his sun rise on the evil and on the good, and sends rain on the righteous and unrighteous. ⁴⁶ For if you love those who love you, what reward do you have? Do not even the tax collectors do the same? ⁴⁷ And if you greet only your brothers and sisters, what more are you doing than others? Do not even the Gentiles do the same? ⁴⁸ Be *perfect*, therefore, as your heavenly Father is *perfect*. (Emphasis added)

carried this little girl back to their hut to die. We had done all we could but so very little for her. But it was just then that a member of our team named Kim pointed out that we had sat this precious child of God on the bare, stone altar of the church sanctuary when we treated her, the altar where the body and blood of Jesus were consecrated every Sunday. All of us, every woman and man on the team, realized almost simultaneously that we had *seen* the suffering body of God in Jesus on that altar that Wednesday morning as that child sat there. We all took a breath and looked at one another in recognition, tears in many eyes. Then we went back to work. It is a moment that is as vivid to me now as if it were happening again. I am tearing up as I am typing this.

Seeing Jesus and God in the sufferers is the needed Ninth Step to being sustained on the Way of discipleship. But it can still be a hard, courageous Step. Few sufferers are like the wholly innocent child who sat on the altar in the church in the Misisi. We who ask God to give us the blessing of purity of heart on the Way are challenged to see Jesus in people who are often partly responsible for their own suffering, often angry and bitter, often vengeful at those who have hurt them, and often ungrateful and entitled. These can be people who are angry at God for not answering their prayers. These are people who sometimes belittle the motivation of our faith for trying to help. It is sometimes hard to see Jesus' pain in the pain of these who are "the least of his" (Matt 25:40).

Over the last eighteen years, we in the justice ministry have tried to help hundreds of women who were wounded by abuse and neglect as children. Their old wounds have led them to self-loathing, abuse of alcohol and drugs, hopelessness, and repeated toxic relationships with wounded men who have further abused them and their children. Each of these children of God has their own stories, but I will try to generalize respectfully about "them." Many of these women were sexually abused as children or teens by a male they should have been able to trust the most. Many of them suffered the betrayal of a mother who chose a continued relationship with an abuser over protecting their children. So they struggle with trust and self-esteem issues for the rest of their lives. Many have turned to alcohol and drug abuse as a kind of anesthesia from their memories and emotional pain. And many have repeated the failures of their mothers to protect them from an abuser when they were children, by failing to protect their own children from an abuser whom they depend upon for their drugs or monetary support. We try to help these women and their children into a resurrected life with their own income, housing, child care, medical care, and supportive community. We obtain for them and their children protective, divorce, custody, and child support orders from the courts and provide them free professional counseling and material support. Often they continue to struggle with addiction, depression, anxiety, damaged self-esteem, monumental doubt, and crushing guilt. Almost all of these women can be very grateful and a joy to help. But some can also be resentful, angry, verbally abusive to our staff, and untruthful to us when we try to motivate them to change their lives, avoid still another toxic relationship, and require that they remain substance free. Some project their anger on us and can be unreasonably demanding and resisting. People who are wounded are wounding. It is sometimes a challenge to see Jesus and his suffering in their suffering.

I once represented a twenty-two-year-old woman who had been shot in the back and face by her husband who was, incidentally, twice her age. She suffered from an intellectual impairment and was subject to extreme mood swings and emotional outbursts. Her parents were undocumented and poor, and she had been passed as a child from relative to relative. She had dropped out of school in the sixth grade. She had no peers as friends. Then this older man found her. She thought he loved and valued her. He gave her a home and personal comforts she had never had. The real basis of their relationship was sex and drugs. This young woman supplied her husband with one of those and he supplied her with the other. She had two children by him. Then she thought she fell in love with a man her own age who was her husband's drug supplier. She abandoned her children, ages three and one, left them with her husband, and moved in with the younger man. Her new man was a pimp as well as a drug pusher, and he required her to engage in prostitution on one of the most dangerous streets in our city in exchange for stronger and stronger drugs. She was hustling on the street around midnight one night when her husband drove up beside her, pointed a handgun at her, and forced her into his pick-up. He took her deep into some thick woods next to a park, shot her, and left her for dead. She crawled out of the woods, blood pouring from her face, and knocked on doors until someone called the police and an ambulance. She required a surgical jaw replacement. She recovered and went to live with her parents and her children.

The husband was indicted for attempted murder. The prosecutor's office referred this young woman to us at the justice ministry. We obtained for her a divorce, sole custody of her two children with no access by the father, a child support order, and a lifetime protective order against his coming within half a mile of her or the children. When she and I walked out of the courtroom after her final divorce hearing, I asked her to see her new start on life as a resurrection. Her parents were there with her, and we all cried together in gratitude and hope. We helped her get into an outpatient drug rehab program, persuaded her to remain with her parents with her children, and helped her find work and subsidized child care. But as time went on, her father reported that she was gone from the house and her children for increasing periods of time, and that he was afraid she was using drugs again. When we tried to encourage her to stay in her new life and asked how we could help, she became increasingly insulting and resentful, denying that she was using drugs again. When we asked her to go into an in-patient drug rehab that we would pay for, she became indignant, refusing to answer our calls or emails. Finally, her father told us that she refused to testify in the criminal case against her ex-husband, had abandoned her children at her parents' home, and had gone back to live with the man who had shot her. Her parents had seen her driving a new pick-up, clearly purchased for her by her ex-husband.

It was impossible to understand her decision to go back to her assailant and his drugs. But we hadn't walked in her shoes. Again, people who are wounded are wounding, particularly of themselves. This young woman was most wounding to her children. *It is a challenge to see Jesus and his suffering in her behavior. It is easier to see Jesus in her pain.*

The male abusers who are so often our opponents in our family violence lawsuits are themselves wounded and in pain, though most are in denial of this. They often share the history of being abused as children with the women and children they are now abusing. They yearn for love, are angry at the love they have been denied, and do not know how to love. Each of these men has his own story, so I will try to be respectful in my generalizations of "them" as well. In my experience, these men have one of two responses to legal allegations against them of repeated abuse. Either they angrily, and I mean angrily, deny the allegations and accuse us in the ministry of being unjust and merciless. Or they cry, apologize, and promise to change for good if the woman will only dismiss the lawsuit and come back to them with their children. When the woman does not relent, they also become angry. Those who have cried, apologized, pleaded, and promised in the past to change have resumed their abuse each time the woman returned. The men who default to anger often threaten us at the justice ministry. Often the men berate us because we are violating our "so-called Christian faith" by trying to break up their family and telling "their" woman not to forgive them. We are called to see Jesus in the suffering of these men. We are called to treat them with courtesy and respect and to give them a vision of hope if they prove over time they have truly changed.

It is a challenge and a blessing to see Jesus and his suffering in the pain of these men, to see the image of God in each of them. Much prayer is required to receive that vision. These abusive men are suffering from their own pain, and they inflict it on those who should be most able to trust and rely upon them. Sometimes it is better to focus on their pain than their behaviors. Seeing and treating them as if they were unclean and beneath our mercy is the way of the kingdoms of the world, not of Jesus' Way. Human history has proven that there is no lasting hope in this response of utter condemnation. But just how do we see the pain of Jesus in the pain of men and women whose lives are so different than his? The pure in heart are those who can see the humanity and divinity in a child abuser and see Jesus' pain in the abuser's pain. That is a seeing that most people do not seek, and a blessing most people do not want.

A person who is blessed with the purity of heart to see God in suffering is Carol Klocek, one of my life's heroes. Mrs. Klocek was the head of the Presbyterian Night Shelter for the homeless when I was chair of the Mayor's Commission on Homelessness. She gave me my first tour of the shelter one day, showing me who slept and ate where and what services the shelter provided. The shelter was all but empty of clients, because of the requirement that the homeless exit the building in the morning for cleaning. (They let their homeless clients remain inside on particularly hot, cold, or wet days.) Carol was keeping up a running explanation of what I was seeing, when she abruptly became silent. I turned to see why she had stopped speaking, and I saw her looking down to the ground dormitory floor from the interior balcony we were on, tears brimming from her eyes and running in tracks down her cheeks. I looked down to where she was looking and saw an elderly man lying asleep on a mat in the middle of the dormitory floor. He was a double amputee, missing both of his legs above the knees. His white hair and long beard were matted. His clothes were torn and filthy. His crutches lay on the floor on either side of him. The shelter let him remain inside during daylight because of his condition. When Carol saw him there, her empathy for him welled out of her in her tears. She was feeling his pain, deep in her beautiful soul. I saw in her at that moment what it is to be pure of heart, seeing the suffering of God in another's suffering, feeling that suffering herself.

People who have hearts like Carol's can be subject to what we moderns call burn out. Many of us crave expressions of gratitude from those we are trying to help. We can let ourselves dwell on the hurt when people we help are insensitive, entitled, and ungrateful. We need to learn over time not to look for appreciation from people who are so deeply wounded. In our interactions with them, we need to focus only on their pain and needs and not at all on our own. We need to look elsewhere for our support, perhaps from other disciples. Those who work daily among the wounded and their many crises can become isolated from their friends and families whose crises can seem so trivial in comparison. And those of us who are among the suffering daily, like Jesus and our four fishermen were in Matt 4:23–25, run a cycle from being so close emotionally to the suffering that it disables and embitters us, to being so necessarily detached emotionally in a kind of self-preservation that we are no longer personally conveying a sense of God's love to those we are trying to help.

And part of the cause of burn out can be disillusionment with discipleship to a God who lets this amount and depth of suffering to continue with entirely too few disciples responding to the call to bring mercy into this wounded world.

Who cares for the caregiver? People called to a discipleship like Carol's need people who look out for them in ways they often will not look out for themselves. We get so close so often to the suffering that we become numb to our own wounds and feel ashamed if we concern anyone with ourselves. Then we reach an abyss where we just can't do it anymore—an abyss called despair. Jesus was fully God but also fully human. He threw himself into a bottomless, shoreless ocean of suffering. Was he ever burned out? He must have been exhausted at times. Given the emotional and physical demands of Jesus' ministry to the suffering, it has always made sense to me that Matthew, Mark, and Luke depict Jesus' ministry as lasting just one year. But how can disciples in our day sustain themselves for longer periods of intimate contact with suffering?

Matthew tells us that Jesus withdrew to pray (14:13). Perhaps prayer was the source of his continuing energy and zeal. But sometimes the communication in prayer feels terribly one way.

On September 10, 1946, a humble nun originally from Albania was traveling by rail to Loreto Convent in Darjeeling, India. She was a teacher in a Roman Catholic school in Kolkata. During that train trip she heard the voice of Jesus, who said to her, "Come. Carry me into the holes of the poor. Come be my light."[27] The nun continued to hear the voice until the middle of 1947.[28] In obedience, she began a fifty-year ministry in the most miserable slums in the world to the poorest of the poor, bringing the touch of Jesus to the unwanted and unloved, the abandoned child, the disabled, the dying, and those suffering from cholera, leprosy, HIV/AIDS, and addiction. In 1950 she gained official church approval for the founding of the Missionaries of Charity, a Roman Catholic congregation of women dedicated to service to the poor. Today, the Missionaries claim more than 5,000 sisters, and run more than 700 centers in more than 130 countries. Mother Teresa, now Saint Teresa, insisted that she and her nuns live in the same poverty as the children of God to whom they ministered. Young women came to Kolkata from all over the world to join with Teresa in lives of poverty to minister to the destitute as she did. When Teresa was awarded the Nobel Peace Prize in 1979, she used the $7,000 that would have funded the customary banquet, plus the million dollar prize for the award, to buy food for the poor in India. In 1952 "Calcutta provided her one of the shelters for pilgrims at the Kali Temple, which she named *Nirmal Hriday*, Bengali for 'pure heart.' . . . There she and her sisters would bring the dying off the streets and offer them shelter in their last days, basic medical care and above all, tender love."[29]

Every day for fifty years when she was not raising funds for her ministry in other parts of the world, Teresa walked the worst slums in India, seeing, touching, and bringing food, water, shelter, medicine, and love to the destitute, ill, and dying. Her writings, speeches, and actions testify that she saw Jesus' suffering in the suffering of "the least of these." Matthew 5:8 and 25:31–46 were obviously central to her life.

But in 2007, her letters to her confessors were published in *Come Be My Light: The Private Writings of the Saint of Calcutta*. These reveal that Teresa suffered a sense of abandonment by Jesus for almost all of her fifty-year mission. She last heard his voice in 1947; afterward she experienced only silence from him. She prayed constantly but felt nothing of his spiritual presence. Where she continued to encounter Jesus was in the suffering of the "poorest of the poor." She came to believe that God was causing the sense of darkness, silence, and abandonment within her so that she would share the darkness, silence, and abandonment suffered by the poor and by Jesus himself. She came to believe that suffering was her way to God, even though her ministry was dedicated to alleviating suffering.

At an address to the graduating class of Saint Thomas Aquinas College in New York in 1997, she told the class about her encounter with a dying young woman in great pain in India. Teresa told the dying woman that her pain was "the kiss of Jesus." The young woman asked Teresa to ask Jesus not to kiss her so much. Teresa had a sense of humor about her belief. But she clearly believed that her pain and sense of abandonment by God was her way to God.

She also at times doubted the goodness or the existence of God. Given her immersion for so long in so much poverty and suffering, how could she not have?

In a letter to her confessor in 1959, Teresa wrote: "In the darkness . . . Lord, my God, who am I that You should forsake me . . . the darkness is so dark. . . . I have no faith. . . . So many unanswered questions live within me—I am afraid to uncover them—because of the blasphemy. If there be God—please forgive me."[30]

That same year, at the instruction of her confessor, she wrote a letter to Jesus, which reads in part:

> That darkness that surrounds me on all sides—I can't lift my soul to God—no light or inspiration enters my soul—I speak of love for souls—of tender love for God—words pass through my lips—and I long with deep longing to believe in them. What do I labour for? If there be no God—there can be no soul—If there be no soul then Jesus—You also are not true. Heaven, what emptiness—not a single thought of Heaven enters my mind—for there is no hope.—I am afraid to write all those terrible things that pass in my soul. . . . I no longer pray—My soul is not one with You—and yet when alone in the streets—I talk to You for hours.[31]

In 1965 she wrote: "If there is hell—this must be one. How terrible it is to be without God—no prayer—no faith—no love."[32]

Teresa walked every Step on the Way of discipleship. She was clearly a disciple who was "pure in heart" and who "saw" God in the poor. But even she struggled with doubt in the existence of a loving and powerful God in the midst of so much evil. Given that Teresa struggled with this doubt, we should have the courage to admit that doubts about God's goodness and power necessarily occur during the Steps of our discipleship. I have not found in any writings of Teresa where she explicitly states that her doubts about the existence of a good and powerful God stemmed from all the evil and suffering which she encountered face-to-face. Instead, she seems to have synthesized the reality of so much suffering and her belief in a good and powerful God into trusting that the suffering is a positive Way to God. But had any of us walked her walk, how could we not at times wonder if our cherished beliefs in the goodness and power of God were true?

How did Teresa stay on the Way despite her pain and doubts? Having read all I can about her, it seems clear that her blessing of love for the suffering children, women, and men she encountered, and for the young women who joined her in her ministry, kept her on the Way. And the joy and satisfaction she experienced at being able to be a conduit of mercy. She clearly had a love for Jesus that surpasses any I have ever encountered. And she was blessed with the capacity to see Jesus in the terrible suffering, to see the image of God and Jesus in each person no matter their faults and failures.

What are the lessons that you and I may learn from Teresa, even if we have not been given the purity of heart to walk her Way? We can learn that empathy, love, and sacrificial mercy for suffering people are themselves experiences of Jesus, that we can "see" Jesus in these. We can pray constantly for the blessing of that urge for mercy. We can pray constantly to see the image of God and Jesus in the life, failures, and yearnings of each hurting person whom God puts in our paths. We can pray constantly for the purity of heart of Teresa. "Blessed are you who have received the blessing of purity of heart, for you are seeing God."

And we can learn from Teresa to keep walking the Way of mercy in the midst of the kingdoms of suffering, even if we sometimes doubt the existence of a good and powerful God in a world of so much suffering.

Please permit me to add a more personal experience to this discussion of Saint Teresa. When I was working in Washington, DC, in the late 1970s or early '80s, I was present at the Basilica of the Shrine of the Immaculate Conception when Teresa was being honored. (I cannot locate a record of the exact date.) Hundreds of religious and lay people attended just to "see" the presence of Jesus incarnate in this woman. I was sitting in the central balcony over the entrance to the basilica, far from the altar area where she and many dignitaries of her church sat. Official after official came to the microphone to tell the stories and sing the praises of Teresa and the Missionaries of Charity. When it came her time to speak, the hundreds in the packed gathering leaned forward to hear her words. She was so small that the microphone had to be lowered more than a foot. She stood at the microphone quietly for a long moment, as if she were praying. Then she said in a quiet voice, "Only God is good," and sat down! That was all she said! People in the gathering gasped. Some began to weep. It was the most heartfelt and eloquent sermon I believe I have ever heard. The officials near the altar with her finally persuaded her to stand and speak further, but her first four words were overpowering. If I had known that this woman we were seeing and hearing that day had been struggling for decades with a sense of abandonment by Jesus, but still persevering on the Way of ministering and living with the destitute, dying, and unloved, my admiration and gratitude would have been even greater. She was purity of heart incarnate. She saw in the poor to whom she was merciful the Jesus whom she no longer heard.

If we are blessed with this purity of heart of mercy and seeing, we will experience the joy and value of this purity, even if God never eliminates the evil and suffering in the world. In fact, we will particularly value this purity of heart while the Kingdom is not yet come, while the kingdoms of darkness continue to reign. Perhaps we will experience in this purity the Kingdom as fully as it will ever be present. And we will continue the Steps of broken hearts, mourning, and hungering for the righteousness of the Kingdom because there is so much more evil and suffering in the world than there are acts of mercy.

The pure in heart are empowered to persist, when Jesus' Way of mercy seems so inadequate to fix the world. The pure in heart have been purified of the propaganda and shallow seductions of the kingdoms of the world. They have gone through the purifying fire of exhausted mercy, and have even been tempted to give up and return to nihilism and comfort. But they have received a renewed capacity for mercy through *seeing* the presence of God in the seemingly small victories of mercy over the suffering. The pure in heart can see God in the things and events that the kingdoms of darkness view as weak and trivial, but which the pure in heart know can and do rescue lives. This is a seeing that is only given and appreciated by the poor in spirit, the brokenhearted and crushed in spirit, the mourning, the meek, the righteous, the merciful and those who have been purified by the suffering of being merciful to the sorrowful and the suffering. The pure in heart are able still to see God and Jesus actively in the world and are still able to sustain the mercy of the Way.

The Ninth Step on the Way of the disciple is to receive the blessing of a heart purely and completely given to mercy, enabling us to see God and Jesus in the sufferers and to continue on the Way.

***

The eight eyes of Sarah, Anne, Janine, and Jazmine saw everything and everyone that could be seen at the mission. They were each spending as much of their days and nights there as they could. Collectively, they were getting to know the stories of all the regular volunteers and all the regular mission clients—the homeless felons, the disabled and the mentally ill, the rejected teenagers thrown out of their homes, the displaced and the undocumented strangers, the drug addicts and the alcoholics, the women and children fleeing family violence. When a new client arrived, one of the four focused in and offered the gentle welcome needed within that particular soul's narrative. When there was a disruptive outburst, Sarah took the lead in talking the person down and if necessary outside.

The numbers of clients coming to the mission's doors increased greatly. Sarah wanted to increase the days that the mission was open to clients, but the logistics of resupply and the availability of volunteers prevented her. A number of young women from the church's women's Bible study group had started coming to the mission to help out, but there still weren't enough volunteers to minister to the increased numbers of clients. And those new young women seemed too in shock at the poverty and suffering they were seeing for the first time to jump in and help. They mostly stood together in their own group and talked about the clients.

These young women volunteers were spreading stories about Sarah, Anne, Janine, Jazmine, and the mission clients through the church as a whole. The church membership was taking an interest in the mission operations as they never had before. The membership saw Sarah, Anne, Janine, and Jazmine either as the hope for the revitalization of the church, or, as Bill Anderson the chair of the trustees called them, "the four horsewomen of the apocalypse." Those who opposed the continuing operation of the mission focused on "all the illegals" being cared for there. Those who supported continued operations focused on Matt 25:31–46. Never in the history of this church had a passage of scripture been so well known by so many of the lay membership.

The personal telephone numbers of the four women were listed in the church phone directory. Each of them received message after message of support from people who gave their names, or anonymous pleas for them to quit ruining the church. Anne's husband was loud and livid at the messages, yelling at Anne for embarrassing him and their family. Sarah's husband was furious as well, but grimly silent. He refused to speak to Sarah, and slept in a separate bedroom.

Sarah and Anne had started staying overnight at their father's house after the long days and nights when the mission was open to clients. When they were together with their dad over a take-out supper, they shared with one another and with him the stories of the clients they had seen that day. John just listened without judgment or even comment, a new world opening to him as it had for his daughters. They even started their meals together with a prayer, which had never before taken place in that home.

John started coming to the mission on Monday and Tuesday mornings to help Sarah with the resupply of food. And he brought clothes that customers to his dry cleaning stores had abandoned. While he was at the mission on Tuesdays, he spent time in the large entry area for clients, directing people to the different service counters and urging people who had already been served to leave the building and make room for more clients to enter. When the weather was bad, persuading people to leave was quite a challenge. When he first started at the mission, he found himself torn between his old self who believed that poor people were to blame for their poverty, and the self being born who saw the tragedies and injustice suffered by the mission clients. At first, John's patience quickly gave out when people did not obey his directions, and he gave into the urge to yell. But as he looked more and more of the clients in their faces and saw the pain of their lives etched there, he became more understanding and gentle. Helping at the mission enabled him to understand his daughters' commitment to the clients and brought the three of them closer than they had ever been before. The newly birthed intimacy among the three of them was a godsend for him, and he kept him coming back to the mission until even he developed his own empathy for the people helped there.

John regularly asked Anne for an update on Eileen Parker and her children, as Anne asked her dad about Obadiah.

"I'm afraid there will never be a 'happily ever after' for that family," said John.

"No," replied Anne. "All they can have is an occasional 'happily ever now.'"

"Ever wonder what their lives would be like if God really answered prayer?"

"Dad, I have thought about that so much. Sometimes it makes me question why I pray at all."

"But you keep praying, don't you. And just what should God do for this family?"

"You mean, if God is really God? Well, first thing, Eileen's lupus would miraculously disappear."

"And the kids' conditions too, particularly the little boy who can't express his thoughts. He gets so frustrated, and who can blame him?" said John.

"And the local housing authority wouldn't automatically ban men who had served their prison time," added Anne. "Hard and fast rules like that can be so cruel."

"Daughter, you are making life less cruel for a lot of people."

"I wish we could do more to help."

"I find myself wishing for more sources of help a lot these days," said John.

"Wishing turns into praying, Dad."

"Not for me . . . at least not yet. So we are right back to where we started this conversation. When does your praying turn into more help?" John paused in thought. "I guess if I do start praying, I need to pray for little things . . . that we can accomplish on our own without God."

Anne said nothing in response. Her father was expressing her own stubborn doubts. But she was amazed, and thankful, at what was happening in him. For most of his business career he had been an employer who would fire a senior worker just to be able to hire a younger worker at a lower wage. He used to speak to his employees in a habitual yell. And he used to say terribly prejudiced things about poor people. Now he was becoming a different person. If only what was happening to her dad would happen to her husband as well. And to the church.

"There's another two prayers. But those would be for no 'little things,'" she thought.

The Thursday morning before the rescheduled Sunday church-wide meeting and vote on the future of the mission, seven of the nine trustees plus Dr. Cotswald showed up at the mission without advance notice. There had been a downpour lasting more than an hour before the opening time of 9 a.m., and steady rain with a strong wind continued through the morning. Fewer of the usual unsheltered homeless clients appeared. Many of the homeless regulars stayed hunkered down under the bridges where they had slept. Many of the regular families seeking groceries stayed away rather than riding the bus and getting drenched when walking the two blocks from the bus stop to the mission. But the

Ninth Step: Matthew 5:8

mothers who needed infant formula appeared in the usual numbers, and many undocumented families with children showed up out of hunger despite the rain.

Because of the weather, Sarah directed that clients would not be kept lined up outside to limit the numbers of people inside at one time. Instead everyone was welcomed in as they arrived. And they were not required to leave the building after they had received what they had come for. The building was packed with clients, and the smell of wet, dirty bodies and clothes was overpowering. Pools of water spotted the floor from the dripping shoes. The first to arrive quickly took all the metal folding chairs, and the rest were squatting and sitting everywhere on the linoleum floor. John moved through the people mopping up the water he could.

When Cotswald and the seven trustees burst in, a kind of shudder went through the volunteers and crowd like a wave. Anne and Janine ran to Sarah's office to ask if some clients should be ushered out to eliminate the crowding. Janine asked if they should start checking for IDs, to weed out the undocumented folk. Sarah forbade both actions. "I'd rather kick out the trustees than the clients. We never check for IDs, so we are not going to pretend that we do now. Particularly given the weather," said Sarah.

Sarah walked out of her office and up to the trustees who were huddled together by the main entrance. They were keeping as much distance as they could from the clients. Bill Anderson was there. Joan Donaldson was there. Of the five other trustees, three were women and two were men. All owned or worked in businesses in the downtown neighborhood of the church. Sarah had seen none of the seven in the mission in the weeks that she had been in charge.

"Welcome. I'm surprised to see you here on a day like today. Let's move out of the entrance," said Sarah. They stood at the entrance to a long hallway leading to the clothing bank, still in view of the main room with the many clients.

Dr. Cotswald introduced Sarah to everyone.

Bill Anderson said, "Aren't you over capacity according to the fire code?"

Sarah ignored him.

Cotswald asked, "Do you have time to give the trustees a tour?"

John and Anne agreed to show them around. Sarah started to go with the group, when Anderson asked her to stay behind with him.

"Are you checking for IDs to make sure there are no illegals here?"

"No, Bill. As I have told you before, it's not practical. A lot of citizens and resident aliens don't carry their IDs around for fear of them being robbed. And just because someone has an ID doesn't mean it is actually theirs. Plus, it wouldn't be Christian to refuse food to hungry people because they don't carry a piece of paper."

"So you have been ignoring the orders of the trustees."

"I'm sorry, Bill. But the church as a whole hasn't voted on the mission operations yet."

"So you don't recognize the authority of the trustees."

"Yes, I do. Except when you don't care enough to see what is going on down here and the people we are trying to help. And except when you give an order that can't practically be carried out . . . and is un-Christian."

Anderson's face became beet red. He was founder and CEO of an investment firm, and he was not accustomed to disobedience. He and his extended family were long-time members of the church and were the largest donors year after year. "Who are you to tell me what is un-Christian, young lady?" he seethed.

Sarah stepped closer and put her face inches away from Anderson's. "I am the *woman* who has been down here every single day since you tried to shove selling this mission down the church's throat. I am the *woman*, with all these other unpaid volunteers, who look these people in the face day after day." Sarah's eyes were spitting fire. "Here's the reality, Bill. We are not employees of the trustees. We're not even employees of the church. We are members and donors to this church just like you are. So quit trying to bully us around."

The other trustees walked up. Donaldson stepped between Sarah and Anderson as Cotswald hung back.

One woman trustee asked why the mission was so crowded. Sarah explained the flow of clients they usually tried to maintain, and why she was making an exception because of the rain. The other trustees seemed supportive of this.

"Sarah, why don't you tell us what you are permitted to do about some of the individuals we see here."

"Glad to. You see that young woman sitting on the floor in the far corner with the two boys?" The trustees turned to look.

Donaldson interrupted. "Why does that one boy have casts on both of his wrists?"

"He was working for a roofing contractor. There were no harnesses provided for the workers to keep them from falling. He fell off a roof, and broke both his wrists when he landed."

"He doesn't look a day over fourteen," said Joan.

"He's twelve."

"Was it legal for him to be working on a roof at his age?"

"No."

"Then why?"

"The family is from Guatemala. They have no papers. People prey on them because they desperately need money and they have no legal protections."

Anderson inserted himself. "So, Dr. Cotswald, you have just heard the acting director of your mission admit that she knows she is serving illegals here."

Cotswald said, "When did it get to be my mission?"

A woman trustee asked, "Why do you serve people illegally in the country here?"

"Because they are in need. Because Jesus tells us to welcome the stranger. Because . . . see that family? Look at them. You want us to turn them away when we have enough food for them? You want us to turn them out into the rain? I see hunger and broken wrists. I see pouring rain. I don't care whether or not I can see a piece of paper."

Donaldson interjected. "Sarah, is it possible for you all to check IDs?"

"It's possible. But whether someone has or doesn't have an ID doesn't prove whether or not they are here undocumented. But to us, that is not an issue. The only issue for us is their need."

"You are shaming this church to this city."

"No, we are not, Mr. Anderson. We'd be shaming this church if we refused to serve anyone in need. But if the city is ashamed of this church because we are feeding hungry people wherever they came from, that is the city's problem. In fact, it would be the city's failure. We are concerned with the problems of these people." She swept her arm across the packed room. "We can't figure out why anyone who calls him or herself a Christian would be concerned about anything else."

Suddenly, an elderly woman with soaked, matted, white hair, a drenched black overcoat, bare legs, and two different kinds of shoes on her feet burst through the front door, screaming, "*Satanas se ha ido! Satanas se ha ido!*" at the top of her lungs. She grabbed a pair of scissors off the desk that was just inside the door, and began swinging them back and forth in front of her. "*El discipulos del diablo!*"

The clients on the floor in front of her jumped up and back. The trustees pressed back. Sarah walked forward toward the woman with her arms spread wide, her palms open and upraised. "*Paz*, Maria," she said quietly as she walked closer. "*Paz.*"

Janine ran into the room from out of the back where she had been translating for clients in the infant formula room. She had heard the ruckus.

"Maria, *donde has estada?*" Janine cried. "*Te hemos extranado mucho.*"

Janine walked without hesitation right up to Maria and hugged her. Maria dropped the scissors on the floor and began to weep in Janine's arms.

The clients in the room began to applaud.

Janine took Maria alone into the women's restroom. Sarah picked up the scissors from the floor and put them inside a drawer for the front desk. She walked back to the group of trustees.

"What was that about?" asked another woman trustee. "Does that happen often? What was that woman saying?"

"When she came in, she said that Satan was here and that we are his disciples."

"How do you know that? Do you speak Spanish?"

"No, but Janine does. That is the volunteer who took Maria into the restroom. Janine taught Spanish for years. She knows Maria well. Maria says the same thing every time she comes in. Janine told me what it means."

"Do you know what Janine said to her to calm her down?"

"I think she asked Maria where she had been and said that she had missed her."

Cotswald asked, "What can you tell us about that poor lady?"

"She is obviously mentally ill. Delusional and hallucinating, probably schizophrenic. She lives on the street. Thinks Satan lives in motels, so she won't stay there even when we give her some money for a night for a bed and a shower. We have called the mental illness outreach team from the county hospital twice for her since I started here. They involuntarily commit her for as long as they can under the law, usually only three days at a time. They medicate her while she's in. She gets more lucid and calm on the meds, so they have to release her. She stops taking the meds, and goes back to this."

One of the trustees asked, "Is she in danger on the street?"

"Of course she is. Mostly from another mentally ill person. But she never has money or possessions to be robbed, and she is not really a target for sexual assault. At least I hope not. But we worry a lot about her and people in her situation."

"Where does she get food?"

"Here. Only place I know is here. She is too paranoid to go to a walk-in shelter where she could get a hot meal and sleep inside. She gets a sack lunch every day from us when we are open. Even when we are not, she comes by and knocks on a window, and we give her some food and let her use the restroom."

"How long can she survive like this?"

"God knows."

"Isn't there something else we can do?"

"Like what?" asked Sarah. "There are dozens of women on the streets around here just like Maria. We are doing what we can. I am afraid that the best thing we do is what Janine is doing for her right now—being a friend and not being afraid of her."

"It's so depressing," said the trustee. "How do you keep doing this?"

"We aren't alone down here."

"What do you mean?"

"Long story. Some other time."

"No. Please. Tell us now."

"Who do you see here . . . now . . . in this room?" Sarah looked at Bill Anderson. "Do you see danger? Do you see illegals? Do you see dirty, hopeless, violent failures? People not worth your worry?"

"Who do you see, Sarah?" asked Cotswald.

"Okay, I'll tell you. Over there, I see Guillermo. He fought in Iraq and has terrible PTSD. He panics in a crowd. I am surprised he can stand to be in here among all these people. He can't hold a job. There I see Ada and her three children. Ada has uncontrolled diabetes and is facing a leg amputation. She is scared she won't be able to work to afford her rent and groceries, and will have to give up her children to foster care. Her kids just soak up her anxiety and are out of control most of the time. So she worries all the more. Over there I see Herbert, the man in the beret. See him? He has terrible cataracts and can't get the treatment he needs. He's getting to where he can't walk on a sidewalk without tripping. That is why he has the bandage on his forehead. See the young woman in the chair there with her coat over her head? She is on the run from a husband who beats her. She is afraid someone will recognize her and tell him where she is . . . I see people who feel all alone, people who feel that no one cares if they live or die. Or how they live or die. . . . Now I'm going to tell you something I will regret saying as soon as I say it. I would never in a million years have said this before I started working down here. . . . Mostly, I see Jesus. In all these people . . . I know that sounds crazy to you, but it is the truth for me. . . . You asked how I keep doing this. It all depends upon what and who you see when you look."

The trustees stared at Sarah as if she were the one hallucinating.

"But with respect. The important question is not how I keep doing this. Or how Anne, or Janine, or Jazmine, or any of the church volunteers keep doing this. The question is how these clients of ours keep doing it. Guillermo and Ada and her children, and Herbert and crazy Maria and all these people you see here. How do they keep surviving—when things never seem to get easier or fairer or kinder for them? I keep doing it because I am able to see them and Jesus in them. Who do they see?"

She paused. "They just flat amaze me with their strength and their endurance."

Tenth Step

Matthew 5:9

⁹ Blessed are you who make peace, for you are children of God.

We continue on the Way. The longer we are empowered by God to walk with the poor and the outcast, the greater grows our hunger and thirst for the Kingdom's righteousness. This hunger and thirst leads to a growing capacity for mercy. This mercy enables us to see Jesus and the image of God in the suffering people. So we are naturally made peacemakers in our next Step—children imitating God the Father incarnate in Jesus. If we see Jesus in the suffering of all people, how can we fail to be peacemakers? Indeed, the seed to the fruit of making peace (5:9) is seeing (5:8).

What is the peace we are called to make? Is it merely an absence of conflict? Or, like the Hebrew *shalom* described by the prophets, is peace found in a community of mercy, justice, and mutual well-being in which all are nurtured and protected?

How can such a peace be made?

Throughout human history, peace as an "absence of conflict" has been made by conquerors and powers defeating by force those who oppose their particular dominance. After victors impose their rule by force, threat, law, societal pressure, incentives to conform, and sanctions for resisting, "peace" is made.

Let us put this saying in its context. During the time of Jesus, Caesar Augustus was proclaimed to be the Son of God and the Savior who had made peace for the entire Roman Empire through military victory.

Monuments throughout the Empire celebrated this peace. The Peace of Augustus was a religious cult. The Peace was declared to be the gift of the gods Jupiter, Mars, and Venus, borne throughout the Empire by Roman legions.

Tacitus, a historian of the Roman Empire, quoted Calgacus, a Britanni describing the Roman conquest of Britannia in 43–44 CE:

> Brigands of the world, after exhausting the land by their wholesale plunder they now ransack the sea. The wealth of an enemy excites their greed, his poverty their lust for power. Neither East nor West has served to glut their maw. Only they, of all on earth, long for the poor with as keen a desire as they do the rich. Robbery, butchery, rapine, these liars call "empire": *they create desolation and call it peace.* (Emphasis added)[33]

Zealots in Israel in Jesus' day prayed for the LORD to bring *shalom* by empowering the Jews to drive the Romans from Israel by violence. So in 66 CE the Jews revolted against Rome's oppression. In 70 CE, after a six month siege, Roman legions under the future emperor Titus destroyed Jerusalem, pulled down the Second Temple leaving only the present day "Wailing Wall," and eventually expelled Jews from Israel.[34]

Peace is described as the product of military victory even in the Old Testament. Until the vision of the Hebrew prophets, peace is presented in the Hebrew scripture as an absence of conflict secured through violence and the threat of violence (Deut 20:10–14; Josh 10:1–5; 10:14–20; 1 Chr 22:9–18). God gave us another vision of peace through the prophets.

In Isa 9, the prophet envisioned that a child would come to Israel and the world. Through this child God would bring peace by justice and righteousness, not by the sword:

> [4] For the yoke of their burden,
> and the bar across their shoulders,
> the rod of their oppressor,
> you have broken as on the day of Midian.
> [5] For all the boots of the tramping warriors
> and all the garments rolled in blood
> shall be burned as fuel for the fire.
> [6] For a child has been born for us,
> a son given to us;
> authority rests upon his shoulders;
> and he is named
> Wonderful Counsellor, Mighty God,

Everlasting Father, *Prince of Peace*.
⁷ His authority shall grow continually,
and there shall be *endless peace*
for the throne of David and his kingdom.
*He will establish and uphold it
with justice and with righteousness*
from this time onwards and for evermore. (Emphasis added)

In Isa 11, the prophet wrote that the child would bring peace not through violence but through the justice and power of his teachings:

¹ A shoot shall come out of the stock of Jesse,
and a branch shall grow out of his roots,
² The spirit of the LORD shall rest upon him,
the spirit of wisdom and understanding,
the spirit of counsel and might,
the spirit of knowledge and the fear of the LORD.
³ His delight shall be in the fear of the LORD.
He shall not judge by what his eyes see,
or decide by what his ears hear;
⁴ but with righteousness he shall judge the poor,
and decide with equity for the meek of the earth;
he shall strike the earth *with the rod of his mouth*,
and *with the breath of his lips* he shall kill the wicked.
⁵ Righteousness shall be the belt around his waist,
and faithfulness the belt around his loins.
⁶ The wolf shall live with the lamb,
the leopard shall lie down with the kid,
the calf and the lion and the fatling together,
and a little child shall lead them.
⁷ The cow and the bear shall graze,
their young shall lie down together;
and the lion shall eat straw like the ox.
⁸ The nursing child shall play over the hole of the asp,
and the weaned child shall put its hand on the adder's den.
⁹ They will not hurt or destroy
on all my holy mountain;
for the earth will be full of the knowledge of the LORD.
as the waters cover the sea. (Emphasis added)

In Isa 32, peace is again described as the product not of force but of justice and righteousness:

¹⁶ Then justice will dwell in the wilderness,
And righteousness abide in the fruitful field.

> ¹⁷ *The effect of righteousness will be peace,*
> And the result of righteousness quietness and trust forever.
> (Emphasis added)

In Isa 57 and 58, the prophet declared: "Peace, peace, to the far and the near" (57:19). But there will be "no peace, says my God, for the wicked" (57:21) who serve their own interests on fast days and oppress all their workers (58:3b) and who "fast only to quarrel and fight and to strike with a wicked fist" (58:4). Peace will come instead to those who "loose the bonds of injustice . . . undo the thongs of the yoke . . . let the oppressed go free and . . . break every yoke" (58:6). Peace will come through those who "share your bread with the hungry, and bring the homeless poor into your house," and who "see the naked and cover them" (58:7). Peace will come through those who "remove the yoke from among you, the pointing of the finger, the speaking of evil," and who "offer your food to the hungry and satisfy the needs of the afflicted" (58:9b–10).

In Jer 8, the leaders and people of Israel claimed *shalom* was present. But the prophet proclaimed that there was no peace,

> ^{10b} because from the least to the greatest
> everyone is greedy for unjust gain;
> from prophet to priest
> everyone deals falsely.
> ¹¹ They have treated the wound of my people carelessly,
> saying "Peace, peace," when there is no peace. . . .
> ¹⁵ We look for peace, but find no good,
> for a time of healing, but there is terror instead.

And in Mic 3, peace is only present when there is justice and mercy to the poor:

> And I said:
> Listen, you heads of Jacob and rulers of the house of Israel!
> Should you not know justice?—
> ² you who hate the good and love the evil,
> who tear the skin off my people,
> and the flesh off their bones;
> ³ who eat the flesh of my people,
> flay the skin off them,
> break their bones to pieces,
> and chop them up like meat in a kettle,
> like flesh in a caldron.

> ⁴ Then they will cry to the Lord;
> but he will not answer them;
> he will hide his face from them at that time,
> because they have acted wickedly.
> ⁵ Thus says the Lord concerning the prophets
> who lead my people astray,
> who cry "Peace" when they have something to eat,
> but declare war against those
> who can put nothing in their mouths.

The Hebrew prophets spoke God's word that true and lasting peace is made not by threat, coercion, and violence, but instead by righteous mercy, justice, provision, and protection for all members of a community.

This voice of God to bring peace by protecting all in the community is also found in Torah. See, for example, Exod 22:25; 23:6; Lev 19:9–16, 33–37; 23:22; Deut 15:11; 24:10–22.

God's peace also sounds loudly and repeatedly in the Psalms: 9:18; 10:2, 9; 12:5; 14:6; 22:26; 34:11–14; 37:14–20; 40:17; 41:1; 72:2, 4, 12; 74:21; 109:16; 112:9; 113:7; 132:15; 140:12.

In our time, our world doesn't hear and heed God's word in the prophets, Torah, or the Psalms about peace or how to make it.

We in the United States claim to make "peace" along our own borders by stringing concertina wire and building walls to keep desperate, exhausted, and impoverished refugees from finding protection and refuge in "the land of the free and the home of the brave." We separate mothers from their children in detention camps to deter these desperate people from seeking refuge. Politicians demonize them in order to gain or keep power. We try to make peace by imprisoning two million people at any given time, and spending $182 billion every year on prisons and jails, as reported by the Prison Policy Initiative.[35] Our political discourse is as demeaning and inflammatory as it has been in our history. Many politicians win election by stoking resentment and fear of the "other." Many of our homes are armed fortresses. Gallup reported in 2020 that 44 percent of all American live in a household with a firearm.[36] Lawmakers in many states claim to be making peace by making it legal for people to openly carry firearms and without requiring training or licensing. Their answer to the lack of peace is for more people to carry more guns in more places.

Internationally we try to make the peace we want by diplomacy, backed by our storehouse of so many weapons of war that no one would be foolish enough to resist us. We try to make the peace we want by exporting enough of these weapons for other nations to make peace by defeating or deterring their enemies. And we export food and medicines along with the weapons to countries with suffering millions, but often to keep regimes that favor us and the peace we want.

Hamas tried to make the peace it seeks by annihilating the nation of Israel through atrocities against Israeli civilians in October 2023 and holding innocent hostages. Israel is, as I type this, trying to make the peace it wants by hunting down all the Hamas forces in Gaza, bombing civilians' homes and hospitals, displacing 75 percent (at last estimate as I type this) of all Palestinian civilians from their destroyed homes, and blockading import of humanitarian necessities.[37]

Putin claims to be making peace across Russia's southwestern border by military invasion and destruction of the Ukrainian infrastructure.

My father was a US Air Force commander of a squadron of B-36 bombers during the Cold War in the 1950s, circling the globe with nuclear bombs in their bomb bays, ready to drop on the Soviet Union on command from the president. The B-36 bombers he flew and commanded were nicknamed "The Peacemaker."

We tried unsuccessfully to impose the peace we wanted in Vietnam with M-16 rifles, mortars, artillery, helicopter gunships, napalm, and carpet bombing.

The kingdoms of the world don't believe the LORD has spoken to us about peacemaking through the Hebrew prophets, the Psalms, and Jesus. Or the kingdoms don't trust the LORD. Or the kingdoms give more priority to profits and power than to *shalom*. Or the kingdoms are too scared to take the risk of hearing and heeding the LORD.

Where Caesar Augustus proclaimed that he had made peace through the military victory, Jesus taught that true peace is made only through mercy, justice, and righteousness. Clearly Jesus' teachings about peacemaking are fruits of the prophets, Torah, and the Psalms. What God had proclaimed about peace through these earlier writings, God said even more clearly and emphatically through Jesus.

"Blessed are you who make peace, for you are children of God" is a summary statement of the entirety of Jesus' life and teachings. While Matt 5:9 is the only place in scripture we find the word "peacemaker" (Greek: *eirenopoioi*), all of Jesus' teachings are about how to make a true and lasting *shalom* he called the Kingdom through righteous mercy, justice, generosity, sacrificial service, and forgiveness.

Tenth Step: Matthew 5:9

Compare the second half of this beatitude: "for you will be children of God," with Jesus' teachings quoted later in Matt 5:

> [43] You have heard it was said, "You shall love your neighbor and hate your enemy." [44] But I say to you, Love your enemies and pray for those who persecute you, [45] *so that you may be children of your Father in heaven*; for he makes his sun to rise on the evil and the good, and send rains on the righteous and the unrighteous. [46] For if you love those who love you, what reward do you have? Do not even tax collectors do the same? [47] And if you greet only your brothers and sisters, what more are you doing than others? Do not even Gentiles do the same? [48] Be perfect, therefore, as your heavenly Father is perfect. (Emphasis added)

Disciples are peacemaking children of God when we are merciful to all, seeing God and God's image in everyone (5:7-8). We are peacemakers when we do not withhold our mercy because of our judgments about who does or does not deserve our mercy (7:1). Jesus tells us in 5:43-45 that God gives God's merciful blessings without regard to such judgments. We will do the same if we are children of this merciful God. God's universal mercy of empathy, generosity, forgiveness, and inclusion is a gift that will lead us children of God to God's peace.

This call for us to be merciful as God is merciful is central to Jesus' teachings. Consider his teaching against anger and insult (Matt 5:21-22). Consider his teaching against violence and retaliation (5:38-41). Consider his teachings about forgiveness (6:12; 18:21-22, 23-35). Consider his teachings against judgment and condemnation (7:1-5; 13:24-30). Consider his many teachings in Matthew's Gospel alone about merciful generosity versus selfish accumulation (5:42; 6:19-21, 24, 33; 10:8; 19:16-24; 20:1-16; 22:1-10; 25:31-46).

Consider now a teaching of Jesus that has broader relevance than its specific words, a teaching that would have a powerful impact on peacemaking if followed.

> [27] You have heard it was said, "You shall not commit adultery." [28] But I say to you that everyone who *looks* at a woman with lust has already committed adultery with her in his heart. [29] If your right eye causes you to sin, tear it out and throw it away. (Matt 5; emphasis added)

Women were powerless in Jesus' time. They are still powerless in much of the world. They were essentially property of their fathers or husbands. A husband could divorce his wife on the authority of Deut 24:1 simply by handing her a paper saying he was divorcing her. As we have seen, most of Jesus' mercy was through his protection and nurture of the powerless and marginalized. So in 5:27–29 he teaches us not to treat women as if they were a collection of objects to be used by men. He specifically taught against seeing a woman as if she were only her sexual parts (5:28). He taught us to see a woman, and everyone, as a child of God in her complexity and value.

There is a broader lesson here, going back to Matt 5:8, "Blessed are you who are pure in heart, for you will see God." When we are blessed with purity of heart on the Way of following Jesus, we are inspired to see every person with God's eyes. We no longer see them as if they were merely a tool to satisfy some need we have. We no longer see them as an object to control. No one is a "thing" in our sight. We see their humanity and their divinity. We see their suffering, their joys, their fears, their braveries, their needs and wants, their tragedies and their triumphs. The sin of men who look at women with lust is that they see the woman not as a child of God but only as an object for their use. They only see those parts of her that will satisfy their lust, not her total dignity and worth.

Jesus taught us a few verses later: "[22] The eye is the lamp of the body. So if your eye is healthy, your whole body will be full of light; [23] but if your eye is unhealthy, your whole body will be full of darkness" (Matt 6). What I hear Jesus telling us is whether our hearts and minds are filled with the truth depends upon who we see and how we see them. If we are blessed to see everyone as a child of God with the image of God within, our lives will be filled with the light of truth . . . about ourselves and about them.

The problem with anger (5:21–22)? Our anger prevents us from seeing the fallible humanity and the enduring image of divinity of the person with whom we are angry.

The problem with violent retaliation (5:38–39)? We do not see the person against whom we are retaliating as God sees him or her, and do not treat the image of God within that person with the respect and mercy of God due him or her. Instead we see them only as an enemy who deserves our hate (5:43–44). We do not see the humanity that caused them to act as they did or the divinity that would enable them to transcend their own failures. We do not see how much they and we have in common.

The root of our refusing to forgive (6:14–15)? Again, our refusal comes from a failure to see the so-called offender truthfully (7:2–3).

The failure of refusing to help one in need because we judge that they do not deserve our mercy (7:1)? The failure is that we do not see the divinity and humanity of that person as God does, and so do not act with God's mercy.

This seeing is a blessing and a gift given by God so that we can be peacemakers, thus showing the world the Father and the Way (5:16). With this gift of divine vision, we begin to see that peace is the Kingdom of Mercy and that the Kingdom of Mercy is God's peace.

Think of what *shalom* would be made if corporate boards of directors and CEOs were to see and therefore treat their employees mercifully and justly as individual children of God, not merely as costs of doing business?

Or if Hamas were to see each Israeli, child, woman, and man, as a child of God, with the same needs, fears, and frailties that they have? Or if Israelis saw each Palestinian as precious in the eyes of God, and not merely as a threat to the future of Israel or mere collateral damage to be sacrificed to destroy Hamas?

Or if Israel and the wealthy nations were to have seen the Palestinian people as children of God as precious as any people, and mercifully ensured them the food, medical care, employment opportunities, self-determination, national identity, religious freedom, and a future for their children that all people need and desire?

Or if Russian soldiers were to see Ukrainians as God sees them? Would they then throw down their arms and refuse to fight Putin's war of aggression?

What peace could be made if every candidate for political office were to see and honor the divinity and humanity of each person he or she is inclined to demonize and use as a tool for election?

Or if all of us were to see and respond with mercy to the homeless men and women in our cities as bearing God's divinity?

Or if every young person trapped in poverty in the inner city, and if every police officer assigned to keep the peace there, were to see God in one another and treat one another with respect and mercy?

Or if the governor of Texas were to see God in the refugees trying to cross the Rio Grande into the safety here?

Or if every potential mass shooter were to see God in each person they were urged by their inner demons to slaughter?

Or if feuding neighbors and divided family members were to see the other and themselves honestly with the eyes of God?

What peace could be made if all of us with more material things than we need were to see the poor as precious to God and as deserving of a generous portion of our plenty?

Or if each of us who live in isolated and protected comfort would seek to see the children of the world who are dying daily of hunger, bad water, and easily treatable disease? What *shalom* would we make then?

Or if each addicted consumer of fossil fuels were to see the earth as saturated with God's loving presence and sustaining power? What *shalom* would we then make with the earth?

There is a deep tension between justice in the world's kingdoms and the justice of the Kingdom of Mercy. One version of justice leads inevitably to conflict; the other version to *shalom*. The source of the tension is how the "other" is seen. Do we see only an individual who has acted wickedly, and who deserves to be punished to deter him and others from the same conduct, or as an obstacle to our getting what we want? Do we see a collection of individuals like the commanders of Hamas or of the Israeli Defense Force who need the justice of "an eye for an eye" (5:38)? Or do we see individuals who have been blinded by suffering, hate, ideology, and threatened nationhood, but who still have within them an image of God that has been wounded? Is the justice that is due to individuals or nations based only upon their terrible conduct or also upon the divinity and possibility within them? What lasting, true peace has "an eye for an eye" ever produced?

Are we at peace with ourselves? Or do we see and treat ourselves as nothing but our body parts, nothing but a conglomeration of physical urges, often out of control and in conflict? If we were to see the amazing complexity of our mysterious combination of divine and mortal as God made and sees us, would we be more at peace with ourselves? Would we be more forgiving of our own human failures, and hungering and thirsting more for our divine possibilities? If we look into our own souls and see God's image of mercy there, would we be better able to live in peace with others and ourselves? And if we were suddenly able to see ourselves as bearers of God and God's Kingdom of Mercy into our communities, would we also be able to see our fellow man and woman as God sees them and then truly become peacemakers and children of God?

That to me is the promise of Jesus' teachings and a culmination of the Way of discipleship. *Seeing* the light of God in the other person is the linchpin of righteous mercy and peacemaking. But, at great cost to the world and its people, only a few of us are ever blessed with the purity of heart to see God in the other, and thus to be makers of God's *shalom*.

> [1] Then I *saw* a new heaven and a new earth;
> for the first earth had passed away....
> [3] And I heard a loud voice from the throne saying:
> "*See*, the home of God is among mortals.
> He will dwell with them as their God;
> they will be his peoples,
> and God himself will be with them.
> [4] he will wipe every tear from their eyes.
> Death will be no more;
> mourning and crying and pain will be no more,
> for the first things have passed away." (Rev. 21; emphasis added)

So the final making of the peace of the Kingdom of Mercy begins and ends with "seeing" God "among mortals."

The Tenth Step on the Way of the disciple is taken when the blessing of the purity of a merciful heart enables us to see God in the other and to help Jesus make *shalom*.

***

The trustee meeting before the Sunday meeting to vote on the mission's future was held on the preceding Thursday evening. Five of the nine trustees voted to invite Sarah, Anne, Janine, and Jazmine to answer questions. The other four trustees were opposed to putting the women through this. The majority wanted to hear the women's defense of their service to illegal aliens.

Dr. Cotswald was inundated with telephone calls and emails from people asking to attend the trustee meeting. He told Mr. Anderson about these requests, and they decided together to stonewall them. Dr. Cotswald absolutely hated conflict. So he agreed with Anderson not to respond to these many requests. The meeting was held away from the church, in a meeting room of Mr. Anderson's investment firm.

The women were kept outside the meeting room for forty-five minutes. They could hear the sound of raised voices through the walls.

Joan Donaldson opened the meeting room door and invited them in. The nine trustees and Dr. Cotswald were seated on either side of a long conference table with Mr. Anderson at the head. The women were directed by Anderson to sit in the chairs at the far end of the table. Instead, Dr. Cotswald, Ms. Donaldson, and two other women trustees vacated their seats so Sarah, Anne, Janine, and Jazmine could sit closer to the head. Cotswald offered coffee or tea all around.

Cotswald opened with prayer. "Let us pray. Lord Jesus, you tell us, 'Peace I leave to you. My peace I give to you. I do not give as the world gives. Do not let your hearts be troubled, and do not let them be afraid.' Lord, help us to find the way of peace in this time of honest and good faith disagreement. Let us treat one another with respect and courtesy. Let us find the way to your peace. Amen."

Anderson jumped right in. "I have a question. Do you three ladies other than Sarah know that the mission has been disobeying the trustees' order to keep out illegal aliens?"

One of the other trustees interrupted. "Excuse me, Bill. We trustees never voted as a board on such an order that I know of. Did we?" She looked around the room at the other trustees. "Does anyone recall our voting on such an order?"

"As chair of the trustees, I am empowered to give that order," said Mr. Anderson.

The trustee turned toward Dr. Cotswald. "Excuse me, Bill. Sorry for interrupting again. Pastor, you are the resident expert on our Book of Governance. Does the chair of a church's board of trustees have any power to issue an order like that without a vote of the entire board?"

Cotswald hesitated. "I don't want to take sides here."

"I'm not asking you to take sides. I'm just asking for information about the Book of Governance."

Anderson turned to Sarah. "You see what you have done here? You are dividing this church. You aren't screening for illegals at the mission. I saw that you aren't with my own eyes. Do you deny that?"

Sarah said, "Do I deny that we are not screening people? Do I deny that we are not refusing food to hungry people who might be undocumented? No, we are not keeping any hungry people out of the mission, no matter if they lack a piece of paper. And we will not deny them some of the food we have as long as we are the ones working down there and looking people in need in their faces every day." She looked to each of the other three women, and each nodded in agreement.

"On what authority do you aid and abet illegals?"

"You call feeding and clothing the hungry and the naked 'aiding and abetting'? We are 'aiding and abetting' them to stay alive. On what authority do you say this church shouldn't feed and clothe hungry and naked people?"

"On the authority of the law."

"I am unaware of any law that prevents us from feeding hungry people in a mission of the church of Jesus Christ. . . . And if there is such a law, I would still defy it."

"So you are in favor of an open border."

"You are talking government and politics. I am talking discipleship and mercy. The sad thing is that there doesn't seem to be much connection between politics and mercy these days for a lot of people. Mr. Anderson, I am in favor of feeding hungry, desperate people whatever path they take to our mission. Whatever the law says about people coming into our country without documents has nothing to do with how we care for individuals who appear at our door. To answer your question, I am not here to discuss the pros and cons of an open border. But as someone who tries to be Christian and who is a member of this church, I am in favor of open hearts for people in need on our doorstep."

Anderson stood and started to point at Sarah. Ms. Donaldson looked to Cotswald to intervene, but he was silent.

"*So much for peace,*" thought Cotswald.

"Bill!" cried Donaldson. "Bill," she said more quietly. "Please sit down."

He sat, but he spoke to all the trustees as if the four women were not in the room. "All these women have brought to our church is conflict. Nothing but controversy and division. People taking sides against one another. Telephone calls and emails to our poor pastor, blaming him for not keeping the peace. Before they," pointing again to the woman, "before they tried to take over our church, this was a beautiful, quiet place to come on Sundays, to get away from all the ugliness out there. The church was our haven and sanctuary. We were all friends. The pastor opened this meeting with a prayer for peace. These women have destroyed the peace of our church."

Sarah spit back. "Whose peace, Mr. Anderson? Whose peace? What about the peace of our downtown neighbors? And you were the one who disrupted the peace of the church by presenting a resolution to close and sell the mission."

"Why do you care more about our so-called neighbors than you do about our church?"

Anne spoke up, "Our church? Who is included in your 'our'?"

"Don't you quibble with us! The families of the trustees sitting around this table have kept this church open and running for years with our donations. Now you are trying to take it over and ruin it."

"I am not quibbling. And don't you speak to any of us like that!" Now Anne raised her voice. "I have been a member of this church myself for decades. My husband and I have always supported this church financially. Why aren't we included in the 'our'?"

"I happen to know that your husband is opposed to what you are trying to pull here." Anderson smirked at Cotswald. "I happen to know that he has kicked you out of the house for it. You have to sleep at your father's now, don't you?"

"You are right. He is opposed to it." Anne looked a bit like a boxer who had been hit below the belt.

Sarah stepped in. "This board is trying to sell the mission. This board took it upon itself to order our church security to call the police on homeless people just for sleeping outside on church property. All they want is some shelter and protection from the weather and the predators on the street. That order resulted in a scared, vulnerable teenaged girl being arrested and separated from her little baby. Thanks to Joan, we were able to undo that injustice. . . . So tell us this, Mr. Anderson. Did this entire board vote on this policy of calling police to arrest these poor people? Or was that something you decided on your own as chair?"

"That is not a mission matter. You have no right to question us about that policy here. And we are not here to answer your questions. You are here to answer ours."

Jazmine spoke up now. "Then why don't we see if any of the other trustees have a voice? Any questions we can answer from someone other than Mr. Anderson?"

Another trustee asked. "Ms. Bodine, please tell us about Maria. The lady we saw in the mission who picked up the scissors. Where is she now?"

"We called the county hospital mental health outreach team again. The scissors decided that for us. Although we hated to do it, we had to think about the safety of everybody, including Maria."

"Is she still in the hospital?"

"Yes. The district attorney's office is probably going to petition a court for a longer-term involuntary commitment for her. The scissors have given them grounds. She had only been noisy before. But she never acted like that. What I regret is that I will need to testify at the comment hearing."

"Weren't you scared?"

"I am more scared of testifying at the hearing."

"Because she might retaliate when she gets out?"

"No. She would never hurt anyone. She's just ill. I am just scared she will think she has lost the only friend she had in the world."

"I was sure scared. I was scared for you. I couldn't believe how brave you were. Don't you think there is a need for security presence at the mission?"

Anderson spoke. "This is one more reason to close the mission. If one crazy person or one of these dangerous illegals injures someone there, this church is facing a million dollar lawsuit. Is that what you want?"

"No, that is not what we want, Mr. Anderson," said Sarah. "But that could happen on any Sunday in sanctuary worship, too. It can happen anywhere in this country, with the guns and the anger and the fear everywhere. Are the trustees going to start ordering security to keep homeless people out of our worship of Jesus of Nazareth? Or pat everyone down for weapons when they enter the sanctuary? Or put up a security system like at the airport? Or keep out people who just appear different? Are you going to turn this church into even more of a private club? This is a downtown church in a big city. Our neighbors include the homeless and the poor and, yes, the untreated mentally ill. And the undocumented refugee. The mission is the one place and ministry of this church that aggressively welcomes all people. And you want to shut it down? And to keep hungry people out for lack of a piece of paper? . . . So in answer to your question, yes, we would welcome security people to the mission, but only if security people are going to stay in the background and take direction from us and not . . . overreact." Her voice trailed off.

Joan Donaldson took the floor. "Sarah, Anne, Jazmine, Janine. Some of us are so proud of the work you have done. And despite what you have heard here tonight, we trustees alone aren't going to decide the future of the mission; the entire church is. So what do you propose the church decide?"

"Joan, we've actually talked about this. And we have consulted the mission's long term volunteers about it. So we have our own alternative proposal to put to the church as a whole, alongside the proposal the trustees previously offered."

Anderson blustered: "This is out of order! These women are trying to make themselves trustees. They are out of control!"

"Bill," said Joan. "They are just answering the question I asked. They know the mission and its operations much better than any of us. Some of us want to know what they think."

Sarah handed copies of a written proposal to each of the trustees. It proposed that the mission building would be kept by the church and that its ministries would continue to provide care for people based only upon need and without regard to race, religion, citizenship, immigration status, national origin, and criminal record. It also proposed to consider expansion of mission operations with a feasibility study for the construction of four floors on top of the present single story mission building, with one of the added floors for a parking facility and three of the added floors to house women and children who were homeless.

The trustees read in silence. "This is ambitious," said Donaldson.

Anderson put his copy on the table before him. "So you ladies aren't satisfied to keep things as they are. You want to turn over the entire apple cart.... This is very irresponsible. If it were to pass, long term members, the backbone of this church, would run over one another getting out the door. You'd lose donations. The only people left in worship would be the homeless and the illegals. You'd sacrifice the peace of this church."

"You started this, Mr. Anderson. Maybe God can turn what you started into something good. We are just proposing that the church as the body of Christ consider this alternative," said Sarah.

"And what about the peace of the church?" yelled Anderson. "You are dividing the church even more deeply. Maybe the trustees will revoke our resolution for the sake of peace."

"Then we will still want our proposal to go before the whole church."

"Then we will go ahead with our resolution," said Anderson.

"You talk about the peace of this church," said Jazmine. "Peace for who? For the homeless folks our security people are calling the police on? For the teenaged girl we had arrested and taken from her baby? For Maria? What about God's peace for all the suffering and abandoned people all around this downtown church? And what about the faithfulness of this church to Jesus? What about discipleship?"

Cotswald stopped the argument. "I think we have gotten as far as we can with this. I guess you ladies have answered our questions. Thank you for coming. And thank you for all your work."

The four women left the conference room. Jazmine asked the other three if they wanted to wait to see what was decided. Janine needed to get home to Estrella and her baby. Sarah and Anne wanted to have a late supper at their dad's.

Two hours later, Dr. Cotswald called Sarah's cell. "The vote of the trustees was 4 to 4 with one abstention on each of the proposals—Anderson's and yours."

"So is the church-wide meeting canceled?"

"No. The vote was also 7 to 2 in favor of presenting both proposals to the church without an endorsement of either one from the trustees as a body."

"Wow. . . . I have to process that. . . . Who will present the original proposal to the church meeting?"

"Bill Anderson and one other trustee."

"Who will present ours?"

"You will. And whoever else you want with you."

"Me?"

"It's not too late for you to turn back, Sarah. If you do, I think the trustees will withdraw their resolution to close and sell the mission."

"How long until they will present the resolution again? . . . I think we want to move forward with our proposal. . . . So the outcome will turn completely on who shows up to vote."

"I think prayer will determine who wins."

"Really? You do? Is all our praying helping the homeless and the undocumented? I don't think Bill Anderson will be depending much on prayer. I think he will call out his hounds."

"Well, it's Thursday night. The vote is Sunday. . . . Self-righteousness will split the church for sure. Whatever you do, Sarah, please don't demonize the members who want to sell the mission property."

"You mean like they demonize the poor and the undocumented? Like Anderson demonized us in that meeting?"

"The way this is conducted is going to decide if this church has a future."

"With respect, pastor, I think that what is decided will determine if the church should have a future."

"And that is precisely the disagreement, Sarah. I wish I still had your passion."

Eleventh Step

Matthew 5:10

¹⁰ Blessed are you who are persecuted for righteousness' sake, for yours is the kingdom of heaven.

Some may consider the next two Beatitudes about persecution misplaced. Why would disciples be persecuted just after we have tried to make peace?

But the order of these Steps is not haphazard. If we take the Tenth Step by helping God make the *shalom* of the Kingdom of Mercy, we will quickly discover that the kingdoms of the world don't want *shalom*. The peace of the Kingdom would be disruptive of the present order of society in which so many people are invested in places of comfort and dominance. In the Kingdom's peace, "the last shall be first, and the first shall be last" (Matt 20:16). Is it surprising that those who are first in the kingdoms of the world don't want to become last when the peace of the Kingdom of Mercy is made? The dominant will not give up their positions without a struggle. It would be too much repentance and too much fundamental change. It would require too much belief and trust in the LORD. There has been and will be hard push back. There has been and will be persecution.

The arrival of the peace of the Kingdom of Mercy would bring a radical reordering of our economy, our social hierarchies, and our personal, national, and international priorities and interactions. The Kingdom's peace would bring an eventual end to the racism, bigotry, xenophobia, greed, class divisions, sexism, violence, and polarization in our society.

Of course there would be resistance and persecution of the bearers of that peace.

Imagine what would happen to the world economy if disciples of the Kingdom of Mercy succeeded in cutting international military spending significantly. Imagine if American politicians couldn't increase their chances of election by promising larger defense spending in their districts? Imagine if politicians weren't getting elected on promises to build more prisons and hire more police, rather than to create programs to address the causes of crime. Imagine if we spent much more on aid to the peoples of the Western hemisphere suffering terrible poverty, hunger, illness, violence, and oppression rather than on walls, concertina wire, and detention centers to keep them out. Imagine if we as a nation spent less money on weapons of war and more on affordable housing, programs to feed and teach hungry, poor children, and adequate healthcare for everyone. Imagine if the uber rich were no longer idolized as celebrities, and if humble servants of the poor and of the common good were celebrated and imitated. Imagine if social media were no longer filled with lies and demonization. Imagine if the comfortable no longer lived completely segregated lives from the poor. Imagine if we created "neighbor"-hoods without class and racial segregation, and without the pervasive fear and distrust that addicts us today. Imagine if people didn't seek meaning and happiness from acquisition of unneeded things and shallow, transient pleasures.

Discipleship advancing the righteous mercy of the Kingdom is a public as well as a personal calling. The kind of fundamental change that would come with concerted attempts of the disciples of the Kingdom of Mercy to make the peace of God's Kingdom would certainly bring persecution.

Notice that the Beatitude that is the Eleventh Step involves work for the Kingdom's righteous mercy without any explicit mention of Jesus. Disciples work for righteous mercy and justice for the poor and suffering by enlisting those who do not share a commitment to Jesus. In this Step, the disciple is merciful "for righteousness' sake" (Matt 5:10), without explicit reference to Jesus. Others who are not followers of Jesus, including members of other faith traditions and people who doubt the existence of a good and powerful God in a world of so much evil, are invited and welcomed into the growth of the Kingdom. Jesus will still be behind and within that growth, but humbly hidden. Given the many hypocritical failures of Christians and the churches over the centuries to be true to the Kingdom's values, many of our fellow citizens who would otherwise join in making our world more merciful would be alienated if such efforts were explicitly made "on my [Jesus'] account" as on the Twelfth Step of Matt 5:11. For example, one of my professors in university in the late 1960s said his only problem with the civil rights movement was that it was breathing life back into the church. But he was an aggressive opponent of racial segregation and marched across the Edmund Pettis Bridge in Selma in 1965 with Dr. King and was bludgeoned by a state trooper.

There were many who joined in the civil rights movement who were not Christian or religious at all, but who were willing to risk and sacrifice for mercy and justice for the oppressed and marginalized. Dr. King always invoked Jesus' name and teachings to the disciples in his many sermons in churches, but not as often to the general public. In his celebrated "I Have a Dream" speech given in Washington, DC, on August 28, 1963, Dr. King quoted as authority for the end of racial discrimination the Emancipation Proclamation, the US Constitution, the Declaration of Independence, and the song "America the Beautiful." He reasserted his strong advocacy for nonviolence, but without identifying its foundation in Jesus' Sermon on the Mount. He referred explicitly to the "persecution" of many present because of their "quest for freedom," but without citing the Beatitudes of Matt 5:10–12 or any other of Jesus' teachings. He quoted Isa 40:4–5 and Amos 5:24, but without identifying the scriptures or naming the prophets. Even though Jesus and his teachings were the critical foundation for the tactics of the civil rights movement for King and the leadership, he never mentioned Jesus' name in that speech. He referred to "all of God's children, Black men and white men, Jews and Gentiles, Protestant and Catholics."[38] He was appealing for the support of all people committed to the mercy and justice of the Kingdom but not committed to Jesus.

Who chooses to be persecuted for any reason, including for the sake of the Kingdom? What sermon have you ever heard that proclaimed that persecution is a blessing to be welcomed or expected on the Way of discipleship? We think that persecution was only for the early Christians. They were hunted, beaten, flogged, and stoned by Jewish authorities for proclaiming Jesus as the resurrected Jewish Messiah (Acts 4:1–3; 5:17–18; 6:8–60; 8:1–3; 21:27; 22:19–20; 23:10; 1 Cor 11:23–25; Gal 1:13). And they were imprisoned and killed by the Romans for disturbing the peace and refusing to worship the multiple gods of the Empire (Acts 16:19–23; 18:12–16; 19:23–41; 22:22–24;

28:17–20). What would motivate Christians in our time to be persecuted? How would that be a blessing?

The Eleventh Step tests whether we have truly accepted the blessing of hungering and thirsting for the Kingdom. Jesus tells us that persecutions will necessarily come to those who hunger, thirst, and pursue the Kingdom's righteous mercy and peace. Why are such persecutions a blessing? Because the Kingdom of Mercy is the greatest of all blessings, and persecution by the opposing kingdoms of the world is the price we must pay to help God bring the Kingdom. Is there any other way to understand the "blessing" of this persecution?

Why should Jesus' disciples expect an easier reception than the one the world's kingdoms gave Jesus? The Jesus who gave us the Way of the Beatitudes was honest with us, unlike the priests and prophets of the world's kingdoms. He told us repeatedly that we who are called and blessed with discipleship will face not just suffering but also persecutions on the Way.

Jesus called his disciples to be itinerant and homeless (Matt 10:5–14; 19:27), to place the Way above family and even above burying and mourning a father (8:18–22; 10:34–37; 12:46–50). Disciples were called to risk their lives (8:23–26; 14:24–26). Disciples were sent out as sheep among wolves, to be flogged, betrayed by their own families, hated, tortured, and killed (10:16–23; 24:9–13). Disciples were to carry Jesus' cross and to lose their life to gain their life (10:38–39; 16:21–26). Why should we expect our "discipleship" to be different than the "Sonship" of the One we are called to follow?

How we want to deny this and pray that it isn't so! Why couldn't our neighbors, captive as they are in the kingdoms of the world, admire and applaud us for our commitment to mercy? Why doesn't God make it so? Within Matthew's progressive Steps of the Way of the Beatitudes, the disciple is making peace, acting mercifully to all, giving to all in need, and seeing God in every human being. She is holding up the light of the Kingdom to those in darkness. So shouldn't the peace of *shalom* be well on its way by now? Shouldn't the kingdoms of the world have already repented of their darkness? If God hasn't accomplished this, how can we by engaging in conduct that will bring persecution?

But the Way requires us not only to hunger for righteous mercy in our personal and private lives but also to hunger, thirst, act, and advocate for mercy and justice in our public words and actions, just as the Hebrew prophets and Jesus did. "[L]et your light shine before others, so that they may see your good works and give glory to your Father in heaven" (Matt 5:16).

The public aspect of our calling to be disciples exposes us to public opprobrium. We may want to be secret disciples in our private lives, while being fully acceptable to the kingdoms of darkness in our public lives. We may want to be conspicuous in our consumption and inconspicuous in our discipleship. We may want the comfort of serving two masters (Matt 6:24). But this is not the discipleship of Matthew's Jesus. The Kingdom of Mercy is fundamentally at odds with the kingdoms of the world. We who seek to live fully in the Kingdom and successfully in these kingdoms deny this. These kingdoms of the world maintain their power jealously and persuasively, with thought control and legal infrastructure. The disciple exposes the darkness of these kingdoms by the light of her life of mercy. People who have been seduced and conditioned into being disciples of these kingdoms are made angry and defensive by words and actions of Kingdom discipleship.

Preachers pack them in at worship by excusing the double mind and the divided heart, and by preaching that Jesus was persecuted so we don't have to be. But that is not what Jesus tells us in the Beatitudes and all his teachings. That is not the hungering and thirsting and the purity of heart of the Way.

Matt 5:10, 11, 12, and 44, and 10:23 are the only verses in which the word "persecute" in some form is used. Our English translations "persecuted" or "persecution" come from the Greek *dioko*, strictly meaning "to put to flight," according to *Strong's Online Analytical Concordance*.

I offer this meaning of "persecuted"—"to put to flight" from the Way of discipleship—as a way to understand and be moved by this Beatitude in our context.

Today, when we try to help Jesus make *shalom* through our public words and mercies, we can expect to be belittled, resisted, and shunned. Even if we do not intend to be self-righteous, our lives will be perceived as an egotistically motivated judgment upon the lives serving the other kingdoms. These kingdoms will "persecute"—attempt to "put us to flight"—from our commitment to the Kingdom. If we go public with our discipleship, as we are sometimes called to do, we will experience resistance and resentment from those who are under the spell of the dominant kingdoms. As Jesus tells us in this Beatitude, then we will know that we are disciples of the Kingdom.

Imagine if we were to campaign for higher pay and more reliable working hours for the poor employees of our private clubs. We should expect attempts to put us to flight with a range of pressures.

Imagine you are the vice president of a manufacturing corporation that is the predominant source of employment in a small town. Imagine that the order comes down from upper management to start to close the plant by terminating workers, with the longest tenured and highest paid employees to be fired first, and to claim some misconduct by each of the laid-off workers that would void a prior agreement to pay them severance. Imagine that you have gotten to know the workers and their families personally and "see" them as individuals. Imagine that you resist the orders, and argue insistently with management to keep the plant open or to delay the closing, to stop the unjust firings and to pay the agreed severance. Imagine that the fired workers take the company to court for violation of their employment contracts. Imagine that you disclose to the workers the orders you have received directing the unjust firings. Wouldn't we expect the corporation to put you to flight for being merciful and just?

Imagine a law firm is hiring a new office manager, that a search firm has presented a list of qualified applicants, and by far the most experienced and best applicant is African American. Imagine that all but one of the partners vote to hire another applicant who is Anglo because of concern that the firm's clients would be uncomfortable dealing with a Black woman in such a prominent position. Imagine that the dissenting partner objected insistently to the decision. Imagine that the other partners threaten to put him to flight from his partnership if he didn't stop objecting. He leaves the firm but has great difficulty finding another position because his old partners identify him as a troublemaker.

Imagine if an Anglo mother in close circle of moms of children at a public school invited and welcomed into the group mothers of children of other ethnicities from homes with much less income. Imagine if this mom invited Black and Latino children into her home for children's parties and sleepovers. What pushback could this mom expect to put her to flight from her mercies?

Imagine that a family provided a home to children from Venezuela who had been separated from their mother in a detention camp on the southern US border. Imagine that this merciful family registered them in their own children's private school? What pressures would come from parents and teachers at the school to put them to flight from their mercy?

Consider if a teacher in a posh private school next to a gated community were to resign to take a teaching position for less pay and much greater stress in an inner-city public school in an impoverished neighborhood? Could she expect to be criticized and put to flight from her decision by her family and peers?

Consider if a physician quit his partnership in a lucrative medical practice to join Doctors Without Borders? And if she urged her partners to open a clinic in an inner-city neighborhood?

Or if a wealthy lawyer left his practice to found, fund, and run a nonprofit to provide free legal representation to refugees from Central America in detention camps in South Texas? Or to poor families evicted from their homes in his city?

Or if a CEO of a wealthy corporation, with a closed circled of friends of like wealth and priorities, resigned his position and salary to found and run for a nominal salary an organization to house and provide services to the homeless? Or to feed hungry children? And what if he talked to his friends at the country club about the poverty and suffering he witnessed in his new job and tried to recruit his friends to help? Could he and his wife expect to remain members of that circle of friends? Or would they be put to flight from the friendships?

What response would all these disciples receive from their peers and their family? Surely not the persecution of physical beating, flogging, or stoning. But ostracism and ridicule? Isolation? In summary: "being put to flight?"

Another way to look at this is whether those of us who have embarked on the Way are ever persecuted—which is to say "put to flight" from the Way—by our own broken hearts, crushed spirits, and mourning at the suffering we are encountering? Does this suffering isolate us from people who are not sharing this discipleship? Do we feel pressured by our family and friends to abandon this Way? Does our constant exposure to the ideologies of the kingdoms of materialism, consumerism, and hedonism make us feel like fools for choosing the Kingdom over their kingdoms?

Or are we persecuted—"put to flight" from the Way—by our doubts about the goodness and power of God to bring the Kingdom of Mercy when so much suffering remains and so much time has passed since God made the promise of the Kingdom?

But if we refuse to be put to flight from the Way, we are empowered to persist because mercy is its own reward, because we see Jesus in the suffering and in the mercy Jesus provides through us, because the Kingdom is unalloyed good in an evil world, and because of the fellowship of the community of the Beatitudes.

The Eleventh Step on the Way of the disciple is the blessing that empowers us to continue to bear the Kingdom despite the persecutions of the kingdoms of the world and our doubts about God's goodness and power.

***

The next Saturday morning, the day before the all-church vote on the mission, a column ran on the front page of *The Metroplex News*, written by its editorial board. The column excoriated four unnamed "well-intentioned but still misguided women" who were leading astray the great and venerable city institution of First Kingdom of God Church of downtown Metroplex with their lawless support and encouragement of illegal aliens who had invaded the city—aliens who had brought a crime wave of break-ins of downtown businesses, who were threatening women and children shoppers of downtown stores with panhandling, who were exhausting the stores of the charity food banks donated for US citizens, and who were the suppliers of much of the fentanyl that was killing teenagers in the Metroplex community. The column credited Bill Anderson and three other named trustees for their heroic efforts to stem the illegal tide, and congratulated them for their attempts to persuade the church to close the mission and sell its property for development of taxpaying businesses. "However much some in this church can claim that the mission is inspired by the teachings of Jesus, it needs to be moved from its location in downtown where it attracts like a magnet homeless illegals, drugs, and crime." The column informed the city that a church vote would be held the next day at noon on the future of the mission, but that only members of the church would be allowed to vote.

Sarah's husband dropped a copy of the newspaper, with his red highlighting of the column, on the front porch of John's house where Sarah had been sleeping for weeks. Into the newspaper Craig Bigelow had inserted a handwritten letter. "Everyone knows you are the ringleader of the 'well-intentioned but still misguided women.' I can't show my face in our clubs or around my friends without being attacked for letting you go out of control. It's not enough that you are dividing the church; you are also destroying our family. I am begging you not to keep pushing this." The letter wasn't even signed.

Anne's husband George telephoned her at her dad's house where she was also sleeping, asking if she had seen the column. Anne interrupted him. "I was at a meeting of the church trustees last night. How did Bill Anderson know that you are opposing me in what I am doing about the mission? And how did he know I am not sleeping at our home?"

"Anne, Anderson keeps his business with my bank. He was blaming me for what you are doing. He threatened to pull his personal and business accounts from the bank. One thing led to another, and I told him where we both stand on this."

"I hope you and Bill Anderson will be very happy together." Anne hung up on him.

The church telephone message center, texts, and Facebook page were filled with objections or congratulations for the women's stand. Many of the opposing messages demanded to know the names of the four women.

The next morning, the Sunday of the church-wide vote to be held after the 11 a.m. worship service, *The Metroplex News* ran a guest column by Rev. Juice Toliver, the senior pastor of Heaven's Rest Bible Church, the largest evangelical church in the city. Rev. Toliver condemned the pastors of First Kingdom of God Church for the heresy of teaching that Christians can reach salvation by trying themselves to create heaven on earth. "The tragic but undeniable truth is that we humans are incapable of raising ourselves to heaven by our own works of righteousness. We are called first, middle, and last to accept our sinfulness, to believe in the Lord Jesus Christ, to depend completely on his atoning sacrifice, to leave the condition of the world to God, and to be good citizens of our communities. Being a good citizen of Metroplex, Texas, does not include aiding and abetting the crimes and addictions of the homeless and the illegal aliens." He added, "Nowhere does the word of God call us to ignore the laws of the state or to welcome and harbor those who are violating those laws and threatening our peace." At the end of his article, he urged "all true Christians to pray that Dr. Felix Cotswald, Sarah Bigelow, Anne Barnes, Janine Bodine, and Jazmine Bodine repent from the error of their beliefs and ways."

The publisher of the newspaper telephoned Dr. Cotswald at 8 a.m. that Sunday to apologize that an overzealous copy editor had left his name and the names of the four women in the published column. He told

Cotswald that he had telephoned the Metroplex chief of police, and the chief planned to have a contingent of uniformed police stationed prominently around the church that morning. The chief himself telephoned Cotswald shortly thereafter to tell him that he was sending a uniformed officer in a marked patrol car to sit outside each of the homes of the four women. Cotswald informed him that two of the women were not living at their homes, and that he didn't know their current addresses.

When the earliest worshipers arrived at the church that Sunday morning around 9 a.m., they saw five marked police cars parked strategically around the church perimeter. More than twenty demonstrators were walking the sidewalk in front of the sanctuary, chanting "Illegals go home" and carrying signs reading "No Sanctuary for Fentanyl Pushers." Another twenty or so demonstrators were walking the sidewalks around the mission building, carrying signs with the same messages. None of the church security or staff recognized any of the demonstrators as members or past attendees of the church.

When Dr. Cotswald arrived at the church, the lieutenant in charge of the police asked him if Cotswald wanted the IDs checked of the people entering the church.

"Why?" responded Cotswald. "We don't have church IDs. What if new people are coming here to worship?"

"Who the homeless are will be pretty obvious. Do you want us to keep them out?"

"No, sir."

"What about the demonstrators?"

"No, sir."

"What if a demonstrator tries to bring in a sign?"

"Hmm. Never had a problem like this in more than forty years of ministry. Maybe it's a good idea if you have a uniformed officer standing outside every entrance, in case our security people ask for help. I'll tell our staff that people have to leave their signs outside."

"Do you want me to assign some uniformed officers to be inside the sanctuary for the worship service and the meeting?"

"No, sir. Thank you, but we have our own security people. But let me talk to the trustees. I'll let you know if we change our minds about that."

Cotswald reversed that decision when he talked to Bill Anderson. Anderson wanted police to be stationed in the sanctuary to help make his point that security would be an increasing problem if the women got their way and the mission stayed open.

When Cotswald was talking to Anderson about possible police presence in the sanctuary, the pastor asked him if he knew how Juice Toliver got the names of the four women to put in his column.

Anderson replied, "Pastor, you leave things like that to me. I'll have dirty hands, not you. The entire future of this great church is at stake here. Millions of dollars' worth of property. The financial viability of the church. This isn't just a game of hopscotch."

Cotswald thought but did not say, *So much for the peace of Christ.* He said, "Bill, you put those women in danger. Do the finances of this church justify that? I really wish you hadn't done that."

"Done what?" asked Anderson. "I was speaking in confidence to my pastor. You can't repeat to anyone what you think I just said."

The 9:30 a.m. sanctuary service attendance was spotty with fewer than the usual number of worshipers. The 11 a.m. service was standing room only in a sanctuary that seats 2,000 people. There was an unprecedented turnout of women under the age of forty for a Sunday other than Christmas Eve and Easter. And to the eye of the church staff, there was a much larger than usual number of people who had never attended the worship services before.

Cotswald had anticipated a large turnout and the difficulty of taking a vote by only church members if visitors were intermingled with members. An insert in the church worship bulletin set forth verbatim the two proposals on the mission, following up on yesterday's email to all church members stating them. The church worship bulletin stated that only members of the church would be allowed to vote, and that non-church members were invited to move to the balcony of the sanctuary to observe when the vote was being taken, but not to speak or participate.

Cotswald gave a short sermon on Matt 10:16: "See, I am sending you out like sheep into the midst of wolves; so be as wise as serpents and as innocent as doves." This was the long-planned scripture in an ongoing sermon series. He tried hard not to sound as if he were taking sides on the imminent vote. Even he thought he succeeded in saying nothing offensive in any context.

As usual at the end of the service, persons desiring to join the church were invited forward to the altar rail. To Cotswald's and the church staff's shock, more than sixty-five people came forward, about a fourth of whom appeared to be homeless. Bill Anderson immediately stood and took Cotswald's arm, whispering in his ear to object to church membership for these people who clearly were joining only to vote in favor of the mission operations.

"We don't know how they will vote, Bill."

"We know how these homeless people will," he replied. "These women probably organized them to come."

"And did you not solicit some of these who don't appear to be homeless to join the church and vote today? Didn't you contact some people who are already members to be sure to attend? You trustees started this, Bill. I do not have the power or the heart to turn anyone away who is asking to join this church."

It took forty minutes, but everyone who came forward to join was welcomed and their names added to forms for the church's registry.

The service then ended, and the church-wide meeting and vote on the mission started.

Mr. Anderson had wanted to run the meeting, but Cotswald took control. He asked everyone who was not a member to move to the balcony. Someone yelled out that this was an issue that would impact all of downtown, and so the entire city should be allowed to vote. A church security guard moved forward to try to quiet the man, but Cotswald called the guard back.

"Sir, with respect, this is our church's mission on our property. We have been operating this ministry for decades. Our members have funded it and will continue to fund it depending upon the vote today. Or we will close the mission and sell the property. All this is up to this church. If you want the community to weigh in on this, I suggest you go through the city council. Now I am going to ask you again to keep the peace and your thoughts to yourself and to go upstairs to our balcony."

The man left the church angrily. About sixty people moved from the first floor to the balcony.

Cotswald continued, "Our church's Book of Governance tells us how we must proceed with a church-wide vote like this. The only persons who may cast votes are those who are members of the church and who are present. I need to say once again that we need to make this as peaceful and orderly as we can. If you are not a member, welcome. But you may not vote. So I ask again that anyone here who is not a member, move to the balcony." A few more people moved upstairs.

"According to the Book of Governance, the two proposals will be read. Then three people will be able to speak in favor of each. Then we will vote twice, first by a show of hands, and then, if the majority is not clearly evident from the raising of hands, we will ask people to vote and be counted by moving to opposite sides of the sanctuary.

"As explained in the bulletin, the board of trustees is not making a recommendation as a body concerning which proposal should be passed. They have voted instead for both proposals to be presented to the church for its determination. Both proposals may not be adopted, because they are in conflict. Only one may be adopted. But both may be rejected. Rejection of both would preserve the status quo. A simple majority will decide both votes.

"Mr. Bill Anderson, the chair of our board of trustees, will come forward to read the first proposal and then to speak first in its favor. Bill?"

Anderson, who was seated in the front row, stood and began to speak in a loud, bass voice. He announced that he was the only person to be speaking in favor of the first proposal and against the second. He then read the same proposal that had been read to the congregation weeks ago. "This proposal is word for word the first proposal that had been approved unanimously and presented to the church before the unfortunate disruptions occurred. I have been chairman of the trustees for more than ten years. The trustees are chosen experts on property and finances, entrusted by the church with the protection and preservation of the church property and the church's financial future. Now we are rewarded for our long, faithful work by this ingratitude and disrespect. Never before has there been any dissent to our recommendations. Who are to blame for this unprecedented ingratitude and divisions? The illegal aliens who were invading the city. That's who.

"This church has always been the solid and totally reliable foundation of rock upon which the entire downtown of this great city is built. But now, because the mission staff and the 'Jennie-come-lately' women who have been running it recently have continued to serve and to aid and abet illegal aliens, the church we all love is a butt of controversy and criticism. Its entire future is imperiled.

"I expect that you are about to hear that the mission cannot serve any of our American citizen poor without also serving illegals, that it is not just impractical to weed illegals out but also impossible. Then how can we keep the mission open to serve anyone? We are violating the law. We would be opening ourselves to multiple lawsuits from people injured by illegals who would not be here except for the succor and encouragement of our mission staff.

"This mission has been in operation more than thirty years. It is to our great church's great credit that we have operated this mission for this long. But surely this has been long enough. And by sale of the mission property, we can assure this great church's existence into the distant future. We all heard the scripture Dr. Cotswald preached from today: 'See, I am sending you out like sheep into the midst of wolves; so be as wise as serpents and as innocent as doves.' The illegals are the wolves. We must be as wise as serpents to protect ourselves and our city from them. We must make the illegals as harmless as doves to us and our downtown neighbors by sending them back where they came from."

Anderson sat down to applause.

Dr. Cotswald then invited Sarah to speak. She stood before the gathering with her head down, too overcome by emotion to talk. She turned to Janine Bodine and asked her to read aloud the second proposal. Janine then did so. But Sarah was still too emotional to speak.

Janine whispered to Estrella, who was seated with her baby and Joan Donaldson. Estrella, the baby, and Joan stood up next to Janine and faced the gathering.

Janine said, "I don't have to introduce Joan Donaldson to most of you. She is a commercial real estate broker with her own downtown firm and a long-time member of our church trustees. And I believe she is intending to vote for the resolution I just read."

Joan said, "Yes, I surely am," her arm around Estrella's waist.

Janine said, "This is Estrella and her fifteen-month-old baby. I am not going to tell you Estrella's last name, because she is one of the illegal aliens Mr. Anderson just tried to make you so scared of. Estrella is from El Salvador in Central America. She is sixteen. She and her husband and baby walked and hitched rides on buses and trains from El Salvador through Guatemala and Mexico to get to the US. That's over fifteen hundred miles. Why? Because of poverty and drug gangs and violence in her homeland. Her husband refused to carry drugs for the gangs there, so their lives were in danger. She is the bravest person I think I have ever met. Imagine what she went through to get here. Imagine how bad things were in her homeland for her to make that journey. Her husband was arrested here just for not having papers. Estrella still doesn't know where he is. She was sleeping with her baby at the bottom of our church's outside basement stairs. The police were called, and she was arrested for trespassing and separated from her baby. Through the help of Ms. Donaldson, Estrella got her baby back. But they were hungry and homeless and unprotected. The mission found mother and child a safe place to stay. I am inviting each of you to see her. Does she look like the demon Mr. Anderson describes?

"Every person who comes to the mission has a story. I've just shared with you some of Estrella's and her baby's story. No mission client we know has a story with fentanyl in it. Fentanyl comes into this country from Mexico in the trucks of smugglers through regular highway entry points, not in the pockets or backpacks of people swimming across the Rio Grande or walking across the Mexican desert into Arizona. If this mission closes, where are the Estrellas going to find food? Do you think it is Jesus' will to close it? Or to stop serving people in desperate need because of where they come from or what piece of paper they don't have?"

Janine, Estrella, baby, and Joan sat down. Sarah had composed herself and stood up. She reported to the congregation the numbers of homeless and poor, illegal or not, whom the mission had served in the time that the four women had been running operations. She told the individual stories of some of the clients, including those whom she knew lacked documents. They weren't drug runners or criminals. They were families trying to escape hell in their homelands. She explained why it was impossible to determine who had documents and who did not. She asked if the church wanted their mission's staff to ask for documents only from Latinos or from everyone. What kind of a welcome would that be? She asked why it should matter to a Christian where a hungry and homeless person is from in order to give them food and shelter when they are in desperate need.

Then she read a portion of Matt 25: "for I was a stranger and you welcomed me." She pointed to Estrella and the baby. "Sitting there," her voice broke, "sitting there, that's not just Estrella and her baby. That's Jesus. It's kind of the Christmas story. There was no room for them in the inn. So the mission took them in."

The sound of grumbling came from the balcony and from many members seated on the first floor.

Sarah looked pointedly at some she saw grumbling. "Discipleship is not easy. It is not supposed to be easy. It takes courage. There is risk to it. Most of the risk is emotional. None of us who have been at the mission the last month have ever felt any real physical risk, but the people we serve there certainly do. Some of the risk we face is to be criticized like we were in the newspaper. But if we as a church community are not living as if Jesus was and is the Son of God, and that what he taught us comes from God . . . then this is not really a church. It's just a club. The truth is that almost all of the members of this church aren't really running any risk from the people we serve at the mission. After all, it's blocks away from the main church buildings. But for some of us in this church and this city, people in desperate need aren't far enough away. So they want us to close the mission.

"There is so much suffering in this world, and in this city. For so long this country and city have been able to keep that suffering in Central America and Mexico . . . and in the low-income neighborhoods of this city. Out of our sight and mind. We can't do that anymore. The suffering has come here. Maybe it's God's will. Did you ever think of that? I hid from the suffering of poverty for most of my life. Now, I can't unsee what I have seen.

"More than ever I now believe that the only possible solution is for us to try to follow Jesus. I am trying to do that for the first time in my life, and I can't turn back. Not yet, at least. All we are asking is for the mission to continue to be a place where Jesus helps the suffering. . . . I know that I have offended some of you in my honesty. I ask your forgiveness for the offense. But I do not apologize for saying what I believe to be the truth. I have to say what I did."

When she sat down, there was a smattering of applause. Some sat in shocked silence. No one there could remember anyone ever talking to the membership of the church like Janine and Sarah just had. But there were many who were dabbing tears from their eyes.

Bill Anderson stood and asked Dr. Cotswald loudly for an opportunity to respond to Sarah. Cotswald refused him and asked him to resume his seat.

The pastor read the two proposals again one after another. Then he directed the gathering to the first proposal in the bulletin. Then he asked those members in favor of the first proposal to close and sell the mission to raise their hands. Then he asked for a separate show of hands for those against. He repeated the process.

"It is not completely clear which side has the most hands. So I want each of you who vote to adopt the first proposal to close and sell the mission to move to your right side of the sanctuary middle aisle, and I want each of you who vote against the closure and sale to move to your left side of the center aisle. Take your time. Be kind to one another."

Once the migration had stopped, Cotswald said, "I want to confirm that everyone over here to your right is a member of this church and in favor of the proposal to close and sell the mission. And that everyone seated over here to your left is a member and is against closing and selling." That confirmed, he walked up and down the center aisle counting.

"I hereby declare that the proposal to close and sell the mission to be defeated."

Then the voting process was repeated for the second proposal, with the additional reminder that it was permissible to vote against both proposals.

Cotswald stood before the gathering and said, "I hereby declare that the second proposal to keep the mission open, to serve everyone in need, and to explore expansion to be passed."

Cheers and booing erupted. People who voted to keep the mission open hugged. Sarah wept. Anne and Joan hugged and kissed her.

Bill Anderson stood up and yelled for quiet. "I hereby resign from the board of trustees of this church and from membership in this church. Three other trustees join me in these resignations."

Silence descended as the four former trustees stalked out. Some members followed them out.

Dr. Cotswald said, "Please join me in thanking these fine people for their many years of faithful service."

A little applause followed.

Twelfth Step

Matthew 5:11-12

¹¹ Blessed are you when people revile you and persecute you and utter all kinds of evil against you falsely on my account. ¹² Rejoice and be glad, for your reward is great in heaven, for in the same way they persecuted the prophets who were before you.

Disciples of Jesus and the Kingdom of Mercy have been persecuted in modern history "on my [Jesus'] account." Consider the persons depicted in the ten statues of "Modern Martyrs" over the Great West Door of Westminster Abbey in London.

St. Maximillian Kolbe's Kingdom discipleship was a threat to the Nazi kingdom of genocide and terror in Poland. He died by lethal injection on August 14, 1941, as prisoner 16770 in Auschwitz because he offered to die to save the life of a fellow prisoner.

Manche Masemola's discipleship was against the kingdom of patriarchy in South Africa. Her father claimed that she had become a Christian because she had been bewitched. He beat her and hid her clothes to keep her from attending Christian worship. In 1928 she was murdered by her father for refusal to abandon Christianity.

Bishop Janani Luwum's discipleship exposed the kingdom of darkness, terror, and oppression of the dictator Idi Amin in Uganda. Luwum was the archbishop of the Church of Uganda. He spoke out in the name of Jesus against the killings and abductions under Amin. In 1977 he was arrested and murdered by Amin's security forces. Amin claimed he was killed in a car crash while being transported to prison, but his body was riddled with bullets.

Elizabeth Hesse-Darmstadt's Kingdom discipleship exposed the darkness of the violence and atheism of the kingdom of the Bolsheviks. Hesse-Darmstadt was a wealthy member of a Russian royal family who gave up her possessions, became a nun, and founded the Sisters of Love and Mercy in Moscow in 1909, funding and staffing a hospital for the poor and providing a haven for homeless women. When the Russian revolution occurred in 1917, the Bolsheviks persecuted the church, destroyed church buildings, and sent hundreds of priests and nuns who refused to disavow their faith to labor camps. Hesse-Darmstadt refused to deny Jesus and was murdered in a mine shaft in Siberia in 1918.

Dr. Martin Luther King Jr. was assassinated on April 4, 1968, because his Kingdom discipleship exposed the evil of racial segregation, racism, poverty, and war. He was stabbed, his home was bombed, and he received daily death threats from 1954 until his murder. Hundreds of other disciples of the Kingdom were killed by disciples of the kingdom of racism during the American civil rights revolution of the 1950s and '60s.

Bishop Oscar Romero was assassinated as he said mass in San Salvador on March 24, 1980, because of his prophetic Kingdom discipleship opposing the violence and oppression of the poor by the Salvadoran dictatorship.

Dietrich Bonhoeffer's Kingdom discipleship opposed the darkness, violence, and idolatry of the Third Reich. He was imprisoned in 1943 and then hung in a Nazi prison camp on April 9, 1945.

Esther John's Kingdom discipleship stood against the kingdom of patriarchy and ignorance in Pakistan. She was murdered in her bed on February, 2, 1960, because she refused to stop her Christian evangelism.

Lucian Tapiedi's Kingdom discipleship exposed the darkness of the kingdom of colonialism and poverty in New Guinea and the kingdom of conquest of the Japanese. He refused to flee when the Japanese invaded and was murdered in 1942.

Wang Zhiming's Kingdom discipleship exposed the atheism and cruelty of the Chinese Cultural Revolution from 1966 to 1976. He was arrested in 1969 and killed in 1973.

To the above discipleships, we should add Nelson Mandela's and Bishop Desmond Tutu's Kingdom discipleships that opposed and exposed the kingdoms of colonialism, racism, and apartheid in South Africa.

Mandela was imprisoned from 1962 to 1990. Tutu was maligned by the African white press and church, and his life was repeatedly threatened.

The *Vatican News* reported on January 13, 2021, that thirteen Christians were being killed each day throughout the world because of their Christian faith, that twelve churches were destroyed each day and that twelve Christians were arrested for their faith each day.[39] I am not sure of their methodology, but it is clear that Christianity is banned and Christians are subject to persecution in nations such as China, North Korea, and theocratic Muslim states in the Middle East and North Africa.

The *Vatican News* also reported in December 2023 that Roman Catholic Bishop Isidoro del Carmen Mora Ortega was arrested in Nicaragua for praying publicly for Bishop Rolando Jose Alvarez Lagos, who had been imprisoned by Daniel Ortega's government for his advocacy in the name of Jesus for the poor and oppressed.[40]

Many contemporary American Christians claim that they are "persecuted" for their faith, but the essence of their objection is that Christianity no longer has the dominant position of influence it once enjoyed.

For instance, in a commencement speech at Liberty University in 2019, the then vice president of the United States said in part:

> Throughout most of American history, it's been pretty easy to call yourself Christian. It didn't even occur to people that you might be shunned or ridiculed for defending the teachings of the Bible. But things are different now.[41]

The speech was at best myopic. The vice president overlooked large portions of "most of American history" if he really thought that Christian disciples in America have not often been shunned, ridiculed, and worse for acting out Jesus' teachings in the public square.

Christians in the south and north in the years before the Civil War who spoke out in the name of Jesus for the humanity of slaves, for abolition, and against returning runaway slaves to their masters were subject to much more than shunning or ridicule. For instance, Elijah Lovejoy established a Presbyterian newspaper in St. Louis, Missouri, in the 1820s. His newspaper was dedicated to opposition to slavery and advocacy of abolition. He was forced by death threats to move his printing press to Alton, Illinois. On November 7, 1837, he was killed there by a pro-slavery mob, and his printing press was thrown into the river. For further instance, a Methodist-Episcopal Church-North minister named Anthony Bewley was lynched by a mob in 1860 in my home town of Fort Worth for preaching and teaching the gospel to slaves during his circuit rides. The state of Texas had made teaching a slave to read the Bible a hanging offense and had empowered vigilantes to enforce this law without trial. In further instance, how many lawless and unpunished murders occurred of Christian slaves who knew Jesus' teachings, spoke against slavery to their fellows, and encouraged their brothers and sisters to flee the slave states?

Many Christians in the nineteenth century spoke out in the name of Jesus against the slaughter and dispossession of Native Americans from their homelands, and they were often threatened and silenced for their stance.

Christians in the post–Civil War nineteenth century and in twentieth-century America who spoke out on the basis of Jesus' teachings against lynching, racism, and segregation might be shot, firebombed, or lynched themselves, depending upon their race and where they lived.

Christians who participated in "Freedom Summer" in Mississippi in 1962 by registering African Americans to vote were subject to real violence, as were those who participated, on the basis of their faith in Jesus, in sit-ins, demonstrations, and the freedom rides. We should never forget the names of the four, innocent young ladies—Denise McNair, aged eleven; Addie Mae Collins, aged fourteen; Carole Robertson, aged fourteen; and Cynthia Wesley, aged fourteen—who were killed in the firebombing of the Sixteenth Street Baptist Church by members of the Ku Klux Klan in Birmingham, Alabama, on September 15, 1963. This church was the center of the Black community's efforts to desegregate the city and to end the intimidations of Black Americans who tried to vote.

I remember well that Christians who demonstrated against the Vietnam War on the basis of their faith were subject to ridicule and threat for being unpatriotic and giving aid and comfort to our enemies. Ministers who spoke out against the war from the pulpit were censored and fired. The same price was paid by some clergy who spoke out against the American invasion of Iraq in search of nonexistent weapons of mass destruction in 2003.

Christians today who demonstrate or speak based upon Jesus' teachings against nuclear stockpiling, the size of the American war budget, lack of adequate health care, affordable housing, food and education for the poor, the cruelty of separating refugee mothers and children at our southern border, the demonization and scapegoating of these refugees, the numbers of young Black men in prison, and the failure to tax the rich at a fair rate to help the poor—all these Kingdom advocates are subject to ridicule and demonization themselves, particularly in today's political climate in America. For instance, in 2023 some members of Congress were highly critical of Catholic Charities, the Lutheran Immigration and Refugee Service, and other faith-based organizations for helping hungry and homeless refugees at the US border, calling for elimination of funding to the organizations. One member of Congress accused Catholic Charities of the crime of "aiding and abetting illegal aliens."[42] So much for respect for the faithfulness of Christian organizations to Jesus' teaching about welcoming the stranger (Matt 25:35, 43): ("I was a stranger and you welcomed me. . . . I was a stranger and you did not welcome me"). The Greek word translated "stranger" in the NRSV is "*xenos*," which meant "foreigner" according to *Strong's Online Greek Concordance*. *Xenos* is the root of our English word xenophobia, or fear of the foreigner. To their eternal credit, these organizations refused to back down in the face of these threats.

The then vice president's speech to the Liberty University graduates was a complaint that Christians might have to face persecution now ("you might be shunned or ridiculed") because of their faith. But many supporters of the vice president want evangelical Christians to have so much power and influence within the American secular kingdom that they never face persecution.

Imagine if we were to organize fellow church members to oppose spending so much of the church budget on the church building and to propose spending much more on ministries to feed, clothe, and shelter the poor in our neighborhoods, based upon the model and teachings of Jesus? We should expect to be "put to flight" by church members who are greater disciples of the kingdom of property.

Imagine if we as members of our church actively recruit and welcome in the name of Jesus poor and diverse racial and ethnic folk to our worship and fellowship, with multi-language worship and songs to truly welcome them? Shouldn't we expect to be "put to flight" from our commitment?

The Twelfth Step is the blessing of union with Jesus and the prophets ("For in the same way, they persecuted the prophets who were before you" [5:12]). At this Step on the Way, the surest resource to persist on the Way is mystical—to be bonded in our minds, hearts, and spirits with Jesus and the prophets. To persevere on the Way in the face of attempts to put us to flight, we need to invest increasing time to prayer, *lectio divina*, and silent meditation, humbly seeking the presence of God that energized and directed Isaiah, the prophets who wrote the poetry of Second and Third Isaiah, Jeremiah, Amos, Micah, and of course, Jesus.

Why is the potential persecution on the Twelfth Step a blessing? It isn't! The blessing comes with the gift of spiritual, emotional, and psychological union with the divine mercy that animated the prophets and was fully incarnate in Jesus. It is that union that is the blessing. The persecution "on my [Jesus'] account" comes because that blessing of union moves us to courageous acts and proclamations of mercy under the threat of opposition.

My experience is that the more someone is faithful to Jesus' call to serve the suffering poor with the mercy of the Kingdom, the less she is likely to trumpet Jesus' name. And, sadly, the louder someone invokes Jesus' name, the less they are likely to live out Jesus' call to mercy for the suffering . . . because they have been taught that invoking the name is all that is needed. It's easy to talk about what Jesus did for us. It's more than hard to live like he did. But we are called to live Jesus, not just to talk Jesus. He must possess us for us to succeed in living him. The more we try to live mercifully as Jesus did, the more reluctant we will be to invoke his name as the source of our actions because of our recognition of how far short we are of living his life.

We live in an age of healthy sensitivity to hypocrisy. The psalmist who composed the poetry of Ps 69:6 wrote:

> Do not let those who hope in you be put to shame because of me,
> O Lord God of hosts;
> do not let those who seek you be dishonored because of me,
> O God of Israel.

What I hear the psalmist saying is "God, don't let me be a hypocrite!" Amen to that. If Jesus' name is always on the tip of your tongue, you best be always carrying his presence in your heart and mind and particularly on your hands and feet. But who can always succeed in that? If you announce Jesus as your model on this Twelfth Step, you will be even more open to charges of hypocrisy.

What Jesus tells us in the Twelfth Step is to expect persecution when we stand up with him for the poor and the suffering against the cruelty and indifference of the world. But Jesus isn't telling us to seek persecution for its own sake.

In the Lord's Prayer, Jesus tells us to ask our Father, "Lead us not into temptation" (Matt 6:13a). This is the translation from the King James

Version, and the language many of us pray aloud together in worship. The NRSV of this verse is: "Lead us not into the time of trial." Jesus tells us to pray to the Father that God not lead us into the kind of trial that could cause us to abandon the Way. I have always been troubled why the Father would ever "lead" us into this temptation or trial. We would all love to know what Aramaic or Hebrew word Jesus used that was translated into Greek and then from the Greek into the English "lead." What I hear Jesus telling us in this prayer as translated is that the Way surely "leads" to persecution because of the deep conflict between the Kingdom of Mercy and the kingdoms of the world. In that sense, when God calls us to the Way, God "leads" us to the real potential for persecution.

But Jesus tells us in the very next verse to pray "deliver us from evil" in the King James Version or "rescue us from the evil one" in the NRSV (6:13b). The two phrases of 6:13 should be read together. Read together Jesus is instructing us to accept that God's Way can and will lead to temptations and trials that challenge us to abandon the Way, but that the Father can and will rescue our hearts and spirits from our loss of courage and trust in the midst of persecution. This describes what Jesus went through in Gethsemane. The Way led him to temptation and trial (Matt 26:37–39), but the Father gave him the courage and faith to stay on the Way to the cross (26:46).

At this end of this discussion of what I see as the Twelfth Step of the Way to the Kingdom of Mercy, I want to bring us back to what makes this Beatitude the last of the Steps up the mountain top of the Way. This Step is the first time in the Beatitudes that Jesus announces the blessing of an afterlife in heaven to the disciples who have made it this far. "Rejoice and be glad, for your reward is great in heaven" (5:12).

But what is heaven? Jesus taught us to pray "Our Father in heaven . . . thy kingdom come, thy will be done on earth as it is in heaven" (6:9–10). What I hear in my mind, heart, and soul in these words of Jesus is that heaven is wherever God is and where God's will is done fully. The motive for us to follow Jesus on the Way to the Kingdom of Mercy is not a self-centered desire for our own eternal life. Jesus makes clear that our motive to follow him should be for us to incarnate and live out the mercy of God that is the image of God within us. The motive is to help Jesus make "thy kingdom come." For me, the reward of heaven that Jesus speaks of in this Beatitude is the mental, emotional, and mystical experience of the presence of God—where God is—in our helping Jesus to bring the Kingdom—where God's will is done fully. The "reward" that is "great in heaven" of this Beatitude is that presence and union with Jesus and the will of the Father.

The Twelfth Step on the Way of the disciple is the blessing empowering us to continue to bear the Kingdom through our union with the prophets and Jesus, despite the opposition of the kingdoms of the world to Jesus and his Way.

***

Sarah Bigelow was appointed interim director of the mission while the search goes on for a permanent hire. She was offered but refused a salary. When she openly began to consider asking for the position permanently, her husband filed for divorce. One of her children refuses to speak to her. Her other child volunteers at the mission when she comes to town. Sarah's husband has already paid her cash for half the fair market value of their home in town, their weekend house on West River Lake, and their vacation house in Red River, New Mexico. She has already received from him half the value of their stock and bonds. She gave up her community interest in his business in exchange for this quick division of the other property. Sarah donated a chunk of the money she received to fund the feasibility study for expansion of the mission.

Sarah moved permanently into her father John's house. They have become close friends as well as father and daughter. She has also become even closer to Anne and to Janine and Jazmine. The four women share a meal weekly in one of their homes. This is a godsend because Sarah has lost all of her old friends. She finds her work isolating and her old friends' lives trivial and sheltered.

Sarah sleeps fitfully at best, because she worries and dreams about the people who come to the mission for help. She remembers without yearning the many days when she was carefree but bored. She is genuinely heartbroken for the people who come for help to the mission daily, but she is deeply satisfied she is able to help. She just wishes the mission could do more for them. Sarah has enrolled in an online college program to become a social worker. She studies Bible commentaries and teaches a Sunday school class at First Kingdom of God Church on the Sermon on the Mount. She prays aloud to Jesus when she is alone in her office, hoping no one hears her and thinks she is a daft fool.

Twelfth Step: Matthew 5:11-12

Anne moved back into her home with her husband. They reached an understanding about her freedom of conscience. She became interim deputy director of the mission when Sarah became director. Anne receives a small salary. This paycheck quiets her husband. Anne has an entirely new group of friends in addition to Sarah, Janine, and Jazmine. These are friends much different than her husband's. He has started attending worship with Anne on Sundays rather than playing golf. But they don't talk about the mission. Anne has all but adopted Eileen and Obadiah Parker's three children. She babysits them, she takes them back and forth to school and to doctor's visits when the parents cannot, and she tutors them.

Anne receives so much energy and derives so much meaning from her work at the mission that she no longer needs her anti-depressants. She worries about how brokenhearted Sarah is about the clients. Anne is not as comfortable talking about or to Jesus as Sarah is. And before all this started, Anne was the more religious of the two sisters.

Janine and Jazmine volunteer at the mission five days a week. Jazmine is learning Spanish to help Janine translate. They speak about the mission to a different Sunday school class every Sunday and at a church women's club meeting at least twice a month. They also show representatives of various funding foundations around the mission when they appear. Janine's health is beginning to fail. Jazmine shields Janine from her own developing type 2 diabetes. They do not know how long they can continue to volunteer so many hours at the mission, but they intend to continue until they are unable.

Estrella and her baby, Esmeralda, still live in Janine and Jazmine's home. Estrella's husband hasn't been located. Estrella may have to return to what's left of her family in El Salvador. She is afraid to leave the house unless she is in the company of one of the sisters. There is no assurance of a happy ending for Estrella and child.

Bill Anderson's dramatic departure from the church removed a heavy yoke from Dr. Cotswald's shoulders. The pastor boldly (for him) wrote a letter to the editor of *The Metroplex News* in response to the column of the editorial board just before the mission vote. He wrote: "First Kingdom of God Church will be true as we are able to the discipleship of Jesus. This is the hill we are prepared to die on. We'd rather follow Jesus in welcoming the outcast and the stranger than make our budget." The church is failing to make its budget because of the departure of so many older and generous donors after the mission vote. Staff for other church ministries are being let go. These people loudly blame Sarah and Anne.

Rev. Juice Toliver responded to Dr. Cotswald's letter with another letter to the newspaper stating that "the sins of the illegals will drive First Kingdom of God Church to its Golgotha."

Dr. Cotswald gave notice that he was retiring from ministry.

Bill Anderson and the three other trustees who walked out of the church meeting joined Juice Toliver's Heaven's Rest Bible Church. Anderson is trying to join its board of trustees in exchange for a large donation.

Many of the older volunteers stopped volunteering at the mission. But many more young women started volunteering, drawn particularly by Sarah's speech at the vote meeting.

Sheriff's deputies started to plant themselves across the street from the mission property to check IDs of the clients. City police officers started issuing citations to the homeless for jaywalking when they crossed the street to the mission—the only such citations issued anywhere in the city. A group of lawyers who are members of the church joined together to complain to the chief of police and the sheriff. But the police chief is appointed by an elected mayor and the sheriff is elected himself. So the intimidation continues.

A number of established customers are boycotting John's dry cleaning businesses because of the actions of his daughters. He had to close two stores. But Obadiah Parker is still employed and is earning more responsibility and pay. His wife and children are doing no better or worse than before. They would be doing a lot worse if not for John.

Sarah is in many ways the most divisive and controversial figure in the city. Insulting, profane, and threatening letters come to the mission. A church security guard is stationed at the mission whenever Sarah is there and remembers to call the main church office.

Sarah was invited to make a presentation about the mission to a downtown lunch club attended by business leaders and city officials. She took Anne, Janine, Jazmine, and Dr. Cotswald with her. Her planned presentation was repeatedly interrupted by hostile questioning about the illegal aliens and drug sellers the mission attracts to downtown. These questioners were organized in advance. Most didn't give her a chance to respond. At first, Sarah was intimidated and unable to a respond. But when Anne, Janine, and Jazmine stepped beside her on the stage, Sarah found her spirit and began to tell stories of the individual clients of the mission. When a particularly nasty questioner challenged her to justify aiding and abetting illegals, she quoted Jesus. This brought a firestorm of conservative Christian rebuttal, until the moderator of the program stopped the presentation, saying that the club's policy prohibited the invocation of religion in any talks. Janine blurted out, "But without Jesus, what we are doing makes no sense."

Two mornings later, another guest op-ed piece by Rev. Toliver appeared in *The Metroplex News*. Toliver was present at the club presentation, although he had not spoken. He claimed to be bringing to public light certain hidden information. Again he named the four women. He presented Sarah and Anne as sheltered and naïve hypocrites for their condemnation of those who did not share their misplaced concern for the mission clients. They were hypocrites because they were wealthy women who claimed to be followers of Jesus while living in the sheltered luxury of a gated community. Toliver repeated his scriptural attack that the women were claiming a righteousness that no one could achieve and certainly not them. What the mission should be doing instead is preaching the good news of Jesus' atoning sacrifice and urging the illegal aliens and the drug pushers to repent their lawbreaking.

It soon seemed that every adult in the city had taken one side or the other about Sarah and the other women. Letters of criticism and support were printed in the newspaper. Threatening emails and letters to the mission increased. Sarah and Anne became afraid to go anywhere other than the mission. They both started shopping at midnight at all-night grocery stores. Anne's husband urged her to carry one of his handguns in her purse, but she refused.

Dr. Cotswald urged all four women to take a break from the mission until the storm blew over. He promised that church staff would keep the mission running in their absence. After all, he said, once we hire a new professional director, your services won't be needed. And the next senior pastor might not be as supportive of the mission as he had been.

Sarah, Anne, Janine, and Jazmine went on a day and night retreat together at Sarah's old lake house. At the urging of one of Sarah's daughters, Sarah's ex-husband agreed for them to use the house. They spent the time together on the patio of the house on a high bluff, sitting mostly in silence and looking over the lake. As the sun was going down, Sarah offered, "Everyone has to make their own decision. I cannot tell you how much I value all you have done for so many. You've done so much; it is more than enough by any reckoning. But for me, I am going to keep going. Jesus has got me by the throat, and he is not letting go. I am not giving him up." The other three women all agreed they wouldn't quit.

Upon return to the city, Sarah informed Rev. Cotswald and the search committee for a new director that she herself was a formal candidate to be the new permanent director of the mission.

The four women continued their work at the mission for another month. Then they were informed by the new senior pastor who had just replaced the retiring Cotswald that the new director of the mission was being brought in from Houston. This man had been director at a mission of the church in Houston where the new pastor had served. Sarah was told confidentially by a member of the committee that the new senior pastor wanted a mission director whom he knew and could control. Sarah had become too controversial a figure in the community, and the church budget was suffering. The viability of the church was more important than the ministry of the mission.

The new senior pastor is a spellbinder from the pulpit, and worship attendance is steadily increasing. His consistent message is "God is good all the time. All the time, God is good." He inspires the church members to see all the good that God blesses all of us with all of the time. He rarely mentions Jesus, and never his Kingdom or the poor.

And all four women were asked to remain away from the mission while the new director establishes his authority and way of doing things.

The decision was made by the new pastor and the new board of trustees not to pursue the feasibility study for expansion of the mission to house homeless women and children. The money Sarah had contributed to pay for the study was redirected to the church general budget to help fill the general budget shortfall. Sarah was informed of this but did not ask for return of her money. She asked instead that the money be reallocated to mission operations. This request was courteously refused.

Janine and Jazmine continue to shelter and protect Estrella and Esmeralda in their home. But they retired from the mission for reasons of age, health, energy, and disappointment in the church's decisions.

Anne continues to care for the Parker family. She is still with her husband and is spending more time with her children. She has retired from her heartbreak and crushed spirit at all the suffering and injustice in the world. She justifies her retirement from the Way by being angry at God for allowing so much suffering and injustice to continue. If God won't do anything, what can she do?

Twelfth Step: Matthew 5:11–12

Since leaving her work at the mission, Sarah is working her way toward a degree in social work at a local university. She is interning at a community center run by a small church in an impoverished, predominantly Latino area of the city. The center has a food and clothing bank and an after-school tutoring program. The church has no board of trustees. Many of the neighborhood residents have lived and worked in the US for decades without documents. Dozens of the recently arrived homeless and undocumented families that had been hounded out of downtown have found refuge in poor homes in this neighborhood.

Sarah is close to achieving fluency in Spanish. She is funding a free infant formula program at the community center. As a caseworker, she helps people find work, medical care, and treatment for addiction. She joined and attends worship at the small church, is its largest donor, sings in the choir, started an "English as a second language" program, and leads a girl's club called "Just for Girls." Young, comfortable, Anglo women who volunteered at the First Kingdom of God Church mission when Sarah was in charge help her mentor the girls in the club. They try to help these young teens from poor families to respect themselves and the image of God within them, to dream big, to avoid pregnancy, and to stay in school.

Sarah has become deeply attached to some of the poor families in the neighborhood. She is lonely at night, even at her dad's house, so she works very long hours. She is thinking of buying and moving into a small house in the inner-city neighborhood of the church, but her father's health is failing and she needs to live with him for now.

Sarah has happily slipped from the public's eye. Day by day and night by night she faithfully and quietly plants and nurtures the seeds of the Kingdom of Mercy as she is able. Sarah prays every dawn and dusk: "Our Father, who art in heaven, hallowed be thy name. Thy kingdom come. Amen." She works and walks the Way while she waits. The Kingdom is already present where she carries it.

Faithfulness for Those of Us Who Remain in Our Boats

Is there a difference between a disciple and a Christian who believes in Jesus? Put another way, is every disciple a Christian while every Christian is not a disciple? I am not sure that Matthew's Jesus thinks we can believe in him and honestly call him "Lord" without being his disciples (Matt 7:21). It may be that one is either a disciple or part of the crowd to this Jesus. "Christian" is not a word Jesus uses in this or any other gospel, and he himself uses the word "disciple" only rarely. Regardless, the contemporary American church denies there is a difference between a disciple and a person who believes in Jesus, because it is too often out to make "churchians" not disciples.

The world needs all the people it can find of any or no faith who exhibit empathy, generosity, gentleness, and honesty—people of good will who are good citizens, employees or employers, parents, children, and friends. This is true whether or not they are trying to follow Jesus. The world needs people who will fill their secular callings with all the excellence, loyalty, industriousness, altruism, kindness, and wisdom they can muster in their roles. Just being a decent human is a 24/7 calling.

The official motto and mission of my United Methodist Church is: "Making disciples for the transformation of the world." "Transformation of the world" sounds like what will happen with the coming of the Kingdom of Mercy. And I believe that Matthew's Jesus would agree that the mission of the disciple is to transform the world ... by helping the Kingdom of Mercy to arrive. But what are the characteristics of the "disciples" being made by the United Methodist Church? A person who professes Christianity, tithes, attends worship, occasionally goes on a mission trip, and brings decency to every setting and role in their lives? Is that person a "disciple" who is going to "transform the world"?

The above traits and actions do not make a disciple according to Matthew's Jesus. Matthew's Jesus taught and showed us that a disciple is someone who repents of his old way of thinking and living, disavows her allegiance and obedience to the kingdoms of the world, and follows Jesus with a purity of heart for mercy and a craving for justice. Such a disciple must be dedicated to bringing the Kingdom of Mercy of healing, feeding, and welcoming, and to protecting and providing for the demonized, suffering, and shunned of the world. Many of us who are immersed in the kingdoms of the world aren't comfortable with this understanding of discipleship, just as we aren't comfortable with the demands of Matthew's Jesus. But Jesus didn't come to make us comfortable. He came to demand that we give our lives to the Kingdom, to him, and to the suffering poor. If we deny this is true, we need to read and reread Matthew's Gospel. We might start with 16:24–25 and 25:31–46.

Maybe Paul can be our more accommodating alternative to Matthew's Jesus. Paul is a favorite of the mainline Protestant and evangelical churches of America. He wrote to the Galatians: "a person is justified not by works of the law but through faith in Jesus Christ" (Gal 2:16). Paul also wrote that the fruits of the Spirit of the Christ are "love, joy, peace, patience, kindness, generosity, faithfulness, gentleness, and self-control" (Gal 5:22–23). This faith is surely essential to embark on the Way, and these "fruits" are exemplary and elusive traits to which everyone should aspire. But Matthew's Jesus taught that *these* fruits do not make a disciple. According to Matthew's Jesus the fruits of his disciples are Steps on the Way of the Kingdom of Mercy (7:13–20; 21:43). Paul barely mentions the Kingdom. He uses the term *"basileia tou Theou"* ("kingdom of God") only nine times in his authentic letters of Romans, 1 and 2 Corinthians, Galatians, Philippians, 1 Thessalonians, and Philemon, and never in connection with Jesus' Kingdom mission to the poor and the outcast. Matthew's Jesus rarely stops talking about this Kingdom, living it, and calling his disciples to repent and do the same. The word "disciple" appears in Matthew seventy-three times, but not once in Paul's letters.

Realistically, given our immersion in the kingdoms of the world and our existing responsibilities to others, is all that most of us can aspire to a part-time or occasional discipleship with Matthew's Jesus? Most people are needed to remain faithfully in their roles of providing the material needs of the human community and caring for their families. But there is also a need for people with different experiences and skills acquired in those worldly kingdom roles to change or add to their careers and callings by serving the poor and the outcast through the Kingdom of Mercy. We are called to look for periods in our lives when we can heed Jesus' call to leave our boats and follow him into the darkness of the world of the suffering.

Some may ask why discipleship requires following Jesus into service to the poor. I was giving a presentation to a Sunday school class not long ago when a woman loudly challenged this, saying that ministry to her friends was no less important than ministry to the poor, the outcast, and the shunned. There was common sense to what she said. There is a need for friendship and mercy in all the kingdoms of world. Human life is touched by tragedy in any role in any kingdom. The job of raising our children and grandchildren to be honest, hard-working, self-disciplined, prudent, and kind is critical and more than full-time in any kingdom.

But as discussed throughout this book, the ministry of Matthew's Jesus was feeding, healing, touching, encouraging, and welcoming the poor, the thirsty, the naked, the sick, the stranger, the prisoner, the homeless, the outcast, the sinner, and the shunned. And he called his disciples to follow him into the same ministry (Matt 10:24). According to this Jesus, it is in that darkness that we will serve and "see" Jesus and God. Maybe Jesus called disciples into this darkness because that is where the most suffering, need, and abandonment live. Maybe he called his disciples there because a kingdom in which the poor are nurtured, valued, and protected is a Kingdom in which all are nurtured, valued, and protected. Maybe he called his disciples there because that is where we, including the rich and the comfortable, can finally encounter and recognize the image of God within everyone. Regardless of God's reasons, Matthew's Jesus says this is what discipleship with him in the Kingdom of Mercy requires.

So can we be faithful to Jesus while we remain in our boats? What ethic applies when we are living most of our lives in our boats in the kingdoms for the world? An answer to that question would require a much longer book. But I will offer here six observations.

First, we are called to be ever aware of the deep chasm between the values and ethics of the kingdoms of the world and the values and ethics of Jesus' Kingdom of Mercy.

Second, just as disciples are called, all Christians are called by Jesus to "see" God's image in everyone. This is essential within every Christian's role in every boat. If we "see" God's image in everyone, we will not be quick to make judgments of condemnation. If we "see" what their challenges have been and are, we will be much more empathetic, merciful, and forgiving to everyone we encounter in every place. We will resist demonization and lies about the vulnerable. We will refuse to see any persons as objects or as tools for our use. We will see them all as ends, not as means. We will help our friends and family, particularly our children and grandchildren, to see God and the image of God in everyone. Seeing God's image in everyone, even from the location of our boats, we will hunger and thirst for righteousness, be merciful as our duties in our boats allow, and make peace as disciples do. Seeing is so critical to faithfulness to Jesus that we might call the "Way" the "See."

Third, in every setting, we are called to advocate and support the poor and the outcast with our time, our expertise, our words, and our money.

Fourth, we are called in our comfortable churches to support with our money, words, and deeds ministries for and with the poor and the outcast, at the cost of reducing the portion of church resources allocated to church property and to ministries that serve only the church's membership. These ministries will enable and empower more and more of us eventually to become disciples bearing the Kingdom of Mercy.

Fifth, we are called in our churches to support, encourage, and nurture proclamation from the pulpit of the plight of the poor and the need for discipleship in the Kingdom of Mercy.

Sixth, we are called to remain open to the possibility that each of us will be called one day to the Twelve Steps of discipleship in the Kingdom of Mercy. We must not let discipleship be reduced to a spectator activity for all of us.

There are not many disciples at a time (Matt 7:14). There are too few mustard seeds and far too little leaven. There surely is not enough light. The kingdoms of the world aspire to be like the black holes in distant space, swallowing all our light so that none is emitted. We must keep shining in their darkness and despite their power. That requires discipleship.

Most of the American church has effectively given up on a final culmination of the Kingdom of Mercy. Comfortable Christians who fund the financially successful churches want the world to remain pretty much as it is. We still repeat without thinking dozens of times every year the words from the Lord's Prayer: "Thy kingdom come." But the Kingdom of Mercy hasn't finally come after all this time. Most of us either believe it isn't ever coming, or we don't give its culmination any priority. If God has the power and goodness to intervene finally and definitively to bring the Kingdom, God still hasn't. "How long, O Lord?" (Ps 13:1).

Perhaps it is better if we give up on hoping for God to swoop down and rescue us in the future. Regardless, we need to hope in the present . . . by moving our feet. The Kingdom *is* here but in too few people and actions. The Kingdom comes when and where disciples are blessed and inspired to carry it. But we have too few disciples, in part because too many preachers have been watering down Jesus' call and denying the fatal clash between the values and works of the Kingdom and the kingdoms of the world.

Thirteenth Step

Following the God Who *Is* Mercy

Whether or not God will finally bring the Kingdom, mercy is the Way of discipleship now and forever. It has its own intrinsic, heartfelt goodness, and unique, positive, nondestructive power. The Kingdom of Mercy *is* present. It is like slowly growing mustard plants that are infesting and fouling the kingdoms of the world. It is like leaven that is rising and making the loaf of human life edible. It is like the salt that is giving flavor and sustaining life. It is the light piercing the darkness, showing the Way to those who will follow, and showing the darkness that it is indeed dark.

But we still must ask, if God is good and powerful, why is there *still* so much random, unjust suffering? Why is the world *still* so dark and in the region of death? Why is the Way *still* so hard? Why is discipleship *still* so needed and so persecuted? Why do so few comfortable Christians care about the plight of the suffering millions? In my interactions and conversations with the abused, the homeless, and with Gen Z-ers and Millennials, the prevailing reason given for unbelief in God and refusal to join a church community is lack of trust that God is good when the world is so full of suffering and random injustice.

I wrote about the Second Step: "*We of course need to take Jesus at his word. But we need to take Jesus at his actions even more*" (p. 29). The same can be said of God. We need to take God at God's words of promise of the Kingdom. But we also need to take God at God's actions and inactions. What actions of God have brought the Kingdom of Mercy since Jesus was resurrected? Have God's inactions been louder and more powerful than God's actions?

I have no satisfactory answers to these questions separate from my experiences. I offer heartfelt responses that are truer on another level for me than any such answer based upon intellect alone. That response is the experience of the goodness and power of God and the presence of the Lord Jesus in mercy and merciful actions. The Kingdom has come in these. The Kingdom still comes in these. The Kingdom will forever be coming in these, perhaps never to arrive fully. The darkness will never become completely lit, but the light will forever shine in the darkness. The darkness will never succeed in extinguishing it. The black holes of the world's kingdoms cannot swallow all of the Kingdom of Mercy's light.

All of us may doubt at times that the God of Mercy exists. But there can be no doubt that mercy itself exists and transforms lives. For me, the goodness and power of God our Father as revealed in the life and teachings of Jesus are best captured, summarized, and limited in the one word "mercy." For me, mercy is the *logos* made flesh in Jesus. For me, God is mercy, and mercy is God. For me, God is as good as mercy is good, no more and no less good. God is as powerful as mercy is powerful, and here is the key for me to the *theodicy* problem, *no more or no less powerful*. There are many forces we might call "god" in this evil world that certainly claim to be more immediately powerful than Mercy. But Mercy is the God revealed in Jesus. Mercy is the God I aspire to trust, follow, and worship.

Skeptics and atheists say that the gods humans have worshiped over time have been no more than projections of aspects of our own beings. So we have projected on to our gods the omnipotence, the omnipresence, and the omniscience we wish we had, as well as the anger, the cruelty, the favoritism, the prejudice, the injustice, the violence, the jealousy, and the selfishness we do have. But all of us have to varying degrees a capacity for mercy. For me, mercy is the image of God within each of us, although life has wounded that image more deeply in some than others. I do not believe that Father YHWH is *merely* a projection of our aspirations, virtues, and vices. But I accept that I project onto my God my capacity and desire for mercy. I also believe and experience that God in Christ "projects" the blessing of a greater desire and capacity for mercy back onto me through the power of the life and teachings of Jesus of Nazareth and of what we Christians call the Spirit.

Paul wrote that love is "patient," "kind," "does not insist upon its own way," and "bears," "hopes," and "endures all things" (1 Cor 13:4–7). The same can and should be said for Mercy. Mercy is patient, kind, hopeful, not insisting upon its own way, and bearing and enduring all things.

Thirteenth Step: Following the God Who Is Mercy

Since God *is* mercy, the same should be said about the goodness and power of God. Perhaps God allows so much evil and suffering in the world because God's eternal nature is mercy—patient, kind, not insisting upon on God's own way, and bearing and enduring all things—and because God cannot change God's nature. However much I might want God to be less kind and patient, more immediately and overwhelmingly powerful and insistent on God's Way, and much less inclined to endure and bear all things—particularly suffering, injustice, and evil—God is still God, and God *is* eternal and incarnate Mercy.

Who else should we follow? To what or who else shall we entrust our hope? Mercy is our only abiding and ultimate hope. Jesus, who was and is mercy incarnate, is the only One who can lead us out of this "darkness" in "the region and the shadow of death" where we find ourselves.

> Hail Mercy,
> Source of grace.
> You are the lord of our hope.
> Blessed are you among all goodness,
> and blessed are all the fruits of your womb.
> Holy Mercy,
> Mother of peace,
> we pray with and for you.
> Amen.

Endnotes

1. "Lethal Combination"; Khatib, McKee, and Yusuf, "Counting the Dead"; "Number of Palestinian and Israeli Fatalities"; Clayton, "New High-Stakes Gaza."
2. Tian et al., "Trends in World Military," para. 1.
3. Bergen, "Opinion," para. 6.
4. "Which Countries?"
5. "Which Countries?"
6. Gowan, "Trends."
7. Alfonseca, "There Have Been."
8. Bushard, "Gunmakers Made."
9. "Firearms Are the Leading."
10. "Threats to American Democracy," 5.
11. Sanders, "Rich-Poor Gap," para. 4.
12. Mendoza, "Almost Half," para. 2. See also Connelly, "Nearly 1.7 Million."
13. Sims, "How Fort Worth ISD," para. 5. See also Allen, "Fort Worth ISD"; Samsel, "Fort Worth ISD."
14. Soucy, Janes, and Hall, "State of Homelessness," para. 3.
15. "Global Homelessness Statistics."
16. "UNICEF and Child Poverty," paras. 5, 11.
17. "UNICEF and Child Poverty," para. 5.
18. "Malnutrition," para. 3.
19. "UN Report," para. 8.
20. "Levels and Trends."
21. "Meek," Cambridge Dictionary.
22. "Meek," Merriam-Webster Dictionary.
23. "Meek," Dictionary.com.
24. Maraniss, *Path Lit by Lightning*, 6.
25. Stark, *Triumph of Christianity*, 112.
26. Stark, *Triumph of Christianity*, 113.
27. Teresa, *Come Be My Light*, 336.
28. Teresa, *Come Be My Light*, 39, 43.
29. Teresa, *Come Be My Light*, 145.

30. Teresa, *Come Be My Light*, 186–87.
31. Teresa, *Come Be My Light*, 192–93.
32. Teresa, *Come Be My Light*, 249.
33. Tacitus, *Agricola Germania*, 19–20; emphasis added.
34. Josephus, *Jewish War*, xix–xxi.
35. Sawyer and Wagner, "Mass Incarceration," para. 2.
36. "What Percentage of Americans," para. 1.
37. "Crisis in Gaza," para. 27.
38. Branch, *Parting the Waters*, 882–83.
39. "13 Christians a Day."
40. "Nicaragua."
41. Groppe, "Vice President Pence," para. 6.
42. Jenkins, "GOP Lawmakers," para. 3.

Bibliography

"13 Christians a Day Killed for Their Faith." Open Doors, Jan. 30, 2024. https://www.opendoorsus.org/en-US/stories/13-christians-killed-day-average/.

Alfonseca, Kiara. "There Have Been More Mass Shootings than Days in 2023, Database Shows." *ABC News*, Dec. 4, 2023. https://abcnews.go.com/US/mass-shootings-days-2023-database-shows/story?id=96609874.

Allen, Silas. "Fort Worth ISD Leaders Say Reading Test Scores Show Progress: Is That the Whole Picture?" *Fort Worth Star-Telegram*, Aug. 5, 2024. https://www.star-telegram.com/news/local/education/article290690439.html.

Bergen, Peter. "Opinion: The Lloyd Austin Incident Sheds Harsh Light on Biden's Team." *CNN*, Jan. 8, 2024. https://www.cnn.com/2024/01/08/opinions/lloyd-austin-biden-problem-bergen/.

Branch, Taylor. *Parting the Waters: America in the King Years, 1954–63*. New York: Simon & Schuster, 1998.

Bushard, Brian. "Gunmakers Made $1 Billion from AR-15-Style Weapons in 10 Years, Lawmakers Find." *Forbes*, July 27, 2022. https://www.forbes.com/sites/brianbushard/2022/07/27/gunmakers-made-1-billion-from-ar-15-style-weapons-in-10-years-lawmakers-find/.

"Child Poverty FAQs." End Childhood Poverty, n.d. https://www.endchildhoodpoverty.org/facts-on-child-poverty.

Clayton, Freddie. "New High-Stakes Gaza Truce Talks Hope to Avert a Wider War." *NBC News*, Aug. 15, 2024. https://www.nbcnews.com/news/world/new-gaza-cease-fire-talks-israel-iran-war-hamas-attend-rcna166693.

Connelly, Christopher. "Nearly 1.7 Million Texas Kids Are at Risk of Going Hungry." Texas Public Radio, May 15, 2024. https://www.tpr.org/news/2024-05-15/nearly-1-7-million-texas-kids-are-at-risk-of-going-hungry.

"Crisis in Gaza: What Is Happening?" International Rescue Committee, Dec. 15, 2023. https://www.rescue.org/article/crisis-gaza-what-you-need-know.

"Firearms Are the Leading Cause of Death for American Children and Teens." Centers for Disease Control and Prevention, May 7, 2024. https://everytownresearch.org/graph/firearms-are-the-leading-cause-of-death-for-american-children-and-teens/.

"Global Homelessness Statistics." Homeless World Cup, 2021. https://www.homelessworldcup.org/homelessness-statistics.

Gowan, Richard. "Trends in Armed Conflicts." Stockholm International Peace Research Institute, 2024. https://search.app/W3cBx8ZCmmErtkRD9.

Groppe, Maureen. "Vice President Pence to Graduates: Be Prepared to Be Ridiculed for Being Christian." *USA Today*, May 11, 2019. https://www.usatoday.com/story/news/politics/2019/05/11/mike-pence-liberty-commencement-speech-prepared-ridiculed/1151252001/.

Harrington, Brooks. *No Mercy, No Justice: The Dominant Narrative of America versus the Counter-Narrative of Jesus' Parables*. Eugene, OR: Cascade, 2019.

Jenkins, Jack. "GOP Lawmakers Once Praised Catholic Charities: Now They Want to Defund the Group." *Washington Post*, July 28, 2023. https://www.washingtonpost.com/religion/2023/07/28/gop-lawmakers-once-praised-catholic-charities-now-they-want-defund-group/.

Josephus. *The Jewish War*. Oxford World's Classics. Translated by Martin Goodman. Oxford: Oxford University Press, 2017.

Khatib, Rasha, Martin McKee, and Salim Yusuf. "Counting the Dead in Gaza: Difficult but Essential." *The Lancet* 404 (2024) 237–38.

"Lethal Combination of Hunger and Disease to Lead to More Deaths in Gaza." World Health Organization, Dec. 21, 2023. https://www.who.int/news/item/21-12-2023-lethal-combination-of-hunger-and-disease-to-lead-to-more-deaths-in-gaza.

"Levels and Trends in Childhood Mortality." United Nations Inter-agency Group for Child Mortality Estimation, Mar. 12, 2024. https://data.unicef.org/resources/levels-and-trends-in-child-mortality-2024/.

"Malnutrition." World Health Organization, Mar. 1, 2024. https://www.who.int/news-room/fact-sheets/detail/malnutrition.

Maraniss, David. *Path Lit by Lightning: The Life of Jim Thorpe*. New York: Simon & Schuster, 2023.

Mendoza, Alec. "Almost Half of Uninsured TX Kids Are Eligible for Medicaid/CHIP." Texans Care for Children, Feb. 1, 2024. https://txchildren.org/report-almost-half-of-uninsured-tx-kids-are-eligible-for-medicaid-or-chip/.

"Meek." Cambridge Dictionary Online, n.d. https://dictionary.cambridge.org/us/dictionary/english/meek.

"Meek." Dictionary.com, n.d. https://www.dictionary.com/browse/meek.

"Meek." Merriam-Webster Dictionary Online, n.d. https://www.merriam-webster.com/dictionary/meek.

"Nicaragua: Another Bishop Arrested." *Vatican News*, Dec. 22, 2023. https://www.vaticannews.va/en/church/news/2023-12/nicaragua-bishop-isidoro-del-carmen-mora-ortega-arrested.html.

"Number of Palestinian and Israeli Fatalities and Injuries Caused by the War between Hamas and Israel since October 7, 2023." Statista Research Department, June 26, 2024. https://www.statista.com/statistics/1422308/palestinian-territories-israel-number-fatalities-and-injuries-caused-by-the-israel-and-hamas-war/.

Samsel, Haley. "Fort Worth ISD Begins Transition to Electric School Buses through $6M Federal Grant." *Fort Worth Report*, Jan. 11, 2024. https://fortworthreport.org/2024/01/11/fort-worth-isd-begins-transition-to-electric-school-buses-through-6m-federal-grant/.

Sanders, Bernie. "The Rich-Poor Gap in America Is Obscene. So Let's Fix It—Here's How." *The Guardian*, Mar. 29, 2021. https://www.theguardian.com/commentisfree/2021/mar/29/rich-poor-gap-wealth-inequality-bernie-sanders.

Sawyer, Wendy, and Peter Wagner. "Mass Incarceration: The Whole Pie 2024." Prison Policy Initiative, Mar. 14, 2024. https://www.prisonpolicy.org/reports/pie2024.html.

Sims, Vince. "How Fort Worth ISD Will Make Sure All Students Are Taken Care of When Online Classes Start." *NBC DFW*, July 30, 2020. https://www.nbcdfw.com/news/local/how-fort-worth-isd-will-make-sure-all-students-are-taken-care-of-when-online-classes-start/2417318/.

Soucy, Daniel, Makenna Janes, and Andrew Hall. "State of Homelessness: 2024 Edition." National Alliance to End Homelessness, 2024. https://endhomelessness.org/homelessness-in-america/homelessness-statistics/state-of-homelessness/.

Stark, Rodney. *The Triumph of Christianity: How the Jesus Movement Became the World's Largest Religion*. New York: HarperCollins, 2011.

Tacitus. *Agricola and Germania*. Translated by Harold Mattingly. London: Penguin, 2009.

Teresa, Mother. *Come Be My Light. The Private Writings of the Saint of Calcutta*. Edited by Brian Kolodiejchuk. New York: Doubleday, 2007.

"Threats to American Democracy Ahead of an Unprecedented Presidential Election." Public Religion Research Institute, Oct. 2023. https://www.prri.org/wp-content/uploads/2023/10/PRRI-Oct-2023-AVS.pdf.

Tian, Nan, et al. "Trends in World Military Expenditure, 2022." Stockholm International Peace Research Institute, Apr. 2023. https://www.sipri.org/publications/2023/sipri-fact-sheets/trends-world-military-expenditure-2022.

"UNICEF and Child Poverty." UNICEF, 2022. https://www.unicefusa.org/what-unicef-does/childrens-protection/child-poverty.

"UN Report: Pandemic Year Marked by Spike in World Hunger." UNICEF, July 12, 2021. https://www.unicef.org/eap/press-releases/un-report-pandemic-year-marked-spike-world-hunger.

"What Percentage of Americans Own Guns?" Gallup, Nov. 13, 2020. https://news.gallup.com/poll/264932/percentage-americans-own-guns.aspx.

"Which Countries Have Nuclear Weapons?" The International Campaign to Abolish Nuclear Weapons, 2024. https://www.icanw.org/nuclear_arsenals.

www.ingramcontent.com/pod-product-compliance
Lightning Source LLC
Chambersburg PA
CBHW052214240426
43670CB00037B/607